ABOUT THE PUBLISHER

The New York Institute of Finance

. . . more than just books.

NYIF offers practical, applied education and training in a wide range of financial topics:

* *Classroom training:* evenings, mornings, noon-hour
* *Seminars:* one- and two-day professional and introductory programs
* *Customized training:* need-specific, on your site or ours, in New York City, throughout the United States, anywhere in the world
* *Independent study:* self-paced learning—basic, intermediate, advanced
* *Exam preparation:* NASD licensing (including Series 7), CFA prep, state life and health insurance licensing

Subjects of books and training programs include the following:

* *Account Executive Training*
* *Brokerage Operations*
* *Futures Trading*
* *International Corporate Finance*
* *Options as a Strategic Investment*
* *Securities Transfer*
* *Technical Analysis*
* *And much more.*

When Wall Street professionals think **training**, *they think* **NYIF**.

Please write or call for our catalog:

New York Institute of Finance
Marketing Division
2 Broadway
New York, NY 10004-2207
212 / 344-2900

Simon & Schuster, Inc.

"Where Wall Street Goes to School" ™

Other works from LeRoy Gross:

PHONE POWER:
Telephone Selling and Prospecting

244 pages, 8½ x 11; illustrations, index;
ISBN 0-13-664350-7

Filled with realistic examples of telephone conversations between securities salespeople and prospects, this new book emphasizes the essential techniques of successful telephone sales:

- how to get past the secretary
- how to overcome the 20 most common telephone objections
- how to use the seven positive words that will increase sales immediately
- how and when to ask the three questions that will help you open large numbers of accounts over the phone.

LeRoy provides new insight into techniques that make actual calling more effective, through work done *before* picking up the phone:

- how to save time by qualifying prospects
- how to know the best times to call attorneys, physicians, dentists, CPAs, and other wealthy professionals
- how to create a referral mine by using present clients
- how to locate prospects with "buy" ability.

PHONE POWER also stresses the four questions that set the stage for the close and shows how to apply the seven examples of phone closes that produce orders.

HOW TO BE A
TOP PRODUCER (video)

60-min. video, full color; all formats

A companion to and enhancement of LeRoy's best-selling ART OF SELLING INTANGIBLES, this 60-minute, full-color video shows how to succeed as a securities salesperson. LeRoy demonstrates and illustrates techniques for organizing the workday, for helping clients and prospects to say "yes," and for successful prospecting. In a walk through the salesperson's day, the video shows how to get organized and stay organized:

- how to start the day on the right foot
- how to use the most important hour of the day
- how to prepare for tomorrow before ending today.

LeRoy provides the words that help persuade people to buy—words that turn prospects into clients and make present clients want to do more business with you.

More than a key tool for new salespeople, this video is a resource for experienced professionals looking for new ideas, new insights, and a fresh perspective.

MINING THE
COLD CALL GOLD (video)

40-min. video, full color; all formats

The ideal companion to LeRoy's new book PHONE POWER, this all-new, full-color, 40-minute video shows how some of the most important telephone selling techniques are used by successful sales professionals. Acknowledging that "most sales are made after the word *no* has been uttered," LeRoy introduces scenarios for getting around the three great NOs: "I already have a broker"; "I don't have any money right now"; and toughest of all, "I'm not interested."

Among the critical telephone-sales skills this video demonstrates: enthusiasm, empathy, thorough product knowledge, and ability to focus on prospect needs. Perhaps most important in emphasis, MINING THE COLD CALL GOLD focuses on closing the order through the *authority close*, the *comparison close*, the *greed close*, the *balancing close*, and the *small-matter close*, among others.

Second Edition

Art of
Selling Intangibles

**HOW TO MAKE YOUR MILLION($)
BY INVESTING OTHER PEOPLE'S MONEY**

LeRoy Gross

NEW YORK INSTITUTE OF FINANCE

NEW YORK • TORONTO • SYDNEY • TOKYO • SINGAPORE

Library of Congress Cataloging-in-Publication Data

Gross, LeRoy.
   Art of selling intangibles : how to make your million($) by
investing other people's money / LeRoy Gross.
     p. cm.
   Includes index.
   ISBN 0-13-049099-7
   1. Brokers. 2. Selling. I. Title.
HG4621.G77   1988   87-27862
322.63'2'0688—dc19   CIP

Printed in the United States of America

10   9

This publication is designed to provide accurate and authoritative information in regard to the subject matter covered. It is sold with the understanding that the publisher is not engaged in rendering legal, accounting, or other professional service. If legal advice or other expert assistance is required, the services of a competent professional person should be sought.
—*From the Declaration of Principles jointly adopted by a Committee of the American Bar Association and a Committee of Publishers and Associations*

ISBN 0-13-049099-7

ATTENTION: CORPORATIONS AND SCHOOLS

NYIF books are available at quantity discounts with bulk purchase for educational, business, or sales promotional use. For information, please write to: New York Institute of Finance, Business Information and Publishing, 2 Broadway, New York, NY 10004-2283. Please supply: title of book, ISBN number, quantity, how the book will be used, date needed.

NEW YORK INSTITUTE OF FINANCE
2 Broadway
New York, N.Y. 10004-2283
(212) 859-5000
A Simon & Schuster Company

On the World Wide Web at http://www.phdirect.com

Prentice-Hall International (UK) Limited, *London*
Prentice-Hall of Australia Pty. Limited, *Sydney*
Prentice-Hall Canada Inc., *Toronto*
Prentice-Hall Hispanoamericana, S.A., *Mexico*
Prentice-Hall of India Private Limited, *New Delhi*
Prentice-Hall of Japan, Inc., *Tokyo*
Simon & Schuster Asia Pte. Ltd., *Singapore*
Editora Prentice-Hall do Brasil, Ltda., *Rio de Janeiro*

DEDICATION

To June, with love and grateful thanks for your warmth, wisdom, steadfastness, and support throughout our lives. Without you and your strength, whatever accomplishments I have achieved would not have been.

And to Linda, Terry, Danny, Paula, and Malka, five wonderful people who each have brought pride and joy into my life!

Contents

Getting the Order: 4 Kinds of Helpful Evidence, 65

Selling Savvy: 6-Way System, 71

HOW TO HEAT UP YOUR COLD CALLS, 81

Prospecting: 11 Greatest Sources, 83

Telling Stock Buyers What They Want to Know, 214

TIPS ON SELLING PRODUCTS, 221

Selecting Common Stocks to Help Sell More Shares to More People More Quickly: 8 Criteria, 223

Foreword

I'm sure you have heard the saying, "Those who can, do; those who cannot, write books about how to." If there is such a rule, LeRoy Gross is the perfect example of the *exception* to it. LeRoy has been a successful salesman, sales manager, and sales trainer for most of his adult life. He has personally used the sales approaches and techniques he discusses in this book, and he has used them successfully. In the years he worked as a securities salesman, he became one of the top producers in his company and in the industry. Not content with that achievement, he created the National Option Sales Department and later became the Director of Marketing for Reynolds Securities Inc., one of Wall Street's leading investment and securities brokerage firms.

I first met LeRoy in 1964 when he was seeking a securities sales career. He had left a successful business in his home town of Asheville, North Carolina, and had moved his family to Charlotte. Having pondered his future, LeRoy decided to pursue a career in the securities business. He joined the Reynolds & Company Account Executive Training Program in April 1964.

It was my privilege to be LeRoy's training director. From the outset it was clear that he was a unique trainee. Though he had the same conventional investment and market interests as his peers, he had some unconventional ones, too. For instance, on many of his lunch hours you could find him at Filer, Schmidt & Company's option trading desk learning everything he could about options. Remember, this was 1964, many years before listed options and the CBOE. In the evening hours, if an investment seminar was being given in or around New York City, he attended, learning everything he could about the right and wrong ways to conduct seminars. Also, his training period was shortly after the Keogh Act (Individual Self-Employed Retirement

Tax Act) was passed by Congress, and few people in Wall Street understood the intricacies of the act and how to market and sell Keogh plans to the self-employed. LeRoy researched the field on his own and discovered that an executive of one of the large mutual funds was the leading expert on the act and on how to set up and market Keogh plans. He arranged numerous meetings with this gentleman and by the time he left New York for Charlotte, LeRoy was as knowledgeable in setting up retirement plans as anyone in the industry.

Behind this all-out effort to develop unusual expertise in such products as options and Keogh plans was a carefully thought-out game plan. LeRoy reasoned that if he became more knowledgeable in selected products than any other brokers in the Charlotte investment community, it would help him to quickly establish an identity as a professional. Also, as a stranger to Charlotte, he properly reasoned that the investment-seminar approach would be the best way to develop personal visibility and credibility.

The fact that he was a rousing success is history. In his first year he sold more Keogh plans than all of the other account executives in Reynolds & Co. combined. He became THE expert in the company on organizing and giving seminars. And, because of his knowledge and success in options he was asked, as of January 1, 1970, to move to New York company headquarters and establish a National Option Sales Department.

Packaging his own option selling strategies and using his rare communications skills, company-wide option sales were soon booming. In fact, after only a few months in his new role, LeRoy had built option sales to a level that was straining the then-existing operational processing capability. The managing partner asked him to direct his sales-development talents in other areas while the option operation was being expanded. We agreed that one of the most constructive things he could do would be to put together his many sales ideas and techniques for use in training both our new account executive trainees and experienced brokers throughout the country. These ideas, which have been honed, refined, expanded, and continuously field-tested over a 10-year period, are the foundation of this book. Frankly, in my 30 years of experience in training securities salesmen, I have not known anyone who has better credentials for writing it.

I foresee the book having an appeal well beyond the obvious audience. Anyone now selling securities and/or related products will find it a gold mine of income-producing sales ideas and techniques, as will anyone involved in any selling of intangibles. Moreover, I think it will be read and appreciated by salespeople of all descriptions. And for those contemplating a career in the challenging world of financial and intangible sales, the book gives a very practical insight into the job requirements and demands. It will help these people make the right career decision.

Glen E. Givens

First Vice President
Director of Training
Dean Witter Reynolds, Inc.

Preface

Selling securities and financial services can be an exciting, rewarding profession for those who respond to challenges, adventure, and annual incomes with *no upside limit!*

This book contains hundreds of workable ideas that show the professional financial salesperson how to:

- Find money, move money, and place money.
- Get past the word, No!
- Overcome objections on the cold call.
- Get prospects to call *them*.
- Pick up on "close now" signals.
- Close a sale and when to close it.

And much more.

The techniques in this book have worked for me and for many of those I've trained. *They have been time-tested and proven in all kinds of markets* over my many years of selling in the securities business.

Successful salespeople realize that they don't have to reinvent proven methods to earn high incomes. From this book you should be able to select, for starters, several ideas and techniques with which you feel comfortable. Then practice them—and practice them some more—until you have made them the sales tools that suit you and your personal abilities.

I am grateful to the many people who helped in formulating the final manuscript. To these wonderful friends, I owe deepfelt thanks: to

Glen E. Givens, Alan C. Snyder, John Olson, Bay Gruber, for their constructive critical reading of the manuscript. To Joanne Marinello and Barbara Heintzelman, for their typing skill. And to Debra Teel Carpenter for her artful caricature.

LeRoy Gross

THE DEDICATED SALESPERSON'S CREED

19 Principles to
Live By, Sell By, Prosper By

By LeRoy Gross

1. *SMILE! People like to buy from genuinely happy salespeople.*

2. *Arrive for work early, leave late.* Clock watchers seldom get ahead or collect big paychecks.

3. *Give more on the job* than the pay seems to call for.

4. *Be punctual* for all meetings and appointments.

5. *Be competitive.* Try to qualify for and win any sales contest your company sponsors.

6. *Be careful, prompt, and precise* about completing all paperwork required of a salesperson moving up the success ladder.

7. *Observe other salespeople.* By watching what top performers do, you can quickly acquire years of experience.

8. *Get interested in other people's financial problems;* try to determine how your services and products can help solve those problems.

9. *Learn all you can about your company and its major products.* From that knowledge will spring the enthusiasm to "light fires" and create sales.

10. *Broaden your horizons.* Attend as many industry- and company-sponsored programs as you can. You'll always learn something of value from other attendees, if not from the speakers.

11. *Be factual and enthusiastic* when selling your company's products and services. Presented properly, the facts are sufficient to make the sales you need and want.

12. *When you don't know, say so.* The customer will respect your frankness and will judge—and possibly reward—you on how quickly and accurately you provide the information wanted.

13. *Do not overstate or misrepresent the facts.* This will only lead to distrust and cancellations.

14. *When things go wrong, politely express your concerns* to the proper superior.

15. *Offer positive suggestions for improvements,* in writing, when you see a need.

16. *Never criticize your company* to clients or competitors.

17. *Plan tomorrow's work* before you leave the office today.

18. *Ignore those around you who have failed* and who try to infect you with negative thoughts about your company, your territory, your goals, or your skills.

19. *SMILE! People like to buy from genuinely happy salespeople.*

GETTING ORGANIZED
FOR SUCCESS

The Making of "Born" Salespeople

Everybody is a salesperson in the sense that we all must persuade others to buy or pay for the products or services we can provide. This is true of secretaries, carpenters, doctors, CPAs, teachers—of everyone who *earns* money. Understanding and practicing selling fundamentals can substantially improve the incomes of people who never think of themselves as salespeople.

The making of a "born" salesperson involves instilling pride in being a salesman. Selling is a respected profession without which our society would be much less affluent. Without salesmen we would not enjoy the many fine luxuries and "necessities" that Americans are so envied for around the world. Yes, selling for a living is honorable, respectable, and a prideful occupation that should be as sought after as zealously as that of a doctor, lawyer, or engineer.

Do you know the one objective all employers seeking people to sell their product or service have in common? To hire "born salespeople." The instruction to do that is blithely given to personnel directors, who then try to teach their subordinates how to recognize, interview, and select this highly desirable, much sought-after commodity, the "born salesperson."

Written tests are devised to unearth this precious creature. Video- and audio tape instruction suggests what to look for in appearance, in verbal responses to questions, and in answers on written tests. Numerous articles and books detail innumerable questions and information-extracting methods that supposedly make it easier to select the "born" prize from all the applicants for the sales job. Special seminars are frequently available, at high cost, that promise to make selectors of salespeople more proficient in their hiring role. Some hirers, on the other hand, simply rely on "gut feel" or look for qualities most like their own.

Unfortunately, as most employers of sales forces have discovered, the "born" salesperson is elusive, difficult to pick out from the throng clamoring for the job opportunity. Effective salespeople come in all sizes and shapes, arrayed in all modes of dress. They may be educated or uneducated, articulate or inarticulate. In voices high pitched or low, they are equally likely to use impressive vocabularies or one-syllable words, including expletives. These highly desirable and much-sought-after salespeople have no distinguishing markings at all! So there's a problem in finding them, right?

There *is* a problem, but it may not be the one you suspect. The real problem with searching for and selecting the "born" salesperson is that no such person exists! This search is fruitless, like the search for the Holy Grail or the pursuit of the Abominable Snowman. The simple fact is that outstanding salespeople are *made—developed—trained*—not born!

Selling is an *acquired skill*, and one that can be developed, at least to some degree, by anyone. People who acquire a high degree of proficiency in the skills of selling are often said to be "born sales-people." They have so smoothly practiced their art that it appears inborn to observers; they seem to have a natural talent. But such skilled salespeople are no more born to their profession than are accountants, doctors, lawyers, engineers, athletes, or other professionals. Top salespeople acquire their skills through study, reading books and articles and attending seminars conducted by talented professional sales trainers. They learn the tools and techniques of selling from films, video-tapes and audio tapes, and other teaching aids. They learn from close observance of other selling professionals. Trial and error is one of their greatest teachers; nothing teaches so quickly and so well as performing the task. Even better is on-the-job performing under a trained person who watches every movement and listens to every word with an attentive ear and then offers constructive help.

Yes, top salespeople are made, molded, developed, trained; they are *not* born at the top. Almost anyone can sharpen their selling skills through good sales training, once the realizations dawn that no one is born to sell, that selling is a learned skill like any other, that profi-ciency comes with constant practice of fundamental selling tech-

Even the best security salespeople often don't recognize a good opportunity *until* they see it working for a competitor!

TWO THINGS YOU CAN DO TODAY TO MAKE YOUR BUSINESS GROW!

1. **Check every aspect of your personal appearance and manner that might keep some prospect from giving you an order. Use this list and grade yourself.**

hair_____	clothes_____	smile_____
nails_____	posture_____	breath_____
shoes_____	handshake*_____	jewelry**_____

*not too hard nor too limp
**not too much/too splashy, or too cheap

2. **Know and present *four* compelling reasons to buy now *for* any product you are selling today. Clearly state any risk or sales cost early in each presentation. Do this and watch your percentage of "yes" answers grow.**

niques. Naturally, some will develop into better salespeople than others. Skill levels will vary from high to low, just as they do in all other professions.

You can read this (or any) book on selling, but that won't make you into a good salesperson any more than reading a book on tennis, golf, or bridge will turn you into a top player. What makes anyone excel at tennis, golf, bridge, or selling is diligent, consistent practice of fundamental techniques. What you *can* gain from reading this book is an understanding of the many fundamentals of selling skill needed to become a top salesperson. If you practice these skills and if you have the desire to reach the top, you may become one of those so-called born salespeople. Some of you may become so proficient that your earnings will double, triple, or even grow to a sum beyond your present ability to imagine.

With the perception that salespeople are *made*, not born, gradually becoming clear at corporate levels, a rather simplistic wishful thought often follows: "If salesmen are made, developed, trained, molded into producing entities, let's do it quickly." The idea sounds so good that great sums of money and countless hours are spent in developing programs, workshops, and seminars designed to produce trained salespeople.

The time allotted to getting this wondrous creature, the "trained professional salesperson," into a production mode may be one day, two days, a week, a month, three months, or, infrequently, six months to a year. The length of training depends upon many factors, including the corporation, the product or service, industry requirements, licensing or regulatory requirements, and, perhaps most influential, the corporate need to have the salesperson in place trying to get orders.

Despite salespeople's obvious importance, their rate of turnover in cornerstone industries like insurance and securities is almost incredible—and frightening to management. Insurance industry statistics purport to show that nine out of ten who enter this field in sales *fail* within three years! In the securities industry, approximately two out of three who enter the industry in sales fail within three years.

The high dropout rate in these and similar industries has two main causes. One is the poor selection of the candidates hired for the job. The second is the lack of high-quality, on-going training in sales techniques. In my opinion it takes *years* to develop a skilled salesperson. Normally, training cannot be acomplished quickly, no more than one can quickly become a doctor, a dentist, a lawyer, or a professional athlete. And without such training, not only will one fail to produce top salespeople, but the turnover rate will stay high, robbing corporations that sell of their greatest potential asset.

Tested under field conditions, the ideas proposed in this book can be used by sales trainers or salespeople themselves to produce more and bigger sales. Reading them once and trying out one or two ideas will not turn a below-average salesperson into a star, however. To achieve star sales status, the sales principles described herein must be applied with disciplined and consistent *long-term* dedication.

Setting Time-Limited Goals

In working toward that powerful measure of sales success, high dollar earnings, you will have to establish goals. Goals serve as prods to spur you onward and upward. Goals serve as measures of attainment—monitors of performance. Goals are instruments in determining accountability. They are invaluable as guides along the pathway to success.

In order to be truly helpful as you climb upward, goals *must have a time limit*. You should establish for yourself three sets of goals: (1) near-term goals, (2) intermediate-term goals, and (3) long-term goals. Each goal should have specific benchmark dates to determine progress.

Goal-setting does warrant two warnings, however. The first is this: do not set goals so high that they border on the impossible to achieve. Too high a goal is likely to discourage you when you perceive it cannot be accomplished. Take a lesson from professional high jumpers and pole vaulters: they gradually inch up the bar when they find they can easily clear a lower setting. If you find you are easily reaching your goals, simply make an adjustment and raise your sights. Keep stretching and seeking higher levels and you will be on your way to attaining them.

The second warning is to set a time limit for achieving a goal. Without the time limit, it is easy to procrastinate and you lose the impetus that meeting a deadline gives. This pressure and sense of urgency is something that most salespeople need and thrive on.

Top security salesmen know that continual prospecting is the key to the continued success of their brokerage business. Twenty-five percent of the average AE's accounts are "lost" each year to attrition. Prospecting at every opportunity is the only way to overcome this normal occupational hazard. Do you have 1600 prospects in your file? Are they regularly contacted?

TWO THINGS YOU CAN DO TODAY TO MAKE YOUR BUSINESS GROW!

1. *Try to get the local bank to sponsor your giving a course: "Teaching Your Wife How To Be a Widow!"*

2. *Call ten strangers (business people) to tell them about the Liquid Asset Fund and the short-term CD unit trust.*

Here are some goals that stockbrokers should consider establishing at the beginning of a career. Experienced brokers or sellers of other investment products can readily adapt the suggestions to fit their particular focus.

Goal 1: Establish a daily minimum goal of phone contacts asking for orders. Don't leave the office until this goal is reached.

Goal 2: Establish a daily minimum goal of direct mail contacts seeking appointments or asking for orders. Don't leave the office until this goal is reached.

Goal 3: Establish a daily minimum goal of seeing at least two people face to face and asking for the order. Don't go home until this goal is reached.

Goal 4: Establish weekly, monthly, and yearly commission goals. After a regular clientele has been built up, establish a narrower goal of daily commission.

Goal 5: To keep enthusiasm high, every month stockbrokers should "fall in love" with a stock that they want to buy for accounts. A goal must be set as to the minimum number of shares to be positioned in a selling period of 20 business days.

Monthly sales goals should also be set for other products: for example, perhaps $50,000 each month for tax-deferred annuities, a specific dollar volume in municipal securities, individual bonds, or unit trusts, closing one tax-shelter sale each month, and so on.

A goal for opening new accounts must also be set. The target I recommend is a minimum of ten new accounts per month. This is the minimum even for established salespeople, who presumably benefit from referrals. Seekers of superstardom should double or triple that number.

Discuss your goals with your manager and with your family. Their knowledge of and interest in what you are trying to do can help you on the road to doing it. Let them know your progress frequently; they may offer some good positive suggestions. The more people you can interest in your progress, the better chance you have to progress.

Using the Most Important Hour of the Day: 3 Sure Steps to Success

"Plan your work! Work your plan!" These perhaps trite, shop-worn phrases are used by salespeople in all industries to incite colleagues to ever-higher levels of production. The message is clear, but the application is often difficult to accomplish.

Sellers of intangibles need a clear head and a clear view ahead each day if they are to succeed in their endeavors. Carrying out the following suggestions will sharply clarify the sales path for you to follow each working day. Accomplish each step at the end of the business day before you leave for home.

Step 1:
Clean Up Your Desk

It is very difficult to be effective at sales if your desk is strewn with hundreds of scraps of paper, two or three weeks' collection of the *Wall Street Journal*, memos from the home office, half-eaten sandwiches, full ashtrays, research reports, annual reports, and countless other "in the way" items. *Every business day before you go home, tidy up!* Put everything in its proper place and prepare your office or desk area as if the richest, most desirable client in the world was going to pay you a visit the next day. Once you form this habit, you will feel better when you leave the office and when you arrive the next morning. The decks have been cleared for action.

Many potential clients are turned off by visiting a salesperson who conveys an impression of sloppiness in handling paper. The thought enters the prospect's mind, "Maybe this person will be as careless with my investments as he (or she) is in keeping this desk orderly."

Step 2:
Spend Up to One Hour with Yourself

Take one uninterrupted hour each day. The secretaries and receptionists should be instructed to take messages only. Take no phone calls unless a true emergency has arisen. During this one-hour period, mentally review every sales attempt you made that day. What was it you said to Mr. Smith that got him to give you that big order? What was it you said to Mrs. Jones that caused her not to buy? What might you have said differently that would have closed the sale? Were your facts incorrect or not convincing enough? Did you fail to radiate confidence and enthusiasm?

After thoroughly reviewing each sales effort for that day, you are now ready for step 3.

Step 3:
Write Down Tomorrow's Sales Plan

One of the best aids in becoming sales-effective is to know exactly what you want to accomplish each day, from the minute you arrive at work. The best way to accomplish this is to write the details of the action plan the night before.

Create a Product Worksheet

With a written plan in hand at the day's beginning, you will find selling a much easier task. The plan makes for a disciplined approach rather than the typical, haphazard, "Let's see what the market is doing before trying to contact clients and prospects" method. Insurance salespeople can easily modify the following list to insurance products.

Here is the minimum information necessary to write down on the planning night.

1. *Favorite growth stock.* Itemize all the meaningful statistics and select a reason for buying now.

2. *Favorite income stock.* Itemize all the meaningful statistics and select a reason for buying now.

3. *Favorite short sale.* Itemize all the meaningful statistics and the reason for selling short now. Include a target downside objective. This coolly chosen selection is necessary for that occasional prospect or client who feels bearish and asks point-blank for a short-sale recommendation. When asked to enthusiastically, confidently suggest a short sale, the average securities salesperson is usually unable to render a logical suggestion. This unreadiness often shows through, and the "impulse order" is missed. By having this information prepared the night before, you will sound smooth, professional, and prepared, able to respond to the request by saying, "I was thinking about short sales last night (true!) and here is the one that looks best to me right now."

4. *Favorite AAA-rated municipal bond.* Itemize all the meaningful statistics, including the dollar price to the client, plus the reason for buying now.

5. *Favorite A-rated municipal bond.* Itemize all the meaningful statistics plus the reason for buying now.

6. *Favorite convertible corporate bond.* Itemize all the meaningful statistics plus the reason for buying now.

7. *The taxable unit trust currently available.* Include the dollar price per unit, all meaningful statistics, and the reason for buying now.

8. *The federal tax-free unit trust currently available.* Include the dollar

When bear markets come, as they inevitably do, good security salespeople become mindful of an old adage: "Hell is truth seen too late!"

Top security salespeople understand the importance of good communication. They make more and bigger sales through their mastery of the three communication skills: (1) simplicity; (2) conciseness; (3) clarity. These apply to phone calls, memos, or letters.

TWO THINGS YOU CAN DO TODAY TO MAKE YOUR BUSINESS GROW!
1. **Put all tax shelter information into a 3-ring binder for quick reference.**
2. **Call 5 people about the next available shelter and its benefits.**

price per unit, all meaningful statistics, and the reason for buying now.

9. *The two most attractive covered call write opportunities.* Include the returns if exercised and if the stock is unchanged at the end of the time period, plus the reasons for buying now.

10. *The most attractive put option to buy.* Itemize all meaningful statistics plus the reason for buying now.

11. *The most attractive call option to buy.* Itemize all meaningful statistics and the reason for buying now.

12. *An interest-rate fact sheet.* List the various current returns on tax-deferred annuities, Treasury bills, GNMA securities, and money-market funds.

Collecting and entering the foregoing information on a product worksheet will normally take 20 to 30 minutes once the daily information resources have been identified. You may want to use a buddy system in which each participant daily digs up certain of the necessary data.

Other product information should be added as your interest dictates.

Once the product information is gathered and entered on a *single, easy-to-read worksheet, that sheet becomes a powerful tool in selling prospects and clients.* You will never again have to interrupt a phone conversation to scramble madly to find a wanted detail or information about a product.

With the completed sheet in front of you, you can always sound like a professional. It becomes easier to flow from one product to another as you talk to clients and prospects. The smooth flow makes sales come easier and enables you to feel much more confident. The transmittal of this confidence to the prospect is what makes the sale. That confidence is generated by the previous night's work.

List Your Phone Prospects

After completing the product worksheet, write down the names and phone numbers of 30 (or more) people you are going to call the next day to attempt to sell one of the ideas on the sheet.

Plan the Direct Mail

When the 30 or more names and phone numbers are listed, complete the direct mail plan. Each night before leaving the office, 10 to 20 "somethings" should be mailed to prospects to try to generate an incoming order, phone call, or information request. These 10 to 20 pieces should be accompanied by enclosed, easy-to-fill-out response cards. Each name mailed should be carefully logged for a call one week later.

When all these plans are completed, you can go home *relaxed*. You have carefully prepared yourself for the coming day. You should rest well, secure in the thought that you are paving the way for future success. You can face work tomorrow with full knowledge of the day's work plan, confidently pursuing orders from prospects and clients.

Each day's product worksheet and list of names to be called should be three-hole punched and filed in a binder. This retained file can then be reviewed and prior suggestions tracked and monitored. In the event of a prospect call-back months later about an earlier recommendation, quickly scanning the sheet can pinpoint the product and the price you recommended it at. The client will be impressed, and that fosters sales. Retaining the sheets is also clear evidence for how hard you have worked, for your daily sales attempts are logged.

All this can usually be accomplished in a quiet hour at the end of the work day. If you do it, and apply the other selling skills and ideas outlined in this book, I am confident success will come your way—and soon!

All that remains to be done is to do it! Start today to make your million investing other people's money.

Good luck!

Achieving Sales Success:
7 Basic Rules

Based on my years of selling and of observing top salesmen, I have formulated seven rules that can help make the salesperson of intangibles a success. Put these rules to use and watch your earnings increase.

Rule 1:
Learn to 'Hate" Other Salespeople in Your Office!

It sounds facetious, capricious, but once you understand the reasons for this particular suggestion, you may agree that it is one of the most valuable in helping achieve sales success. When newly trained completely registered brokers (or sellers of insurance, tax shelters, bonds, or other intangibles) return to the office (assuming they were trained someplace other than at the branch office), they will normally be warmly welcomed by the office manager as well as by their selling coworkers. Everyone wants to hear the latest rumors afloat at the home office as well as wanting to bring the returning salesperson up to date on local happenings. These people all appear to be friendly and nice, and that makes it difficult to refuse the time to carry on those oh, so interesting discussions.

New salespeople, not wanting to make enemies or hurt anyone's feelings, often surrender a good part of their potentially productive work time carrying on discussions that cannot lead to a commission! These friendly overtures are so insidious that neophytes rarely realize so-called friends are *stealing* that most precious commodity, selling time.

New salespeople may accept lunch invitations from office "buddies" (during which neither can earn a dime in commissions) and successfully kill an hour, maybe two. Or perhaps a colleague will extend an invitation to have a drink late in the afternoon, further robbing the new salesperson of valuable selling time.

Successful professional salespeople know that selling time is their most valuable asset and must not be recklessly squandered on non-prospects! A difficult but crucial lesson to learn is how to abbreviate time spent with coworkers and maximize time spent with prospects and clients.

New salespeople must constantly be aware that their most ferocious competitors for business are often their own associates on the sales force. Such people are looking for, fighting for prospects in the same market area. Secretly, the older salespeople root for the new ones to fail. And why not? Every failure lessens the competition and offers positive proof to the manager, spouses, and higher-ups of how tough it really is out there. Besides, should a new salesperson succeed, that very success might suggest that the older, more experienced people on the sales force aren't working hard enough, might even cause some people to think that the veteran salesmen should be replaced!

Each multi-manned office usually contains bitter, unhappy, and relatively unsuccessful salespeople *who can infect others* with their

If you are ever inclined to imbibe to relieve your worries, pay heed to Thomas Edison who said, "As a cure for worrying—WORK is better than whiskey."

TWO THINGS YOU CAN DO TODAY TO MAKE YOUR BUSINESS GROW!

1. *Contact one or more list brokers and purchase a tax-shelter buyer's list for your area (and any others that you and your pocketbook might want).*

2. *Sell a buddy on sharing the cost of subscribing to the Value Line convertible service, if your office doesn't get it.*

bearish opinions and outlook if given the opportunity. Often they even try to create opportunities to spread their "disease."

Understanding the "learn to hate the other salespeople" concept, taken in the sense that your coworkers are really not your friends but are often (subconsciously if not consciously) seeking your failure, can be a life-saver. Be courteous at all times, of course, but learn to say "good morning" and "good evening" at the appropriate times and spend the rest of your time making prospecting calls and sales attempts.

Rule 2:
Work Long, Effective Hours

Sales success rarely comes easily in the field of selling intangibles. Sales of securities, insurance, tax shelters, mutual funds, commodities, and so on, can often be consummated early in the morning or at night, before or after the normal working day.

Aggressive, eager-to-make-it salespeople normally pay a price for success. The price is that precious commodity, time: time spent away from family and from recreation, time spent planning, arranging appointments, seeking prospects, calling prospects. It is not unusual for a new broker to log sixty or more hours each week, month in and month out, trying to get a foothold in the community. The nine-to-five mentality usually does not find success in the brokerage business or in any sales business where the income potential is unlimited but depends solely on sales commissions.

Just putting in the hours, however, does not ensure success. Many people work long, hard hours and earn very little for their efforts. It is what you do with your time that counts. Many so-called salespeople fritter away valuable selling time—reading, filing, doing many varieties of nonselling activities so that they can fool themselves and their supervisors into thinking they are working. The true measure of the value of hours worked is eventually counted in commission dollars earned, in actual sales presentations made, and in "asked for" orders. Reading, studying, keeping informed is very valuable and necessary, but these activities do not produce sales. What produces sales are the calls you make *asking for the order*.

Work *is* a four-letter word, but not a dirty one. It's the kind of four-letter word that can put big dollars in the commission salesperson's pocket. Work in the sales game is the *constant* day-in, day-out solicitation of orders from prospects and clients.

Good security salespeople know they have no time to waste: they have to arouse interest immediately. Their first words and actions must be planned to capture the prospect's complete attention. Options, with limited risk and unlimited profit potential for buyers, can capture the prospect's attention perhaps better than any other product!

TWO THINGS YOU CAN DO TODAY TO MAKE YOUR BUSINESS GROW!

1. **Call 2 of your firm's top producers to see if you can get an idea—psyche yourself up.**

2. **Meet with the Mercedes salesman. You might exchange leads and get access to their list of late model foreign car owners.**

Rule 3:
Keep Good Records

If you aspire to success, to sales stardom, you must discipline yourself into being a good record keeper. Records must be kept on each prospect. Information must be recorded when the prospect is called, sent mailings, seen. You should note what was discussed and when the next contact is to be made. All transactions, consummated or proposed, must be carefully recorded and filed so as to be easily recoverable. All signed documents necessary to each account must be copied and retained in a file in the event that the client or the home office misplaces their copies. All verbal or written commitments concerning future service must be placed in a "tickler" file or entered on a desk calendar so that they are not forgotten. Your efficiency and attention to detail breeds confidence and loyalty in your customers, and pleasing clients helps to develop referrals.

Any complaints or errors should be promptly written up, with copies of pertinent documents for the file or to the local manager. Unresolved problems or adjustments that drag on uncorrected in your customer accounts drive business away. Prompt notification to the right authority, along with correct documentation to support the claim, speeds the process and makes for happier clients and more business.

Top salespeople want to know how they are doing, so they constantly keep records of their own progress. Daily commissions, monthly commissions, monthly new accounts, and daily sales calls are the minimum of personal records to maintain. Typical record-keeping includes the following:

1. Prospects: names, addresses, phone, occupation, income
2. Prospect contacts: mail, phone, in person
3. Documents: authorizations, agreements
4. Complaints
5. Errors
6. Customer statements and order confirmations
7. Commission statements

Rule 4:
Develop Enthusiasm and Confidence

Developing enthusiasm and confidence in the product or service is one of the most important factors in determining the future success of the seller of that product or service. Getting that enthusiasm and confidence is not such an easy task, however, especially for stock or commodity brokers who deal in risk investments. Adverse markets *do* occur, and they can cause the best-researched, most carefully thought-out investment position to deteriorate and, at least temporarily, erode a client's capital. How do brokers stay confident, and show it, when a price move against their recommendations makes their judgment look bad? How do brokers get enough enthusiasm and confidence to even make risk recommendations?

Confidence and enthusiasm are created through *in-depth knowledge of the product or the service* being sold. That knowledge is often obtained by attending product seminars conducted by experts, from extensive reading of analyst reports, or through contact with a knowledgeable industry executive.

Thorough study of the investment situation, along with the strong opinion of a recognized expert, gives broker salespeople the enthusiasm and confidence necessary to sell their viewpoint to others. The more you know about the proposed investment, the more confidence you will have. Natural enthusiasm will then grow from your knowledge. Regardless of what people purchase, they feel more comfortable and reassured if the seller is enthusiastic and confident. Customers also tend to buy more and refer friends to a confident, ebullient salesperson.

The study involved in building a *story book* is one of the greatest ways for stockbrokers to obtain knowledge and confidence and increase sales. A story book is simply a three-ring binder containing the annual report, the quarterly report, the Standard & Poor's sheet, and, if available, the Value Line report. You should also include your firm's research report, newspaper clippings, the prospectus (if any), and the company's brochures on its products. This book should be compiled on those stocks you truly believe to be suitable recommendations for a large percentage of investors. The objective is to build a large position that will eventually be sold at a profit, making available proceeds to put toward another chosen situation.

Once compiled, the story book is a powerful tool to help close face-to-face sales, for prospects get the opportunity to see the story as well as hear it. It also provides instant reference on a company, and serves as a compliance function by proving that you have done your homework.

Story books can also be compiled on a variety of other products, such as options, tax shelters, annuities, municipal securities, mutual funds, commodities, life insurance, and financial planning. They are wonderful aids in achieving sales success. They take time and effort to build and maintain, but you will find they pay back golden dollars for your investment.

Sales Tip

Don't go anywhere without a story book under your arm. Whenever you meet anyone, a friend or a stranger, work the conversation around to your profession—investments. Inevitably you will be asked, "What looks good now?" With the ammunition in your story book, you are on your way to a show-and-tell session that can lead to an order.

Rule 5:
Complete 30 Selling Phone Calls Per Day

The measure of how hard you work in selling investments is not how many piles of mail are addressed and sent out each day, nor how many minor details have been attended to, nor how much reading and filing has been finished. The sole measure is how many calls were made asking for orders.

Your goal is to build a clientele whose commission-generating business will propel you into the ranks of high earners. Except for those rare few whose prior connections provide an almost immediate pool of clients and prospects, salespeople starting out have no clientele. Similarly, many older salespeople have lost clientele through normal attrition, poor judgment, or adverse markets. In either case, the answer to achieving high income lies in *contacting strangers daily* and asking them to buy a product or service on the first contact.

If you want high income, strive *each day* to reach 30 new people and ask each for an order. That may sound brash and nervy. Many people find it difficult to understand how people can be expected to entrust their money to a completely unknown—and unseen—salesperson and, moreover, to do it at the first phone contact. But that scenario of first contact–first order is replayed daily. What you must realize is that selling is a numbers game. The more contacts made and the more orders asked for, the greater the possibilities for success.

Many salespeople are hard workers who make the suggested number of calls and still fail. One reason for their failure may be that their verbal and selling skills are not great. Most often, however, they fail because they are *timid*. The reluctance to ask for an order still exists in many salespeople. They want the client to make the decision to buy, to roll over or play dead, to place an order and hand over their money voluntarily. Salespeople who think that way are usually destined to remain at lower earning levels. Making the daily quota of calls is not enough unless you can state after the call is completed, "I asked for an order, and I asked for an appointment."

Top security salespeople know that Wall Street has many brilliant AEs who start out in a blaze of glory but lack the sticktuity to be a continuing success. Their accounts and business are eventually taken by patient, hardworking AEs who never stop prospecting and asking for orders regardless of market conditions!

TWO THINGS YOU CAN DO TODAY TO MAKE YOUR BUSINESS GROW!

1. *Review your cross-reference file and see how many people you can get to trade up to 1000-share positions from lower amounts.*
2. *Send a note with new information to each holder of shares in your biggest position.*

Each day of 30 completed selling phone calls should produce one or more "live prospects" who will eventually become clients, if not at the first contact.

Take the pledge:

1. Complete 30 calls each day to strangers for 30 consecutive business days.
2. Ask each person for an order or an appointment.

At the end of 30 days, review your results in terms of new accounts and business done, and I believe you will find the effort paid off, especially when compared to any previous effort. I predict you will make the 30-call practice a daily habit.

Rule 6:
See Two Prospects Each Day

Constantly trying to create sales and develop prospects through phone contact alone eventually becomes boring. Besides, many salespeople are better at "one on one" than they are at making their sales points over the phone. To create a mental uplift and provide new vigor to the task of prospecting, create a daily discipline of seeing *quality prospects* face to face each day. Please note that I said "prospects," meaning people who are not yet your clients.

These "face to face's" can be accomplished during lunch hour, on the way to or from work, or on a simple prospecting tour of the other business places in and around your office. Meeting people face to face tends to pump up your enthusiasm, and it provides you with an opportunity to use your story book to get the order. Good salespeople also recognize that many wealthy prospects *only* do business with people they have met and with whom they feel comfortable.

In addition to providing a breather between phone calls, face-to-face meetings can produce referrals, and they typically result in larger initial orders than those gained through phone prospecting. These face-to-face presentations can be of three types:

1. Scheduled appointments in your office
2. Scheduled appointments in the prospect's office or home
3. Nonscheduled appointments in the prospect's office

Establish a goal of meeting at least two qualified prospects face to face each day and asking each to do business with you. If you do so, you will be amazed at how rapidly your business and referrals grow.

Sales Tip

Make time for daily "facials," not excuses for avoiding them.

Rule 7:
Send Out 10 to 20 Personalized Mailers Each Day

Salespeople well versed in selling fundamentals constantly try to keep a steady stream of prospects coming to them to seek advice and place orders. A great aid in strengthening the flow of incoming calls and requests is in the proper use of direct mail.

Mail-produced leads, in my experience, consistently generate more and better-qualified prospects than do newspaper or magazine insertions. Mail can be pinpointed to a narrow geographic area densely populated with the affluent investors who are the desired targets.

Using the mail to produce a sufficient supply of qualified prospects at a low cost requires a lot of thought and planning, as follows:

1. The area to receive mail coverage should have a demonstrable concentration of wealthy prospects.
2. The area should be close enough to the office to enable you to visit the prospect easily and for the prospect to visit you at the office.
3. Send no more mail than you can follow up with a phone call approximately one week after the mailing. Mass mailing is an expensive burden on the office and will not normally be tolerated by the local manager unless sales results can be documented. It is also a waste of time, because you cannot possibly follow up on each piece.
4. Each piece of mail should have a business card attached or be stamped with your name, address, and phone number. (If you stamp, use red ink. It is a better attention-getter than the typical black ink.)
5. Personalize each piece of mail with a *handwritten note* block-printed in large, easy-to-read letters. (Again, the use of a thick-writing pen with colored ink helps gain readership and lessens the chances of your mailing becoming a quick throwaway.)

A typical general use personalization might read:

> *Dear Leroy:*
> *Call me right away as soon as you have read this.*
>
> *(Your name)*

6. Never send out *any* direct mail unless you enclose *at least two response cards* for the prospect to complete and return. Response cards that request a specific item are the most rewarding, because they pinpoint an area of interest that you can zero in on. You should further instruct your assistants to include two or more sales darts in all your outgoing correspondence that, when returned, can lead to an order or new client.

7. Log all outgoing mail for a follow-up phone call one week later. Use the phone call to make sure the information was received and to solicit the order. (Never forget that getting the order is the object of the game.)

   To make your mail program work, you must always have on hand a supply of response-card enclosures of various types to appeal to any interest. Use paper in different colors; bright, light shades of yellow, blue, green, and pink are recommended.

   Don't leave the office each day until at least ten "somethings" are in the mail, personalized, containing sales darts.

   Do see that preaddressed return envelopes that carry your name or identifying number are enclosed to ensure that any leads generated get directed to you. If the response card needs no envelope and is preaddressed, mark your initials or identifying number on the card to properly ensure the lead assignment.

Creating Success:
6 Surefire Ideas

Stockbrokers seeking to make it big should recognize that the great majority of the industries' big producers create significant portions of their revenue from "position building." They zero in on a particular stock, research it carefully on their own (even if the stock is extensively covered by their own research departments) and become sold themselves before recommending a single share to clients. Once having found a desirable stock, they tell and retell the story about that stock to as many people as possible each day. Of course *they ask each listener to buy!*

Top producers know that they have a responsibility not only to select suitable recommendations but also to follow them until the position is eventually sold. Good salespeople also realize that they can know well and follow only a limited number of issues. Knowing this, they carefully restrict the number of stocks they follow usually to no more than 10 or 12 in any given year. All of which leads to six surefire success ideas.

Success Idea 1:
Familiarize Yourself with Products

Each month, *select one stock* to learn thoroughly, and then sell the story to as many people as possible. The natural enthusiasm generated by a new idea builds sales quickly. However, any story you tell and retell dozens of times every day will become old and boring to you. After a time, your enthusiasm wanes, and along with the decline in enthusiasm, sales begin to slow. After a period of concentration on the chosen stock, *stop actively promoting it!*

Learn a new stock. Follow the procedure for researching and documenting. You will find the constant need to keep your enthusiasm at a high level. One way to ignite enthusiasm in yourself and in others is to learn something new each month. This procedure keeps position-building within reasonable compliance limits and also permits prudent diversification among holdings in clients' accounts.

Success Idea 2:
Ask for Referrals

Nothing warms salespeople's hearts so much as the account and commissions earned through a referral. Having a friend or client refer another prospect to you not only brightens the day but usually so charges you up that you will probably find yourself making more calls and selling more enthusiastically. Salespeople *love* referrals, yet many are so timid that they will not directly ask for a referral. They want their judgments—their stock, option, or commodity recommendations—to perform so impeccably that satisfied clients will automatically disclose an unending list of referrals.

What a wonderful dream world! The real world, however, is full of risk as well as the possibility of profit. No matter how carefully a situation is chosen or researched, it can deteriorate substantially after the client has invested. Erosion can occur with a general market fall or because of unforeseen circumstances affecting the particular situation. Certainly a loss in value won't help make the client eager to recommend others to the same broker's ministrations. Sometimes, as in 1973–74, a protracted stock market decline dries up referrals. So much for referrals generated by the broker's flawless recommendations to clients.

If you know anything about investor psychology, you should understand that the best way to get referrals in regular, large numbers is to ask for them. The two best times to ask for and get referrals are as follows:

Referral Time 1

Ask for a referral when you report the executed price of a transaction in a stock, option, or commodity. Once investors know they are

Top-earning salespeople know:
"Beginning is the most important part of work."

"in," their natural instinct is to root for that position to move favorably and produce a profit. They also realize that the greater the number of people assuming the same side of that trade, the more pressure is brought to move the position in the desired direction. If asked for referrals at the time of a price report, these clients are likely to surrender two, three, or more names of people who might want to test the same water. Investors' enthusiasm is high at the time of entry into an investment; good salespeople press this advantage and ask for referrals at this point.

A typical price reporting conversation might go like this: "You bought 300 ZXY at $18. The outlook really looks great for increased earnings, a dividend increase, and a higher stock price. I have three extra reports on my desk right now. Who do you suggest I mail them to, people who might also be interested in this excellent opportunity?"

Referral Time 2

Whenever you have investors enjoying a winning recommendation, ask for referrals. Call each winner and say that you can handle a few additional accounts and would like to place selected friends of theirs on your mailing list. This approach is usually very effective and helps build a prospect file.

Sometimes prospects will allow you to use their names in contacting others (most desirable, of course), and sometimes not. Always ask permission *after* you have the referral names.

Don't put off asking for referrals. The market action of your recommendation may do you in. An immediate decline may occur even

27

before settlement, creating a "nonreferral" situation that may last for a long time—maybe forever.

I once sold the bulk of an entire syndicate new issue stock offering just by asking for referrals. The issue was "cold," "sticky," hard to move at the $12.50 per share offering price, enabling interested salespeople to get a lot of stock and earn a good commission for each share placed.

With the prospectus information in hand, I called a local merchant, a stranger to me, who handled the products sold by the particular company making the offering. I extolled the potentials (and outlined the risks), stressing that it was an opportunity to purchase shares at the same price available to any public investor, no matter how wealthy. I also stressed the "no commission to the buyer" aspect of the newly issued shares. The prospect, who was well acquainted with the company and its products, gave me an order to buy 100 shares at the $12.50 offering price. No big deal, sure, but a new account was on my book and a commission in my pocket.

I then asked this prospect for the names of people he knew who might want these new shares. He suggested a cousin and a friend in different towns. I called them and opened an account for each, using my new client as a reference. Each of my new clients then gave me several other names to call, which I did. The chain of referrals and orders grew and grew. I eventually opened 45 new accounts in seven different states and sold over three-quarters jof our entire syndicate allotment myself. All as a result of asking for referrals!

Seek referrals from these main sources:

1. Existing clients
2. Close friends
3. Acquaintances
4. Other salespeople not in competition with you

Finally, always remember that "no sales," people who do not buy, for whatever reason, can still give referrals.

Success Idea 3:
Learn the "Apology" Sales Technique

The *apology sales technique* is a sales fundamental that can add thousands of dollars in commission income each year to its skilled practitioners. Here is the principle behind the apology sales technique: when salespeople obtain an order for an investment (stock, bond, annuity, life insurance, mutual fund) and confirm the price to the investor, they normally experience a moment of joy (sometimes exhilaration, depending on the size of the order), and then continue their routine of calling other clients and prospects, having "finished" with the client who gave the order. What many salespeople fail to understand, however, is that clients, particularly new ones, rarely place an initial order representing all, or even a significant part, of their available cash or assets. First and second orders are usually tests. If the salesperson's recommendations work out favorably, more orders, and larger ones, will be placed. Initial orders are trial votes of confidence in the salesperson's story.

You can often get increases in initial order sizes with the apology sales routine. Assume the following scenario: Joe Salesman calls John Prospect about a research-selected stock, XYZ, selling at $20 per share. The stock is rated A-plus and currently yields 10 percent from a dividend that has been raised annually for 20 consecutive years. The future outlook for more dividend and earnings increases looks good. John likes what he hears and agrees to buy 200 shares at $20. After executing the order and reporting the purchase price, Joe feels great. His hard prospecting work has paid off with a new client and an order.

The next morning, just before the market opens, Joe calls John: "John, this is Joe. I'm calling to *apologize* about your purchase yesterday of 200 XYZ at $20." Joe then pauses while his words sink in.

Typically, John Prospect is jarred. He might stutter: "What happened? How far down is it?"

Joe continues: "Don't get upset. Nothing bad has happened. *I just wanted to apologize to you* for my poor sales presentation. Yesterday I told you about the attractive features of XYZ and you did buy 200 shares. I must not have made clear to you that this stock is rated A-plus by Standard & Poor's—that is the highest possible rating. It yields 10 percent from a dividend that has been regularly increased for 20 years. The future is bright not only for the payment of higher income, but this stock offers potential capital gains as well. My story was so poorly delivered that you only bought 200 shares. I am calling this morning to make up for my lack of enthusiasm yesterday and see what else you might have that you could transfer into 300 (or 800) more shares while the price is low and the yield high. If you place an additional order right now before the opening, you might be able to get shares at or near where they closed."

A conversation of this type usually brings a response from the prospect such as "You really must like this stock to call me back so soon after my first purchase. If you are really that strong on it, get me 300 more shares."

Experienced sellers of investments know that frequently people understate, misrepresent, or lie outright about the funds they have available for investment. But at the drop of a good investment story, they suddenly "discover" or remember about money available. By calling the same client back the day after a purchase and forcefully, enthusiastically presenting the same sales points, an original order frequently can be "lifted" to a much higher level.

I conducted a sales meeting early one morning in Syracuse, New York, for 16 established salespeople. The apology sales technique was one idea that attracted Mike C. He said, "LeRoy, that sounds terrific. I'm going to try it today!" Mike went to his desk and called a client to recommend the purchase of 200 shares of Continental Telephone. He stressed the high yield, the dividend increase record, the quality. Mike got the order for 200 shares.

Mike then asked if I was going to be around the next day to supervise him in the implementation of his first try at using the apology sales technique. I told him I was leaving that day after the market close. Mike was disappointed that I would not be around to monitor his attempt at apology selling. He frowned for a moment, and then his face lit up: "Hey, I'll just *wait an hour* and call my client back and try the apology sale while you're here and can watch me."

An hour went by, and Mike called the client who earlier bought 200 Continental Telephone: "John, this is Mike, and I want to really

One step in cracking the high-earnings barrier is to realize that the first order only converts a prospect into a client. The next step is to convert the client into a steady, repeat-business client through your service and attention.

TWO THINGS YOU CAN DO TODAY TO MAKE YOUR BUSINESS GROW!

1. *Contact a load Mutual Fund that does not have a wholesale representative covering your territory. Study the fund's holdings and performance record. If you like what you see, make an effort to get at least one order for the fund's shares from an existing client or prospect.*

2. *Contact the fund (start with the president) to obtain all current literature and tell of your interest in promoting the fund's share. Ask for all leads in the area to be sent to you. Ask for the statement copies of all fund holders in your area not presently being serviced. Tell the president you would like to try to contact each holder to encourage them to make add-on purchases. You may just fall into a bonanza! (You will never know if you don't try!)*

apologize to you about the 200 Continental Telephone you bought this morning."

"What happened, Mike?"

"Nothing yet. The stock is just where you bought it. But I really must not have turned you on. You only bought 200 shares. Maybe I didn't make clear to you that the dividend has been raised each of the last 10 years, the yield is high, and your opportunity for a future profit looks great. If I were any good as a salesman you would have gotten at least 500 shares. I am calling back while the stock is still low to try to get you to buy 300 more shares of this high-quality, high-yield stock."

"You really must like this stock to call me back only an hour after I bought!"

"You know I believe it or I wouldn't be trying so hard to get you to buy more," Mike replied.

Said John, "Well, if you feel that strong about it, buy me another 300."

The apology sale worked for Mike as it had for me. The second request for an order soon after the first creates the client's conviction that the salesperson really believes in the recommendation!

Mike was so excited about this success that he excitedly exclaimed, "I am going to wait another hour and try it again with the *same client!*" Another hour went by and Mike called the client who had twice that day bought Continental Telephone shares: "This is Mike again. I want to apologize to you. In my hurry to encourage you to buy more Continental Telephone because of its high quality, high yield, and capital-gain potential, I forgot to tell you that if you buy 1000 shares today, you are entitled to a much lower commission charge per 100 shares. With a conservative investment like this, one that offers the potential for more income each year plus the opportunity for a capital gain, you should put more dollars in it now while the price is low. What do you have that you could transfer into another 500 shares and take advantage of our lower commission rate?"

Mike's client, certainly surprised at the third call that day, exclaimed, "Well, if you really like it that much, sell 500 XYZ and get me 500 more Continental."

Mike hung up the phone, wrote the orders with a big smile lighting his face, and said, "LeRoy, you taught me a lesson I will remember all my life."

The apology sales technique worked for Mike and it can work for you, too. Give it a try! Let it help you make big sales out of little ones.

Most salespeople's commissions are greatly affected by their mood. When they feel up, they can close sales, prospect enthusiastically, do the work of several people. But when they feel down, sales-people can't even sell the best quality investments at sacrifice prices.

Nowhere is this mood swing clearer than in stockbrokers who trade securities for a significant portion of their income.

In euphoric periods like the late 1960s and up-market times in the 1970s, brokers excitedly sold new issues, little-known secondary stocks, and established growth stocks to eager investors. They convinced themselves and others that 30, 40, 50, and even 60 times the latest 12-month earnings was a "cheap" price to pay for shares. Prestigious institutions, pension plans, and investment advisors also participated in the frenzy. The up mood created by large profits caused large and small investors alike to pay little heed to risk. It was easy to make sales due to the mood of the moment.

When down markets hit in 1969–70 and 1973–74, brokers in general could not get up enough courage to recommend A-plus utility shares yielding 15 percent, even when they were offered at a net price to the client and the salespeople paid double, even triple, the normal commission rate. Brokers made only fainthearted efforts to sell old clients and prospect for new ones. People were reluctant to buy well-known companies like EXXON and General Motors, even though their shares sold at historic low prices.

Learning how to psyche yourself is a fundamental selling skill that you must develop in order to reach the income level you desire, no matter what the selling climate. All the above is background for my next idea.

Success Idea 4:
Plan Appointments for Big Ticket Sales
for Friday Afternoon or Saturday Morning

Selling face to face requires different skills than selling by phone. Personal appearance becomes an important factor, as do exhibits and documentation that can be used as convincers to close the sale. Also helpful are attractive surroundings, a professional-looking office.

In addition to using all the foregoing to your advantage, make the appointment for a Friday afternoon or a Saturday morning. If the appointment results in a sale, your weekend mood will be elevated.

You'll feel great! Even though the rest of the week may have been torture, ending the week with a good sale helps create a better, happier weekend environment for you and the people you're close to. When Monday morning arrives and you enter the order ticket for the good sale, you will feel much more up than those associates struggling for the first order of the week. The up feeling will provide some equanimity in the event that Monday's market moves adversely for your special situations. The feeling you get from the weekend close is that you have the new week made. Feeling that way enables you to seek more orders and make more appointments on the wave of optimism caused by the sale. Making weekend sales is one of the best morale boosters in the world! I must warn you, though, they're addictive. But that type of high is entirely beneficial.

Success Idea 5:
Prospect 7 Days a Week

Sellers of intangibles understand the necessity for getting new accounts. They know that new accounts are their life blood, and in order to get new accounts on a regular basis, one or another form of prospecting is necessary. Salespeople who don't make it fail because they have not made themselves prospect-conscious 100 percent of their waking hours.

Always be on the lookout for prospects. Search for new clients among friends, acquaintances, strangers. Always keep yours eyes, ears, and mouth open. Trying to open up a stranger and get the conversation turned toward investments is a constant challenge.

If you are looking for them, prospect can be encountered almost everywhere you go. You can strike up conversations in airplanes with a captive audience. In restaurants it is often possible to strike up a conversation with a prosperous-looking fellow diner and steer the conversation to investing. Bars may be productive meeting places. Cocktail parties and other social functions like weddings and birthday parties are great for meeting new people who are prospects for future solicitations for business. Always be alert for prospecting opportunities at civic affairs, church-group meetings, club functions. Let people know what business you are in, what services you can render. Don't be afraid to start and steer conversations toward your favorite topic, investing!

Wherever good sellers of intangibles spend money, they concentrate on trying to get some of it back by selling to the salesperson, the manager, or the owner. For example, when you buy a car, get the salesperson (who earned a commission from selling you the car) to become your client for investments. The folks are usually talkers and, as clients, are likely to refer a stream of others to you.

Eliminate the thought that prospecting is done only during working hours. All your waking hours can be prospecting hours, and the sooner you realize this and eagerly pursue the opportunities to present yourself and your ideas wherever and whenever people congregate, the quicker your commission checks will increase.

Success Idea 6:
Set Up "1000 Up" Prospect Files

Getting accounts on the books is the necessary beginning to building a large production base. In order to develop a book of accounts quickly and maintain a high level of opening new accounts, skilled salespeople establish a prospect file.

I have come in contact with thousands of salespeople seeking to climb the ladder of success who are not yet successful. These people invariably buttonhole me and ask me to review what they are doing and perhaps put them on the path to sales stardom. My first question to these success seekers is, "Could I see your prospect file?" More often than not, they don't have a prospect file. Many who do show me a file box or rolodex on a shelf or in a drawer that is sparsely filled with some heavily notated, soiled cards. Others drag out coffee-stained lists from seldom-used drawers. Still others offer up as prospects old coupon leads heavily inscribed with hieroglyphics of some type.

Here are my ideas of what a prospect file should consist of and how it should be maintained:

Qualified Names Only: Each name that goes in the prospect file should represent an investor with potential as determined by either of two things: where he or she lives (in an affluent area) or what he or she does. Don't waste time and money calling or mailing prospects with little buying ability.

Screened Names: Have your local manager screen each name in your prospect file prior to your making a sales effort, to prevent time wasted in your prospecting an associate's account.

Lined Cards: Use lined cards only, so that all information can be neatly aligned. *Unlined* cards encourage sprawling, illegible note-writing. Make sure the card is sufficiently large to contain a lot of information and that the back of the card is lined also.

Top security salesmen know that many other Account Executives have good ideas and work plans but fail to achieve good results. The big producer understands that success stems from following through on a work plan for today . . . tomorrow . . . next week . . . next month?

TWO THINGS YOU CAN DO TODAY TO MAKE YOUR BUSINESS GROW!

1. Put all the annuity information into a 3-ring binder for quick reference.

2. Call 5 people to tell them how to:
   —earn high untaxed interest
   —run no principal risk
   —have all principal $ available on demand

Quarterly purge: Every three months the entire prospect file must be reviewed card by card. Prospects repeatedly contacted and found to be unresponsive or deemed to have low potential should be culled and put into a special file for an annual mailing (the "dead" sometimes do come to life!).

Weekly additions: To keep a prospect file "live," it is necessary to feed it new names. A minimum of ten new prospects a week must be placed in the file in order to keep it up to strength, since the quarterly purge weakens it.

Placement near phone: To be effective, the prospect file should be situated next to the phone as a constant reminder that there are calls to be made, appointments to be sought. The prospect file that is hidden from view is a file that never lives up to its potential for getting business. The file constantly in sight puts subtle pressure on you in dull or despondent moments: it reminds you constantly that there is sales work to be done!

A prospect file that is too small is quickly used up and seduces you into slowing down your efforts to seek new accounts. That is why building the file to large numbers is important. Then the excuse "I don't have anyone to call!" can never be used truthfully. Contact each name in the file at least once a month by phone, by mail, or in person. *Consistent prospect contact builds clients.*

Finding Money,
Moving Money, Placing Money

To people who have never sold intangible investments but think they'd like to, the idea of talking to others about money and how to use it to better advantage has great appeal. Possibilities for talking about unlimited earning potential make the salesperson's work seem attractive and somehow easy.

However, experienced purveyors of stock, commodities, bonds, insurance, tax shelters, mutual funds, and other investment products know that getting and keeping a clientele is not easy. The failure rate is high, and a substantial number among those who survive more than three years do not earn attractive incomes.

An important cause of the high failure rate and low earnings is the failure of many in the field to grasp what their job entails. The investment salesperson's job has three main aspects:

1. Finding money
2. Moving money
3. Placing money

Properly understanding these three aspects of the job can help propel you toward the higher earning level you desire.

Finding Money

The first task is finding money—locating the pockets of wealth in the community you serve. (Remember that with the help of the phone, the community you serve can actually be nationwide.) Finding money is a never-ending quest for aggressive, high-income-seeking salespeople. They constantly have to find more and more money from which commissions may flow, to replace dollars that get frozen or flow away. The building of a prospect file, as previously discussed, is the first step in the money-discovery process. The second step is contacting individual prospects to ascertain whether investment dollars are actually available, either in cash-equivalent forms or in other liquid assets. Prospects who have neither cash equivalents nor liquid assets may still have the use of money by means of their borrowing power.

The best place to search for money is among the *known* wealthy. Attendees at investment lectures, or direct-mail respondents are sometimes extremely wealthy. People who have acquired wealth through marriage, divorce, or inheritance are fine prospects. Such people may live in areas that seem unpromising, so you must have an eye open and an ear tuned to every individual with whom you come in contact. Money is often discovered where you least expect it. Furthermore, people who *don't* have investment dollars may lead to and influence those who do.

Moving Money

Once you locate money, you must make your strongest effort to move it under your control. Moving money is the objective of all the selling skills discussed in this book. Moving money may require home or office appointments that take hours and hours of your time. Conversely, money sometimes moves quickly by phone, with just a nudge from you, because the prospect has been thinking about moving money and is simply activated by the timeliness of your call.

In order to turn a prospect into a client, the *money must move.* However, just finding and successfully moving money do not *always* insure sales success in respect to commissions earned. I met a broker once who was not doing well enough although the total capital represented by accounts on his books was over $5 million! He had been successful in finding money and successful in getting the money moved to his firm. Yet all that work and effort was rewarded with very little in the way of commission dollars. One client kept over $1 million in a money-market fund because it was convenient and earned high interest. Nice for the salesman's firm, but no immediate commission for the salesman and only the hope that some day some of those dollars might flow to a commission-producing product.

Another of his clients had transferred a portfolio from another firm to his. Here was a $1 million stock account with a $300,000 debit balance. The salesman had worked hard to find this money. He worked even harder to convince the individual to give up allegiance to the other broker and transfer the account. The big sales hook to influence the transfer was a one-half-percent lower interest charge on the client's debit balance. What a joyful day for my friend when that account transfer was effected. A million dollar client was his, all due to hard work in prospecting and employing selling skills to cause the money to move.

A year later, the salesman had not earned one cent in commissions from this account! The portfolio consisted of stocks, each with an extremely low cost basis—stocks the individual *never intended to sell.* The total dividend income was being used to pay the interest and reduce the debit balance. A good account for his firm because of interest profits the firm might earn, but not a winner for the broker.

It's not enough, then, to find money and make it move. The money must be so positioned as to create a commission flow.

Placing Money

One of the great secrets to selling securities successfully is the concept of money placement. Many salespeople flunk out of the industry because they are simply poor at placing money. After working hard to find and move money, they either lock it up in one-time commission sales or select investments that lose a significant portion of their client's assets, thereby turning off not only future commission flows but referrals as well.

I believe that ambitious securities brokers should concentrate on trying to place the bulk of a client's money in products that will deliver repeat commissions. If the money you find can be made to turn over periodically, each turnover creating a commission, you get an earnings-producing effect denied to our friend above with the virtually useless million-dollar client.

It goes without saying that the client's account should not be churned. Within the bounds of prudence and good money management, many opportunities for beneficial changes dictated by the vari-

Top security salespeople know that prospecting efforts have to be doubled in bear markets. They also know that loss-burdened investors are more receptive to new ideas from other brokers in depressed markets. Are you contacting 10 new prospects daily?

TWO THINGS YOU CAN DO TODAY TO MAKE YOUR BUSINESS GROW!
1. *Set up a 3-ring binder to hold a form file and procedures for handling estate securities.*
2. *Call on 3 attorneys in person to show this estate security valuation service, and seek their personal and estate business.*

ous investment markets as well as by changes in client circumstances will arise. These occasions should be utilized. Sometimes, brokers are so governed by fears generated by their compliance departments that they fail to recommend appropriate changes; as a result, their clients are not well served.

The same reluctance to suggest changes often causes security salespeople to lock up money in the purchases of mutual funds, utility stocks, long-term bonds, or unit trusts. All of these may or may not be "good" investments, but they reduce the turnover of money to a base trickle, necessitating the finding and moving of *new* accounts in order to earn commissions.

My concept of building success in the securities industry revolves around the development of repeat commission business. Try to place found money into the four categories discussed below: Note that the percentages suggested are for the *total* money under your control, not the money in each individual account. The percentages recommended can be altered to suit the individual salesperson's preferences.

Money-Placement Plan

Covered Call Writing: 25 Percent. Approximately one-quarter of all the money you can find and influence to follow you should be placed in a covered-call-option-writing program. This placement generates *repeat commission business* from that same money as stocks are sold due to exercises of the calls, as calls expire and new ones are written, as calls are purchased, and as new calls are written at higher or lower strikes or for longer time periods.

Covered call writing is one of the simplest to understand option activities and, if properly conducted, is quite often recognized as prudent by investors, brokers, and compliance departments.

Customers to whom you recommend this activity must, of course, be suited to it and the type to be satisfied with seeking a high annual return. The proper prospect for covered call writing is a percentage-minded, securities-oriented, active investor who enjoys following the market and is content not to try to get rich quick.

Experience leads me to suggest the following guidelines for the writing of covered calls:

1. *Recommend the purchase of quality stocks that pay at least 4 percent in annual cash dividends.* Make sure that the dividends have been maintained or increased over the most recent five years and that the outlook for future increases looks good. Clients find it easier to retain their equanimity in falling markets if their unrealized losses are eased with the balm of receiving dividends and premiums. Panic action is lessened by this steady influx of money to the client.

2. *Recommend the writing of the longest-term call possible.* (Sometimes the middle month is acceptable if there's not a respectable differential in time premium of the far month over the middle.) I recommend this practice, first, because writing the far-out call brings in the greatest number of advance premium dollars, which gives more instant stock downside protection while lessening the amount of dollars the client invests in the position. Second, writing far-out calls normally reduces the number of decisions required of the investor, which tends to make the procedure more attractive to the busy, sometimes unavailable investor. Third, writing far-out calls sharply reduces the overall commission dollars in comparison to the commission dollars for a consistent investment practice of writing near calls. Finally, writing far-out calls generally results in fewer completed transactions that must be reported for federal taxation purposes. Consequently, the long-term call writer's transaction recording is simpler and potentially less expensive. These four advantages, to my mind, more than offset any potentially slightly higher annualized gain from writing near-term calls.

3. *Recommend writing out-of-the-money calls.* By establishing for the call written a strike price above the stock purchase price (usually

the nearest strike over the stock purchase price), the combination of cash dividends, premiums, and favorable strike price differential increases the potential for profit.

Special Situation Common Stocks: 25 Percent. Approximately one-quarter of the money you find and influence should be committed to special situation common stocks that investors buy intending to sell at a profit some time after holding them longer than one year (the period currently necessary to gain long-term capital gain tax treatment).

Position building for a broker is an important ingredient for success. The security business holds no greater thrill for a broker than building a large (100,000 or more shares) position in a stock, watching it reach a target profit level, and then calling clients and saying those soothing words: "Let's sell now and take a profit!" The clients are served well, and they enjoy the money made, as well as the successful completion of their venture. And the broker has earned a well-deserved commission. Funds from the sale can then be put to work in a new special situation. And hopefully so on ad infinitum.

Such common stocks should be well chosen, research-endorsed, and merchandised in a way to build a significant position. The expectation of a future sale at a profit should be built into the sales presentation. When you truly believe in such a stock and are yourself sold on the recommendation, build into your presentation the recommendation of a future purchase at a lower price if the stock goes down for market reasons (as opposed to a fundamental change in the outlook for the company). Averaging down is not always an investment no-no; many times it results in lowering the average cost of a position that later works out.

Special situation stock investors are often itchy, anxious for the expected force to come and move the stock up. If the stock simply remains stable or drops a little, many investors become bored with the insignificant price fluctuation and want a new recommendation. The turnover occurs, and along with it commissions.

Knowledgeable brokers teach their clients not to fall in love with stocks per se, but to understand that they are simply pieces of paper by means of which profits are sought. Teach your clients to understand that changing one piece of paper for another may provide tax benefits, better profit possibilities, lower risk potential, or higher annual income.

In selecting special situation common stocks for position building, the focus should be on low-risk, high-potential situations as opposed to high-risk, high-potential situations. Why? One reason is that no broker really enjoys the commissions earned from clients' losses, especially those derived from the broker's suggestions. The more important reason is that losses, although traumatic events to the broker and client alike—part of the game—reflect the everpresent risk of being "wrong."

Diversification in an individual's account is also important. If no situation represents a large part of an investor's assets, then a single declining stock—even if not sold in time to prevent a major loss—will not greatly affect the overall portfolio.

Clients will stay with a broker year after year and provide a steady stream of commissions if they make a lot of money or make a little money or even *lose* a little money. But they will leave a broker and cut off commissions *if they lose much money*. Investors stay with brokers often because stock trading provides an interest, excitement, a feeling of involvement outside their usual sphere of activity that can last *as long as the major part of the capital is not lost*. Good brokers avoid high risk. Stock risk cannot always be measured in advance to determine the exact degree of risk to the share buyer. But reasonably accurate downside calculations can be computed for many stocks widely held. Mental (or actual) stop-loss points can also be used as exit points for stocks that fail to move favorably.

Managed Money: 25 Percent. The third quarter of the money you find and influence should be placed in managed-money accounts. Guided commodity accounts are a typical depository for a small per-

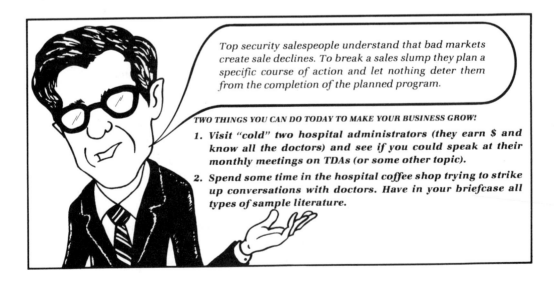

Top security salespeople understand that bad markets create sale declines. To break a sales slump they plan a specific course of action and let nothing deter them from the completion of the planned program.

TWO THINGS YOU CAN DO TODAY TO MAKE YOUR BUSINESS GROW!

1. Visit "cold" two hospital administrators (they earn $ and know all the doctors) and see if you could speak at their monthly meetings on TDAs (or some other topic).

2. Spend some time in the hospital coffee shop trying to strike up conversations with doctors. Have in your briefcase all types of sample literature.

cent of a *wealthy investor's assets.* A $1 million portfolio might have $50,000 dedicated to a guided commodity program where experts provide a diversified commodity portfolio seeking a high annual return. Guidelines about leverage, stop-loss points, breadth of diversification, and order entry procedure are all provided by the manager. You are free to prospect and find new money instead of being tied to the desk watching pork bellies fry or orange juice get squeezed.

Other managed-money accounts are available for equity investments, for option writing, and for risk arbitrage. Commissions from these accounts flow in whether you are sick or well, on vacation or in the office. Commissions generated on a regular, recurring basis provide some degree of security in a very insecure business.

Typically, a broker who places 20 accounts, averaging $50,000 size, with commodity advisers would normally receive $150,000 to $200,000 in annual gross commissions and normally would obtain pretax earnings of $60,000 to $80,000 *each year* the money stayed in the advisers' hands. The potential for even greater commission flow exists if the assets increase substantially in value. The one-time sale of the idea coupled with on-going commissions is a pleasant conjecture and even more pleasant when realized.

One million dollars placed with professional money managers in a normal call writing program might be expected to provide you $50,000 a year in gross commissions (pretax income approximately $17,500). Before you conclude that managed-money accounts in commodities are so lucrative that you should concentrate your efforts in money placement solely in that area, let me hasten to assure you that the risk associated with commodities makes them much more difficult to obtain. Moreover, there are fewer suitable candidates for managed accounts in commodities than for managed accounts in equities. Generally, the amounts placed in equity-managed accounts represent a much greater portion of an investor's assets.

Single Commission Sales: 25 Percent. The fourth quarter of the money you find and can influence should go into a potpourri of single-commission sales that pay a handsome one-time commission and normally result in the money's being locked up in that investment for a long, long time. Such sales are not likely to produce more sales commissions from that same money.

In this category I lump tax shelters, mutual funds, tax-deferred annuities, unit trusts, and long-term bonds (occasionally tax swaps can cause these to turn over). All are good products and certainly play a part in a broker's product mix. They frequently provide additional commission revenue from add-ons or additional purchases, but not from the initial investment dollars.

If you try to build a business on the fourth 25 percent (making it a more dominant factor in your product mix), you will be dependent on constantly finding new clients and new money. If the emphasis is placed on putting money into products that generate repeat business (such as those in the first three money placement suggestions), you are likely to remain in the industry and develop into a large producer.

BUILDING SALESMANSHIP

Increasing Your Sales Power and Income: 3 Magic Words

All sellers of risk investments (stocks, options, commodities, bonds, mutual funds) recommend situations that sometimes produce capital losses for clients, rather than the hoped-for, sought-after capital gains. Sometimes these losses are merely due to general market declines that carry the specific investment to a lower-than-purchase price. Sometimes the losses are due to some specific change in the fundamental aspect of the investment.

Whatever the reason for the decline in value, the investor is less happy with losses than with profits. As long as the loss goes unrealized, the investor can hope that the investment value will increase back to or above the original purchase level. Losses in investment value are often transitory and of short duration; other times they worsen and the investment value appears permanently impaired.

Dealing with an investor who is holding a loss is not the easiest of jobs, especially if the position was entered into at the salesperson's recommendation. Many times sellers change their opinions about the future prospects of an investment they once thought superb. When you find yourself in this situation, contact the investors and tell them exactly why you no longer like your previous choice. Most investors understand risk and appreciate your staying in touch, keeping them informed. Countless clients are "lost" or move on to other salespeople simply because when a client suffers a loss, the salesperson is so uncomfortable that he or she fails to call the client or keep the client properly informed as to what's happening with the investment.

Like most humans, salespeople hate to face the music and admit the error of their ways. Their first bad judgment was in the original recommendation. The second is that, instead of calling clients who have the loss, they often neglect them, thereby making these clients a rather easy target for other salespeople. Occasionally, a seller will compound the problem by offering false hopes of recovery rather than advising acceptance of the loss.

How should you handle a client enmeshed in a losing situation, particularly one that you originally recommended?

First, be honest and straightforward. Call the client and say that the value of the investment has changed, and say why the situation is different. Salespeople with integrity make the same effort to get a client to accept a loss and move the money to a more attractive investment as they expended to get the client to invest originally.

Many clients, however, will not sell anything at a loss. They don't want to give up the hope of making money on a particular investment, or perhaps they want to get even before they get out. The "getevenitis" disease has probably wrought more destruction on investment portfolios than anything else. Rather than recovering to an original entry price, many investments plunge sickeningly to even deeper losses. Investors are also reluctant to accept and realize losses because the very act of doing so proves that their first judgment was wrong. Buying high and selling low is certainly not the way to build assets!

Investors who accept losses can no longer prattle to their loved ones, "Honey, it's only a paper loss. Just wait. It will come back." Investors who realize losses must admit their folly to the IRS when they file that itemized tax return. For all those reasons and more, investors as a whole are reluctant to take losses, even when they feel that to do so is the right course of action.

Sometimes you will prevail with an investor, gain the order to liquidate the losing position, and then hear the investor say, "Send me the proceeds." That phrase signals the eventual termination of your relationship with this particular client.

When you suggest that the client close at a loss a transaction you originally recommended and invest the proceeds in another position you are currently recommending, a real act of faith has to take place. That act of faith can more easily be effected if you make use of some transitional words that I call "magic selling words."

The words that I consider to have magical power in the sense that they make for a more easy acceptance of a loss are these: *"Transfer your assets."* The words by themselves, however, have little force. You must prepare the ground for these magic words.

Top security salespeople know the surest way to mishandle a problem is to avoid facing up to it.

TWO THINGS YOU CAN DO TODAY TO MAKE YOUR BUSINESS GROW!

1. *Get out of the office and see "face to face" two affluent businesspeople or professionals and ask them for an order.*
2. *Call a local charity, such as the YMCA or United Way, and volunteer your services as a solicitor. This gives you the opportunity to meet new people and do a civic good deed.*

"Buy" is a pressure word. If you understand that, you will see that sales are easier to make when the word "buy" is avoided. "Sell" is also a pressure word, and "sell at a loss" is even worse—a depressing, sometimes terrifying, phrase. If those words are avoided and more appealing words substituted, you have a greatly improved chance to consummate additional sales.

To show you how to ease into the magic selling words, "Transfer your assets," look at the dialogue that follows. Assume a broker is talking to a client (or prospect) who owns 500 XYZ bought at $30 and now priced at $20. The broker wants the client to sell 500 XYZ at $20, accepting the loss, due to a changed outlook for XYZ's business. Upon completion of the sale, the broker would like to have the client buy 500 PDQ at $20. PDQ is a company whose prospects appear much brighter in the eyes of the salesman.

Joe Salesman: "John, I have been reviewing your portfolio of securities, particularly your common-stock holdings. What you have invested in XYZ is your assets. I assume that what you want from your assets is the *best chance to grow in value* from the current level, combined with the *least risk of loss*. Isn't that what you are really after?"

John Prospect: "Sure, that's what I want. More gain possibility and less risk. That happy combination isn't so easy to get. Look at my XYZ, for instance."

Joe Salesman: "I have been looking at your XYZ [valid reason for the call], and that's why I'm calling you today. At the time you bought XYZ, earnings were increasing, and prospects looked great. However, unexpected contract cancellations and cost overruns turned an expected increase into a loss [reason for suggesting the transfer].

The near-term future prospects look rather bleak at this time. I called you when the price declined from 30 to 25, but you decided to wait for a possible up-turn closer to your purchase price."

John Prospect: "I was hoping to get out of XYZ at a price closer to even."

Joe Salesman: "I know how you feel [Empathy]. Often I have done the same thing. With XYZ now about 20 it appears to me that you would have a better chance to accomplish what you say you want [client's objective mentioned again], a better chance for your assets to grow in value from the current level combined with a lesser chance of loss. You can meet that goal if you simply *transfer your assets* [the magic words] from 500 XYZ into 500 shares of PDQ. PDQ has none of the current problems affecting XYZ, and the earnings prospects are bright. [The close] They are both approximately the same price. If you make the transfer now you won't have to put up any additional money."

John Prospect: "Well, if you think I will be better off, and since I don't need to put any additional money to make the transfer, go ahead and do it [the order given]."

Read the scenario carefully again and note these crucial elements:

1. The word *sell* was never used.
2. The word *buy* was never used.

Avoiding those two pressure words whenever possible makes sales easier to come by. The two separate transactions (moving out of the loss and moving into a new position) are made to flow together by the magic words "transfer your assets." The prospect thought he was making a single decision, switching one investment into another. He was not being asked to think in terms of selling XYZ and collecting the proceeds, then having to think of many different ways to reinvest the proceeds. Joe Salesman simplified the process and made it easier for John Prospect to make the move by focusing John's attention on the following key sales points:

1. Increasing the gain potential of his assets
2. Decreasing the risk of loss possibility
3. Avoiding the investing of additional funds to make the transfer

Sales Hint. (Whenever possible make the purchase amount the same as or lower than the sales proceeds.) If necessary, as additional sales power you can bring the tax deductibility of the loss to the prospect's attention.

In 1973 I was asked to conduct a special sales meeting in my firm's Birmingham, Alabama, branch. The branch had 16 experienced salesmen. Their mood at the time was one of despair, due to a sharply declining stock and bond market. The regional manager brought me in to motivate, stimulate, and energize the loss-stricken account executives.

I presented my sales techniques and ideas with remarkable clarity in an exhilarating manner. The presentation certainly counted as one of my best—an A+ rendition. (Bashful I am not!)

When I told the assembled group of the power that lay in my magic words, "Transfer your assets," and how those words might produce sales the very next day and forever after, there was a general wave of enthusiasm. However, one man in the back of the room obviously did not share the group's delight over my suggested phrase. He stood up and, in a deep Alabama drawl, said, "LeRoy, that's nonsense!"

Calmly, trying to keep him from destroying the meeting's effectiveness, I said, "Jimmie, I have found this phrase to work wonders in all of the other 49 states. Tell me, why do you think it won't work here in Alabama?"

Jimmie replied, "I'll tell you why it won't work here in Birmingham. It's because I have financially killed every investor in and around Birmingham who had any significant amount of money. I sold my clients real-estate investment trusts that came out at $20 per share and later went to $1 per share! And I sold them others that did even worse! I have had the unique ability to select the worst performing stocks recommended by our Research Department."

He continued, "I happen to be one of the best amateur golfers in the state of Alabama, and I can't get a foursome to play golf with me any more. I have really *destroyed* people. Following me, my former friends have lost their kids' education money, seen their retirement plans disappear. When it comes to stocks I've just been snake bit. *Your magic words* won't work on my clients!"

"Jimmie," I said, "that is a mighty sad tale, but I believe my words will work even with your clients and their sadly worsened financial condition."

Jimmie said, "You meet me in the office tomorrow morning at 9:00, and I will show you my account book. I'll prove to you that your phrase won't even make them budge."

Who could resist a challenge like that? I agreed to meet Jimmie the next morning. At 9:00 A.M. I was sitting at his desk, leafing through the ledger pages where his clients' trades and positions were itemized. As I poured over the pages, tears came to my eyes. He really *had* financially damaged everyone. The best looking of his stock positions was down 50 percent in value!

Jimmie looked at the expression on my face. "I told you I was snake bit. Now do you believe me?"

"I believe you have had bad luck, bad advice, or bad judgment, Jimmie. I also believe that my magic words will work here in Alabama, just as they have elsewhere."

"Okay, let me call this guy. He used to be my buddy. Played golf with me every Saturday and Sunday, but now he doesn't want to talk to me. He owns 1000 XYZ bought at 20, and now 9."

"Call him, Jimmie, and give the story on PDQ. Tell him to *transfer his assets* from one to the other and why you think he should."

"All right, I'll give it a try, but you sit right here, 'cause I just feel uneasy about talking to him, considering all he's lost."

Here's a recap of the conversation between Jimmie and his erstwhile friend and client, good buddy Joe:

A wise man once said:
Anyone who stops learning is old, whether this happens at 20 or 80.

TWO THINGS YOU CAN DO TODAY TO MAKE YOUR BUSINESS GROW!

1. **Review all the names in your prospect file. Have you called each or written each within the last 30 days?**

2. **See that all recent names of prospects from ad leads or whatever source are properly placed on prospecting cards in your desk-top file.**

Joe: "Hello."

Jimmie: "Joe, this is Jimmie. How ya doing? I am sittin' here with a vice president from Noo Yawk. He likes a stock, PDQ, and he's done looked at the thousand XYZ you got that's giving you a pain. He says you better transfer your a— out of that one, into this one right now!"

Joe: "Well! if that's what he thinks I should do, Jimmie, go ahead and do it."

After Jimmie had written and entered the two order tickets to sell 1000 shares and to buy 1000 shares, I made the following observation: "Jimmie, you thought my magic words wouldn't work here in Alabama, but they did, just as I told you they would. You have two good orders to prove it. But Jimmie, you would have gotten the order just as easily if you had used the phrase I taught you, *'transfer your assets,'* rather than your abbreviated version."

You who sell intangibles will, I hope, forever remember Jimmie and his sad tale of woe. I hope you will also remember that you can make a lot more sales when you say "Transfer your assets" than when you use the higher pressure, two-decision phrase "Sell this. Buy that."

Making a Sale: The 4-Gs Method

In order to sell an investment product, there are four simple steps to master.

Step 1:
Get Someone to Listen

This, of course, is the step on which most failures or low producers stumble. They don't get enough people each day to listen to their sales pitch. You can't expect to achieve sales success unless you talk about the merits of your investment products to a large number of prospective buyers—either current accounts or new prospects. Without an audience no one can build sales success. If you really want to make it big, be sure each day you get 20 or more people to *listen to you* tell them about an investment idea.

Step 2:
Get Their Interest

Just talking to a large number of prospective buyers each day will not produce substantial sales unless the salesperson gets their interest. The biggest interest-getting device available is the idea of the prospect's potential profit as a possible result of the investment you recommend. The appeal to greed still is the most powerful sales approach, and the one that most often works. Staying within compliance guidelines, point out the profit potential and you will rivet the prospect's attention. Any risk associated with the proposed investment should be presented fully and clearly, but that does not mean you have to de-emphasize the profit potential. To make the sale, prospects must be made to see sugarplums dancing in front of their eyes.

Step 3:
Give Facts and Benefits

Prospects who invest hard-earned, retained dollars want to reassure themselves of the correctness of their judgment in making the investment. The reassurance is gained from the salesperson's concise, accurate, enthusiastic presentation of *the facts* about the investment and listing *the benefits* that may accrue to the buyer. Constant repetition of the facts and benefits is usually necessary to make an imprint on the prospect's mind. Give the benefits and facts many times over in a single sales presentation. Follow up by asking the prospect to repeat the salient facts and benefits. Selling is not a one-sided undertaking. Get the prospect involved in the conversation by asking questions and you will be on your way to making sales.

Step 4:
Get the Order

No matter how many people listen to an investment idea, get their greed level up, and understand the benefits and facts, *no* commissions are earned unless an order is obtained. Many salespeople do a fine job in advancing through the first three steps to sales success but then trip and fall on the fourth step. Getting the order is the objective, yet many salespeople fail to get orders because they (1) are afraid actually to ask the prospect to buy, (2) they wait for the prospect to voluntarily commit funds, and/or (3) they don't know the many different techniques for asking for orders.

The fear of being told "no" influences many sellers of investments to talk too long or to become repetitious to the point that they actually alienate would-be buyers. The trick is *always* to ask for an order after making sure that the prospect clearly understands the facts and benefits of the proposal. (Asking for an order more than once is a selling fundamental.)

In order to accomplish these four steps, you must become a good question asker. Politely asking pertinent questions may open up a prospect who will disgorge reams of information that you can file in your memory bank (and later on the prospect information card) to use in getting the order.

Here are some great questions I have used or seen others use that help loosen the prospect's tongue. Listen carefully to the answers; they will give direction to your sales effort.

Super Questions for Prospective Investors

1. Can you use *tax-free* income?
2. What stock worries you the most right now?
3. What is your tax bracket?
4. What was the most profitable security investment you ever made?
5. What do you think a really good broker should do for you?
6. Are you satisfied with the return you are getting on your investments?
7. Would you like to pay less in income taxes?
8. Would you like a Standard & Poor's sheet on every stock you *now* own?

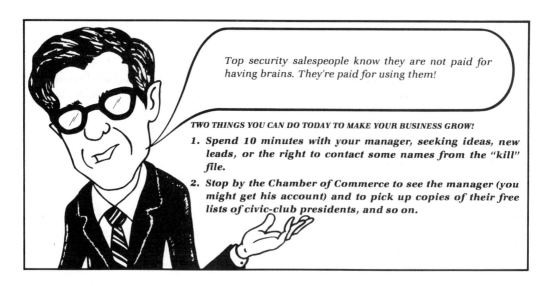

Top security salespeople know they are not paid for having brains. They're paid for using them!

TWO THINGS YOU CAN DO TODAY TO MAKE YOUR BUSINESS GROW!

1. Spend 10 minutes with your manager, seeking ideas, new leads, or the right to contact some names from the "kill" file.
2. Stop by the Chamber of Commerce to see the manager (you might get his account) and to pick up copies of their free lists of civic-club presidents, and so on.

9. What are you doing to protect your assets against inflation?
10. Would you like a free portfolio valuation?
11. Would you like to have all of your municipal bonds priced at current market and graded as to quality?
12. How did you get where you are today?
13. When you retire, how much do you think you will need each month in *after-tax* dollars?
14. Do you have enough insurance to take care of your loved ones adequately when you die?

Your own ingenuity can add to the above list. The main idea is to learn to ask questions bearing on the needs and wants of the prospect's investment program.

Be a good listener. Prospects' responses will guide you concerning the products they might need and their receptiveness to a prosposal. The more you can learn about prospects, the easier it will be for you to sell, and the very best way to learn is to *ask questions!*

The Super-Powerful Appointment-Getter

Many securities salespeople know their products well and can be very persuasive in presenting their ideas to a prospect. However, a great many of these same securities salespeople are not as financially successful as they might be, due to their inability to get a constant flow of highly qualified prospects to grant face-to-face interviews.

Readers should certainly be aware that selling securities successfully is basically a "numbers" game in the sense that the higher the number of actual daily prospecting contacts you make by phone or in person, the more accounts you will open—and the greater your flow of commission dollars will be.

Of course, the number of contacts made daily isn't the sole determinant of financial success. Knowledge of product and skill in presenting the facts and benefits plays a major role also. But no matter how knowledgeable and skillful a securities salesperson happens to be, if only a few hear "the story," the commission flow will be weak. So learning how to get qualified prospects to agree to see you face to face is the subject of this short chapter.

In January 1982, a young man attended my sales training program. He had a burning desire to succeed and was willing to work as much and as hard as possible to attain success. He decided to make the telephone cold call his primary prospecting tool. With that in mind, he honed and refined a prospecting call around a *specific investment* product—a call that was designed to get him a face-to-face interview in either the prospect's office or his own.

His consistent, daily effort using this *particular phone approach* enabled him to open an average 35 to 45 accounts per month! By the end of his second year in the securities business, he had produced over $1,000,000. That was the finest production performance of any trainee I have ever coached in my brokerage career. Superlatives like "fantastic" and "outstanding" are not really adequate. To draw an analogy, it would be like a rookie baseball player batting over .400 or a high school runner doing a 3:50 mile.

The following is his approach. Learn it well, and see that it is delivered to 30 or more qualified prospects day in and day out, and perhaps you will experience appointment success that will please you, even if it doesn't result in a record as outstanding as his.

Broker: "Mr. Morgan?"

Prospect: "Yes, this is John Morgan."

Broker: "John, this is _____ at _____. We are calling key business people (retirees) like you today about an excellent investment opportunity. Before I describe the opportunity, I need your answer to one question. Do you mind if I ask it?"

Prospect: "No, go ahead and ask."

Broker: "Do you have any money anywhere now earning you less than _____?" (Fill in the current GNMA rate.)

Prospect: "Yes, I do."

(Almost everyone has money in a money fund, money-market deposit account, savings account, or CD *earning less than the GNMA rate*.)

Broker: "Would you like to earn _____ (fill in the current GNMA rate) on your money that you say is now earning you less, if your principal and interest payments were guaranteed by the United States Government?"

Prospect: "Certainly, I would, but I am not aware of any government return like you mentioned."

Broker: "What I would like to do is meet with you at your convenience *this week* to explain to you all of the benefits and details of a particular U.S. Government-guaranteed investment. When would be the best time for you?"

Prospect: "How about tomorrow afternoon at 4:00 P.M. *at my office?*"

Broker: "I'll be there, and I am sure you will like what I will show and tell you."

Good security salespeople spend time and effort preparing their sales presentations to make them effective. They have learned to adhere to the three important rules for successful sales presentations: (1) prepare a good opening; (2) prepare an excellent close; (3) keep the two very close together!

TWO THINGS YOU CAN DO TODAY TO MAKE YOUR BUSINESS GROW!

1. **Get approval to take the 144 examination.**
2. **Read the 144 material so that you can become a "miner" of 144 gold.**

Readers should note carefully that at no time is the term "Ginnie Mae" used. Those words are not well understood even by many sophisticated investors. Instead, the whole phone call was geared to try to obtain three "yeses" from the prospect.

Yes #1: The investor admits to having some funds earning less than the current GNMA rate.

Yes #2: The investor expresses a desire to earn a higher return if interest and principal are safe from default risk.

Yes #3: The investor agrees to meet face to face and learn more about the opportunity.

All securities salespeople should be aware that GNMAs are complicated investments, whether packaged in a unit trust or purchased in individual certificates. To meet compliance department guidelines, a full explanation of benefits and risks should be delivered verbally and preferably backed up with available literature.

Once the appointment is granted, half the battle is over. Face to face, my young sales star "closed" over 90% of the prospects. Many bought GNMAs; others, not liking certain aspects such as taxable income, opted for municipal bonds or municipal investment trusts.

Remember: When trying to emulate the successful efforts of this sales star, his calling was *restricted to highly qualified people*, people that he judged qualified by where they lived ("high rent" district) or their occupation (brain surgeons, corporate presidents, and the like).

Many brokers fail to achieve their lofty financial objective simply because many of their prospecting efforts are spent on prospects with very little financial expertise or "wherewithal." When orders are obtained, they are usually small in size. The better qualified your list of prospects, the greater your chances of success in developing substantial accounts.

Using "Chair Position"
to Help Make the Sale

Face-to-face selling can be the most stimulating, demanding, and challenging of the various selling techniques. Insurance salespeople, stockbrokers, sellers of commodities, and mutual fund salespeople normally close their biggest accounts at personal meetings with prospects. Face-to-face selling was, for me, the most rewarding and exhilarating of all.

There are many advantages of being "eyeball to eyeball." Observant sellers can carefully watch the facial expressions and body action of prospects. Observations can clue sellers in to alter a sales approach or try an entirely new one. The great flexibility of using visual displays, exhibits, and various third-party proofs to help convince the prospect to buy simply isn't available except in face-to-face sales encounters.

Once the face-to-face appointment has been granted, and the salesperson is in the prospect's presence, the real work of trying to obtain an order begins.

In the Prospect's Territory

When appointments are in prospects' homes or offices, it is quite likely that prospects will place a barrier between themselves and you. Such barriers are meant to place you in a position inferior to the prospect. Sometimes a barrier is there to show the prospect's power and authority. The barrier, most often, is a desk or a table. Frequently a desk is in an elevated area, the chair behind it, again to try to make you constantly aware of the prospect's power and superiority. The barrier is intended either to prevent a sale from taking place or to produce a sale with the most favorable terms possible—for the order-giver.

Whenever you are faced with such surroundings, ask the prospect for permission to move your chair *next to the prospect's chair*. Most often, permission will be granted, especially if you carefully explain that by sitting together at the desk or table (or on a couch), the prospect will be in a better position to see, and to interpret, the visual data in the presentation.

If necessary, take pains to show how hard it will be to see the material if you and the prospect are not seated side by side. Sell this "we" approach as your participation in helping the prospect better his or her financial situation. By breaking down the social distance created by the barrier, you can take a friendlier, less aloof attitude as both you and the prospect, shoulder to shoulder, pore over the details of the prosposal. *Note: Be sure to keep yourself immaculate.* Heavy body odor or bad breath can destroy the impact of a well-presented idea.

In Your Territory

If the face-to-face appointment has been scheduled to take place in your office, arrange the chairs side by side (or use a couch if one is available) before the prospect arrives. The "together we decide" approach is a powerful closing technique.

If you are trying to sell two prospects (usually a husband and a wife) try to place your chair *between their chairs* so that all three of you can easily see the visuals while you are extolling the virtues of the proposed investment.

By placing yourself between the prospects, you divide their united resistance to your proposal. They can't kick one another under the table (at least not without alerting you!), squeeze a hand, or easily exchange a warning look. "Divide and conquer" is a good way to win a battle or a sale!

Too many offices give little thought to the chair position of client and account executive. Firms invariably plan desk layouts so that the prospect is opposite to the broker in a standard adversary pose. In my view, this layout is totally wrong, and one that leads to other problems. In the typical brokerage office, the salesperson's desk and chair face the ticker tape and the client's chair faces the broker. This not only makes the "we" approach impossible, but the running tape is constantly in the broker's sight. What a distraction! The broker's tape watching often makes prospects or clients resentful.

If the purpose of the appointment is to sell the client, arrange for a side-by-side presentation to be made in a conference room, if one is available; or arrange your private area so that you and the prospect can work closely together to shape the prospect's financial horizon without the distraction of tape happenings.

Getting the Order:
4 Kinds of Helpful Evidence

In trying to persuade prospects to commit money to the offered product or service, skilled salespeople bring in all the evidence they can muster. Yet the sellers of intangibles face peculiar problems when presenting a specific type of evidence. Their problems are different from those facing sellers of autos, houses, boats, typewriters, television sets, and the like. Yet if the evidence is strong and logically presented, more orders will result.

Evidence comes in several varieties. For the seller of intangibles, some types of evidence are more effective than others. These are the main types of evidence that can bring the prospective buyer of an intangible to a successful close.

1. Samples of the products
2. Anecdotes about users of the products
3. Statistics
4. Endorsements from third parties

Samples of the Products

Sellers of tangible products get terrific mileage from demonstrating their product to prospects. They want prospects to get their senses involved. The smell of new leather, the feel of seating comfort, the beauty of a paint job, the sound, the look and feel of fabric all are artfully presented to make prospects want the offered item more than they want to hold onto their money. Demonstrating investment products is not so easy, but it can be done.

If you can involve prospects in using their senses, even intangibles become more "real" and thus more likely to interest prospects.

When I was a broker trying to establish a large position in a common stock, I would contact the company and ask for samples or miniatures of products they made or sold. I used these in demonstrations to my prospects. Most companies are extremely cooperative; after all, they want to acquire more shareowners.

At one point, Cooper Tire and Rubber Company shares looked very good. Our analyst loved the company, earnings were good, and the dividend yield was high. But I was having difficulty in getting investors to purchase shares because the name Cooper was just not as familiar as General Tire, Goodrich, and Goodyear. I called the company and asked the public relations people to send me a cross-section of a belted bias tire, at that time a hot item in the replacement tire market. Familiar as I was with Cooper's financial data, I wouldn't have known a belted bias tire if I'd tripped over one!

A few weeks after my call, a truck pulled up to the front of the office and the driver entered, announcing, "I have a delivery for Mr. Gross!"

The receptionist pointed me out, and the driver asked, "Where do you want it?"

The secret of selling is to show prospects that your product could help them obtain something they really want.

TWO THINGS YOU CAN DO TODAY TO MAKE YOUR BUSINESS GROW!

1. *Select a heavily available muni bond and fill out 10 muni bond mailers to mail to prospects. Be sure to record their names to follow up with phone calls in one week.*
2. *Call 10 clients to sell them about the muni bonds that you are going to suggest to prospects.*

"Tax-free" is a magic phrase!

I pointed to a spot near my desk. He went out and came back rolling a dolly holding a huge, six-foot-high wooden crate! He rolled this monster off the dolly, placed it on the floor near my desk, got his receipt, and was on his way, leaving me to struggle with my "demonstrator." With the help of a chisel, a hammer, and three friends, I was able to uncrate it and view my lovely piece of evidence.

There it was! A life-size new tire mounted on a wooden display emblazoned with the Cooper name! The top part of the tire was cut away to show different colored belts, each clearly labeled and self explanatory.

What a piece of evidence! You could see it! Touch it! Smell the new rubber smell! At a glance you could understand what the company made and how the tires were constructed.

With some rearranging I was able to keep that display near my desk. As prospects and clients came to my office for appointments, they would look at this awesome piece of evidence—feel it—sniff if—look at the various colored belts. When I then told them the financial data about Cooper, they bought the shares, for they had gained an immediate understanding of belted bias tires and the replacement market. The product sample helped get orders that words or fact sheets alone could not.

Showing a product sample has subsequently been used to market hundreds of thousands of shares of different stocks.

Think about how a piece of evidence relates to the intangibles you sell—evidence that can be felt, tasted, heard, smelled, or seen. Product samples are one of the most powerful forms of evidence and should be used at every opportunity in trying to make a sale.

Anecdotes about Users of the Products

User stories are another powerful form of evidence put to work by sellers in all fields. Telling true stories about how others have benefited from a particular product goes a long way toward convincing new prospects to buy. Buyers everywhere want to know that others have bought, used, and are satisfied with a product they are considering. Buyers are usually aware that there are dissatisfied owners of the suggested product, but the reassurance of hearing about the good experiences of others is often the evidence necessary to close the sale.

Brokers featuring stocks will benefit any time they can relate user stories about investors who bought ZYX when it was low and are now sitting on a handsome profit. Or they do well to point out an analyst's past recommendations that brought success to those who followed the advice.

The seller of tax shelters should gather a collection of user stories built around dollars saved for particular clients and potential profit possibilities retained. Prominent sports figures and other nationally known investors who committed some of their funds to these investments are often mentioned in magazines. Local buyers often give permission for their stories to be used.

Sellers of insurance should store up a supply of user stories, such as those about people who bought policies providing certain policy benefits that were later paid as promised. People who are being encouraged to buy an intangible need, want, and love the support of user stories. The stories are pieces of evidence that make sales presentations more credible.

Warning:

User stories properly presented build sales, but false user stories lead to loss of credibility, order cancellations, even law suits. Make sure any user story you relate is accurate, true, and supportable. Equally important is adequate stress on any risk of loss. Selling fairly is the only mode to pursue in building a quality, long-lasting business.

Statistics

As long as people have been selling, statistics in one form or another have been a highly favored type of evidence. Statistics are the chief weapon in the arsenal of the seller of intangibles.

By themselves, statistics can be boring, meaningless, and actually counterproductive. If you throw too great a volume of numbers at the prospect, a turnoff is the most likely result.

To be effective, pertinent statistics must be separated from non-pertinent surrounding data. The statistics you show to a prospect must be easily understood, clear to the ear or eye. If you are using printed data, make sure they appear in bold, easy-to-read numbers.

Charts, fact sheets, income statements, balance sheets, earnings, dividends, hypothetical proposals, and past results are all statistical evidence available to help you in your search for that "yes" answer to a prosposal. Colorful, large, clear illustrations bearing on a single point are usually the most effective.

Used in conjunction with the other selling-skill techniques, statistics help make sales come easier, but don't become so statistic-

Good security salespeople know that success comes in can's, failures in can'ts!

TWO THINGS YOU CAN DO TODAY TO MAKE YOUR BUSINESS GROW!

1. **Call the convertible trader for a possible merchandisable idea about a good value or new risk arbitrage opportunity you could sell to suitable investors.**

2. **Call at least 10 people with a convertible arbitrage idea while it's fresh and you are enthused.**

conscious that you deliver numbers and facts machine-gun fashion to the point that little actually gets through to the prospect. Under these conditions, what does get through is often negatively received.

Keep statistics simple and few in number. Use them judiciously to spice up your presentation. Use statistics to quantify *the benefits* and *respond to the needs and desires of your prospects* so that the prospect can justify spending money.

When you are presenting statistics for the prospect to read, make sure they meet the following conditions:

1. Bold, easy-to-read type
2. Color contrasts
3. Spotlights on single statistics
4. Simple to understand
5. Relevant to the product being offered

When you are telling the prospect statistical evidence, make sure it meets the following conditions:

1. Clear and easy to understand
2. Concise (brevity makes for a more receptive client)
3. Relevant to the product
4. Narrowly focused on a specific topic or feature
5. Stated slowly and forcefully

Endorsements from Third Parties

The endorsement of a product by some third party, preferably a person or source well known to the prospect, is powerful evidence.

The third-party endorsement is often a written testimonial by a happy user or a favorable article by a writer in a prestigious magazine or newspaper. Evidence of this type usually stresses all key points and advantages (sometimes the disadvantages) of the proposed investment. Messages of this kind usually get across to prospects.

Keep a three-ring binder with tab dividers for the various products that provide your commission revenue. Whenever you receive written testimonials and are given permission to use them by the writers, copy them and file them in the binder. Favorable articles about a product are reinforcement for your suggestions for the prospect's money.

You can let prospects take a ring binder home to read. Or they can go over the endorsements in your office. Either way, written endorsements immerse prospects deeper into the product, and that is a positive step.

Selling Savvy: 6-Way System

One of the more difficult things salespeople have to learn in order to ply their trade successfully is to organize the sales presentation in a logical sequence so that it becomes easy for a buyer to say yes. Selling investments, intangible products that put the client's own savings at risk, requires a subtle approach. It takes careful conceptualization and speech to gain that wanted order. Making your sales presentation conform to the six-part format discussed below can improve your average at getting the buyer to say yes.

Point 1:
Point Out a Profit Potential

The preceding chapter emphasized trying to get a prospect interested in the offered product. *Nothing* captures interest faster or keeps it at a higher level than the mouth-watering thought of a profit. If the potential gain is large, your prospect's interest focuses sharply on your next comments.

Be sure that you lead off with your big gun in the sales pitch: the possible profit for the prospect. Do not, however, overstate the possibility of gain. To stay in business you must build credibility and live within the boundaries established by compliance departments, regulatory agencies, and simple good business ethics.

Here are some typical interest-generating openers:

Illustration 1: Common Stock

"John Prospect?"

"Yes."

"This is Joe Salesman with [the firm]. Our Research Department has just come up with an idea that *might make money for you—maybe as much as 50 percent or more* over the next 12 months. I need just a couple of minutes to tell you why our analyst strongly recommends that this high-quality stock be bought now."

Illustration 2: Tax-Deferred Annuity

"John Prospect?" "Yes." "This is Jill Saleswoman with [the firm]. We have an idea that might make money for you. Many of our clients are now earning over *10 percent annually, free from current income taxes*, without risking a single dollar of principal. You might want to learn what they are doing to legally avoid current taxes while keeping their *savings safe from risk*."

Point 2:
State Three Essential Facts

Unless you back up your talk about profit potential with some supporting facts, prospects will normally not believe you. They will

Enthusiasm is refreshing. It's the magic ingredient that makes one seller stand head and shoulders above competitors. And how easy it is to be enthusiastic about options, TDAs, muni bonds, or undervalued stocks!

TWO THINGS YOU CAN DO TODAY TO MAKE YOUR BUSINESS GROW!

1. **See that all of your prospects are on cards in desk file—not on lists in your drawer or file cabinet. Remember, out of sight—out of mind.**

2. **Delete names from your prospect file of the deceased, moved, or just no possibility. A prospect file, to be rewarding, must be filled with real possibilities.**

just dismiss the potential, and you, from their presence and from mind.

In order to soften the direct approach of pointing out the profit potential, it is absolutely necessary to furnish the prospect with at least three incontrovertible pertinent facts to add believability to what you say about the reward potential. These facts must quickly follow your statement of the profit possibility.

Illustration 1: Common Stock

"Here are some of the reasons why our analyst likes the stock right now. *The shares at 20 are selling 30 percent below book value* and near the low for the year. *The earnings have been higher each year for the past 10 consecutive years. And the dividend has been raised each year for 10 consecutive years.*"

Illustration 2: Tax-Deferred Annuity

"Our clients, who hate paying current income taxes as you do, like the fact that they *can earn currently untaxed income, at a high rate* [*specify the rate*] *guaranteed for at least one year*. In addition to avoiding current taxes and getting high interest, they love the security of knowing that they can get all or part of their money on demand to meet any sudden need and that they are *guaranteed against loss of principal*. A lot of people today are earning taxable interest at a rate lower than they could earn in currently untaxed interest. They pay more in taxes simply because they are not aware of how to pay less, earn more, yet be absolutely safe."

Point 3:
Give Two Primary Benefits

After carefully imprinting on the prospect's mind a few key facts about the product being offered, shift the flow of conversation to the benefits that will accrue to the prospect once the money has been turned over to you. In stressing the benefits, strive to speak *slowly, distinctly, forcefully* so that the message really gets across to the prospect.

Remember, *repetition* helps the prospect understand and become convinced! See that the benefits are voiced at least twice in each sales presentation and you will be on your way to more closes.

Illustration 1: Common Stock

"Getting the stock at this low level will provide a *real benefit to you* in terms of locking in a *high return on your money of 10 percent* from a dividend that has been increased in each of the last 10 years. Another benefit to you is the *potential low-taxed, long-term capital gain* should the stock reach our analysts' target."

Illustration 2: Tax-Deferred Annuity

"Putting money into this tax-deferred annuity right now provides a real benefit to you in being able to *get a 10-year guarantee* that your money can *never* earn you less than 8 percent a year but *could* earn you more. Another benefit to you is in *not having to pay federal or state taxes on your interest earnings* while your money is at work."

Point 4: Point Out Risk

In selling intangible products it is paramount that you avoid damaging your credibility. To develop repeat commissions and a flow of referrals, you must give the prospect confidence in you. Prospects must feel that what you say is honestly presented without omitting any possible negatives. Failing to note any potential risk adequately is a flaw that is most often found in sales presentations made by unsuccessful representatives.

Most salespeople mistakenly believe that pointing out risk or disclosing a sales charge will kill the prospect's interest. Nothing could be farther from the truth. A prospect who has been properly educated as to the risks as well as the reward potential is always a more satisfied client. (Such prospects also have little basis for complaints or lawsuits.)

The message should be quite clear: point out all the risk you can foresee under the *worst imaginable circumstances.* The worst-case possibility can then be softened by restating the potential profit probabilities based on your own or your firm's best guesstimates.

Illustration 1: Common Stock

"*The risk looks low* as the shares are *selling near their lowest price of the last 10 years,* while the per-share earnings are highest in their

Top security salespeople learn to answer objections before they are raised. They present their sales ideas in a manner that kills off negative thoughts before they become implanted in a prospect's mind.

TWO THINGS YOU CAN DO TODAY TO MAKE YOUR BUSINESS GROW!

1. *Call your college alumni office and get a current list of local alumni to prospect.*
2. *Draw a circle on your daytimer and enter the number of prospects you asked for an order today! (It had better be a double digit!)*

history. No one can guarantee any stock's future price, but judging from historical price action, your downside risk looks minimal if you buy now."

Illustration 2: Tax-Deferred Annuity

"Very few areas are available where you can put your money to work at a high rate of interest, avoid paying current income taxes, yet *run no risk of losing even one dollar of principal.* Yes, you heard me correctly! With a tax-deferred annuity, your principal is absolutely guaranteed safe against loss by the issuing insurance company."

Point 5:
Compare the Benefits Potential Versus Risk

When investing money, careful investors try to assay the potential risk versus the potential reward. If the foreseeable risks are greatly outweighed by the potential benefits, an order is more easily obtained.

Visually or verbally offer the prospect a comparison, a comparison that *fairly* shows all degrees of risk that might exist and then compares the potential loss to the potential gain. This approach tends to clarify in the prospect's mind the wisdom and prudence of the suggested money placement (assuming, naturally, that the comparison points out a clear case for accepting the risk).

Illustration 1: Common Stock

"When you weigh our *downside risk estimate of approximately 15 percent, based on historical prices, versus the potential gain in value, over the next year or two, of 50 percent or more,* you might want to buy more than 1000 shares. Consider also the fact that you would *be getting 10 percent in annual dividends* versus the 5 *percent you are now receiving* on your bank savings."

Illustration 2: Tax-Deferred Annuity

"I want to *compare for you the difference,* in your 50-percent tax bracket, in *earning 7¼ percent in taxable interest* on your time deposit *versus earning 7¼ percent in untaxed interest* from a tax-deferred annuity. Using the $20,000 you have available now, in 20 years you would have over $100,000 more, all without undertaking any greater risk."

Point 6:
Ask for the Order

Salespeople dependent upon commissions know that in order to survive and thrive, they must get orders. Skilled sellers of intangibles understand that to get orders, they must ask for the order rather than wait and pray for the prospect to buy. A concept that seems difficult for many people to accept is that most securities and insurance contracts are *sold by the efforts of the sellers,* not passively selected by prospects.

In learning the selling process and in developing and delivering sales presentations according to the system set forth in this chapter, you can perform well in the first five parts and then dissipate the value of your effort by not boldly asking for the order.

Prospects like to be sold! They like being asked to buy, encouraged to make decisions. Don't blow future sales simply because you get cold feet at the very end and lack the courage to ask for an order. A useful technique is to ask for an order several times during a sales presentation. Many sales are closed only after asking the client to buy two or three different times in the same selling interview.

Illustration 1: Common Stock

"Now that you have carefully weighed the potential in this stock versus the risk, *do you want to get 2000 shares or 1500 shares?* Keeping in mind the annual yield of 10 percent as well as the gain potential, I would suggest that you acquire 2000 shares. Which quantity is better for you right now while the stock is low?"

Illustration 2: Tax-Deferred Annuity

"Judging from your comments, you clearly understand that your money in this tax-deferred annuity will earn high interest untaxed until you later take it out. Knowing that your money is guaranteed safe and available, would you prefer to transfer $50,000 or $40,000 from your savings to take advantage of the current high rate? Which amount do you think is best for you right now?"

Putting It All Together

Now let's put all six parts of our illustrated sales presentations together and observe the flow, the continuity. The proper construction and sequence of a sales presentation greatly improves the possibility of getting the order. Good preparation followed by a good delivery will provide commission dollars (the level of commission dollars determined generally by the number of presentations given). The more you talk about your products to qualified prospects, the greater your opportunity for success.

Top security salespeople have learned the value of their time. They segregate their work into two categories: (1) sales activities, (2) nonsales-producing duties. All items in (2) must be done before the selling day begins or after the selling time is over.

TWO THINGS YOU CAN DO TODAY TO MAKE YOUR BUSINESS GROW!

1. *Clean up your desk area! Throw away old, out-dated papers. You will feel better and work better.*
2. *Check your prospect file to see that it contains at least 1000 names and phone numbers on cards. If not, start building that number.*

Illustration 1: Common Stock

Broker: "John Prospect?"

Prospect: "Yes."

Broker: [Potential Profit] "This is Joe Salesman with [your firm]. Our Research Department has just come out with an idea that might make money for you, maybe as much as 50 percent or more over the next 12 months. I need just a couple of minutes to tell you why our analyst strongly recommends that this high-quality stock be bought now."

Prospect: "All right. I have a couple of minutes."

Broker: [Facts] "This stock is LRG Corporation. Here are the reasons why our analyst likes the stock right now. The shares at 20 are selling 30 percent below book value. The earnings have been higher each year for the past 10 consecutive years, and the dividend has been raised each year for 10 consecutive years."

Prospect: "That sounds pretty good."

Broker: [Benefits] "It is good, in my opinion. Getting the stock at this low level will provide a real benefit to you in terms of locking in a high return on your money—10 percent—from a dividend that has been increased in each of the last 10 years. Another benefit to you is the potential low-taxed, long-term capital gain should the stock reach our analyst's target."

Prospect: "Look, it sounds okay, but I've heard good stock stories before. What's the risk?"

Broker: [Risk] "The risk looks low to our analyst and to me as the shares are selling near their lowest price of the last 10 years, while the per-share earnings are the highest in their history. No one can guarantee any stock's future price, but judging from historical price action, your downside risk looks minimal if you buy now."

Prospect: "You make it sound very attractive."

Broker: [Comparison of Risk versus Benefits] "It not only sounds good, John, but it is good when you compare our downside risk estimate of 15 percent versus the potential 50 percent or more gain over the next year or two. Consider also the fact that you would be getting 10 percent in annual dividends versus the 5½ percent you are now receiving on your bank savings."

Prospect: "What are the shares selling for now?"

Broker: "The last sale was at $20."

Prospect: "And what did you say the dividend rate was?"

Broker: [Asking for Order] "Two dollars per share annually and paid fifty cents quarterly. I want you to keep in mind the annual yield is 10 percent plus the capital gain potential. Now that you have carefully weighed the potential benefits versus the risk, do you want me to try to get you 2000 shares or 1500 shares while the price is low? What quantity is better for you right now?"

In the second illustration the product is entirely different, yet the six-part sales presentation is the same. Once you have learned the six-part presentation, you can make it fit any product or service that you have to sell. It takes a little planning and effort, but the payoff is easily measured in commission dollars you can earn.

Illustration 2: Tax-Deferred Annuity

Broker: "John Prospect?"

Prospect: "Yes."

Broker: [Profit Potential] "This is Jill Saleswoman with [your firm]. We have an idea that might make money for you. Maybe a lot of money. Many of our clients are now earning over 10 percent each year free of current income taxes, without risking a single dollar of principal. You might want to learn what they are doing to legally avoid current income taxes while keeping their savings safe from risk. I need just a few minutes to give you the basic information that might help your dollars earn a lot of money for you."

Prospect: "Okay. It sounds interesting but make it quick. I am busy."

Broker: [Facts] "Our clients, who hate paying income taxes like you do, like the fact that they can earn untaxed income at a high rate, guaranteed for one year. They love the security in knowing that they can get all or part of their money on demand. They also like being guaranteed against loss of principal.

Prospect: "I like the thought of not paying current income taxes and being guaranteed against loss. But it really sounds too good to be true. What are you talking about?"

Broker: [Benefits] "I am talking about your putting money to work in a tax-deferred annuity where the benefit to you would be in getting a 10-year guarantee that your money could never earn you less than 8 percent a year but could earn you more. Another benefit to you would be in not having to pay income taxes on your interest earnings while your money is at work."

Prospect: "What is the catch? There must be some risk?"

Broker: [Risk] "You heard me correctly. With tax-deferred annuities your principal is guaranteed absolutely safe against loss by the issuing insurance company. I am sure you know that there are very few investments available where you can put your money to work at a high rate of interest, avoid paying current income taxes, yet run no risk of losing even one dollar of principal."

Prospect: "I like that safe aspect because I have lost plenty of money in speculation. That's why I am out of the market now."

Broker: [Comparison of Risk versus Benefit] "When you compare the difference in earning taxable interest on your money versus earning this percentage of tax-deferred interest, you will want to transfer a significant dollar amount of your savings into a tax-deferred annuity. The dollars you won't pay Uncle Sam can earn thousands of extra dollars for you to spend later, when you need them. This extra benefit is all earned without incurring any risk."

Prospect: "What is the minimum amount I can invest and what sales charge do I have to pay?"

Broker: [Asking for Order] "The tax-deferred annuity I am recommending is no-load! That means you do not have to pay anything initially in order to put your money to work. The minimum amount you can purchase is $5,000. Judging from your comments you clearly understand that your money in the tax-deferred annuity will earn high interest untaxed until you later take it out. Knowing that your money is guaranteed safe and always available, would you transfer $40,000 or $30,000 from your savings to take advantage of the current high rate? Which amount do you think is best for you right now?"

HOW TO HEAT UP
YOUR COLD CALLS

Prospecting:
11 Greatest Sources

Every seller of intangibles who aspires to be a big earner is constantly on the lookout for quality prospects. Unfortunately, many of these aspirers to wealth fail because they don't uncover enough prospects nor understand how prospects can be ferreted out. The failures normally have not been exposed to the prime, easily available sources of prospects in their particular communities.

Without a steady stream of different people to subject to a sales pitch, the salesperson's commission revenue often declines to a trickle. Learning where to find an endless number of qualified prospects is one trick of the trade that can be mastered by anyone willing to work the established mother lodes listed in this chapter.

Prospect Source 1:
The Daily Newspaper

Daily papers in every community are studded with names of likely prospects for you. The best names to collect and add to your prospect file are the names of people just promoted to a higher job. Usually the promotion announcement is accompanied by a photo and is planted as a news release. The free news write-up serves three basic functions: (1) it recognizes a valued employee; (2) the article possibly attracts new business; (3) the article serves as a free ad.

The following story illustrates the power of collecting these free leads.

I sat at the desk side of a successful account executive in our Denver, Colorado, office. Gene O. was a mature (fiftyish) salesman who had spent 20 years in military service, retiring as a colonel. Gene chose Denver for his adopted home because of the climate, his love for skiing, and the growth of the area.

When he entered the brokerage business for his second career, he was faced with the challenge of learning all the rules, regulations, and various details about investment product details. In addition, he was trying to build a clientele in a town in which he was a complete stranger. Within three years, Gene was netting over $50,000 a year!

Between Gene's phone calls, we chatted about how he had gone about finding prospects. *Gene told me that he used the newspaper as his sole source of leads!* He daily perused the business section and clipped articles about executives who were being promoted or recognized for some particular accomplishment. Gene then taped each clipping to his stationery and sent it to the executive with a simple note saying something like this: "I thought you might like to have an extra copy of your recent write-up in the paper. Congratulations!" Then he simply signed his name.

A week later, Gene would follow up with a phone call. (He almost always got through by telling the secretary this call was in reference to his letter and the newspaper article of the previous week.) Most often he was warmly greeted and thanked for his thoughtfulness. Gene carefully would work the conversation to investing and mail the prospect some interesting investment ideas. Another follow-up phone call was made, usually followed by an appointment where an order was obtained.

That prospecting process alone was sufficient (augmented by inevitable referrals) to propel Gene to a high level of earnings within 18 months. You might want to follow Gene's lead in building a prospect file.

Prospect Source 2:
Dun and Bradstreet "Directory of
Million Dollar Corporations"

In 1972 I conducted a sales training program attended by Jerry H. Jerry was an aggressive young man in his twenties with an MBA and a stong desire for the finer things in life. Jerry listened and learned in

Top security salespeople have had to learn one of life's most valuable lessons: "Lost money may be recovered but lost time is gone forever!"

TWO THINGS YOU CAN DO TODAY TO MAKE YOUR BUSINESS GROW!

1. *Try to meet with the Welcome Wagon or New Neighbor hostess in your area. She may become an account and could refer you to lots of people. Try to speak at a monthly luncheon.*

2. *See two attorneys face to face to show them the benefits of an estate security valuation report.*

class. After completing the sales training program, Jerry began to sell in one of our northern New Jersey branches. At the end of his second year, using the sales ideas he had learned, he was earning at a $35,000 annual rate! Not bad, but not good enough for Jerry. Jerry began to feel a geographical restriction due to being surrounded by competing offices of his own firm. In addition Jerry had a hankering for the faster business pace of New York City as opposed to the more tranquil suburban life.

Jerry decided to change firms and go to work for an old-line respected firm that had comparatively few retail branches. He left behind his established accounts and set about the task of prospecting and building a new clientele. Within four years' time Jerry's net earnings exceeded $300,000 annually.

I asked Jerry where he obtained his prospects. Jerry told me that his main source of prospects was the Dun and Bradstreet *Directory of Million Dollar Corporations*, a book that is normally available in every public library to those who can't or won't pay the annual fee for their own copies.

Jerry thinks that book is an absolute gold mine! It lists the name, address, and phone number of every corporation that has more than $1 million in revenue annually. It also gives the names of the key officers. "All I do," said Jerry, "is call these business people at their place of work and present a timely idea. I make sure to ask for an order! I get plenty of turndowns, but enough 'yeses' come through to make me one of the highest-paid people in Wall Street!"

Not bad for a young man now in his thirties! Perhaps you can take a clue from Jerry and develop a lot of high-quality prospects into clients from this exciting prospect pool.

Prospect Source 3:
Fine-Arts Patrons

Almost every city has a little theater, an art museum, or a symphony orchestra that is supported by local people who appreciate and patronize the arts. These kind people want their children and friends to acquire culture, a love of various art forms. They generously give time and money to make art appreciation available to the general community.

Often the only recognition they receive is to have their names printed on a program at a performance or included in some publication acknowledging their contribution. These names usually include many of the wealthy people in the area and are a prime source of prospects. You only have to take the time to gather the names and look up the addresses and phone numbers for your prospect file. Making regular contact with the patrons on these lists, and asking them for orders will produce substantial commission revenues.

Prospect Source 4:
Contributors to Charity

Every community conducts annual charity drives. Wealthy people invariably are asked to make substantial contributions to such community fund-raising campaigns. Most charities, like United Way, the Heart Fund, or the American Cancer Society, use volunteers who offer their time and expertise. These volunteers are supplied with names, addresses, phone numbers, and the amounts of contributions in previous years.

These charity drives are a double-barreled opportunity for you. They give you a chance to do a civic good at the same time you are presenting yourself to wealthy prospects who could be substantial sources of new business and referrals. I have met many fine people who later became clients while soliciting donations to local charities. Offer your services as a solicitor for charity drives in your church, the YMCA–YWCA, Red Cross, Community Chest, or any of hundreds of charitable organizations that solicit contributions.

Another aspect of working for a charity is to offer the use of your

Top security salespeople have learned how to defeat the four biggest time wasters: laziness, procrastination, distraction, impatience. Make up your mind to join the ranks of top producers and conquer these four enemies.

TWO THINGS YOU CAN DO TODAY TO MAKE YOUR BUSINESS GROW!

1. **Send each phone prospect contacted a note (enclose a return info request card).**

2. **Offer a free S&P sheet on every stock owned by any prospect you have solicited for the first time. This service can lead to an appointment or an order, and it also extracts the number of holdings.**

office for a telephone contribution call-a-thon on some Saturday or Sunday. Of course, this can only be done with your branch manager's approval. This also assumes that you have 15 or more phones available for the solicitors to use.

In addition to providing a civic good, you will find excellent prospects among the solicitors themselves. (Don't forget to arrange for free coffee and cookies, and to clean up after they leave!)

Often the solicitors will leave you with copies of lists naming last year's givers, which are an outstanding source of prospects. A little effort in the right place may pay off in obtaining the finest clients.

Prospect Source 5:
Annual Reports

Another great source of prospects often overlooked is the annual report. Particularly valuable are annual reports of companies located in or near your workable territory. Each of these reports invariably lists the names of the members of the board of directors. These people are influential, and usually affluent enough to serve as directors. They make ideal prospects. These prime prospects are used to making decisions, they are familiar with dealing in large dollar amounts, and they fully understand risk. Their grasp of investment ideas is quick. Approaching such people consistently and logically will give you a chance at big commission prospects who could become long-term clients.

I told one of the attendees at a sales course about this magnificent source of prospects. He was excited at the idea of zeroing in on this high-quality market. Perhaps some of his excitement stemmed from the fact that he was only 23 years old, and selling securities was his first full-time job.

We discussed in detail how he was to approach this particular market segment. His branch office was in Fort Lauderdale, Florida. This particular area abounds in publicly traded securities of small local banks and insurance companies.

Here are the steps I outlined for him:

1. Compile a list of all the companies headquartered in the area whose stock is publicly traded.
2. Obtain an annual report from each company.
3. Make up a prospect file consisting of the names of the members of the board of each company.
4. Systematically call or see each board member.
5. Ask each board member to make any open-market purchase of company stock through him or sell shares through him.
6. Follow the companies' stock prices on a regular basis; also become familiar with its business fundamentals.
7. Alert the OTC trading department to notify you when blocks of stock become available for purchase or sale.

In just three years' time this young man, at age 26, was netting $75,000 per year from clients obtained from this one prospecting source!

Prospect Source 6:
City Directories

One of the finest sources of quality prospects easily available in every community is the city directory for the area. This wondrous book lists names and phone numbers of the residents on each street. If you do not already know them, get someone to point out the streets where the most affluent people reside. Then you can construct a prospect file with the names of people who live on those streets, and each person is mailed, called, and, preferably, seen. This source alone led me to a high annual income in less than 24 months.

Yearly updates of the directory keep a flow of new prospects available. Here is a special sales hint that you might find valuable. If you are selling in an area where competition is strong, work your city directory prospecting street by street from Z *to* A rather than from A to Z. Those people living on streets beginning with the last letters of the alphabet are usually not subjected to as many sales attempts as those people who live on streets beginning with the early letters of the alphabet.

City directories are usually available in every public library. In the event your firm does not furnish you with one, just visit your library.

Prospect Source 7:
Yellow Pages of the Telephone Book

The telephone directory should be one of your most valuable sources of prospects. Normally, I recommend avoiding the white pages as they contain too many unqualified prospects. The best candidates for conversion to clients are from the listings of lawyers, doctors, CPAs, dentists, and other licensed professionals. To those lists can be added the heads of the companies that advertise in the Yellow Pages.

Some of my best clients were acquired by calling a place listed in the Yellow Pages and asking to speak to the boss. One of the best approaches for securities salespeople is to examine any current research reports carefully and determine what prospects might be familiar with the researched company or its product. After compiling a list of people who might be interested, I'd call each one and offer to send a copy of the research report for them to read. If the answer was "no," I'd tell them that after they read the report they very well might concur with the analyst and want to invest in the shares. If the answer was "yes," I'd make a pitch to add to the existing position.

All in all, the Yellow Pages are as filled with gold as their color indicates.

Prospect Source 8:
Welcome Wagon

One of the most underutilized sources of prospects in most communities is the name list compiled by organizations like Welcome Wagon or New Neighbors.

Such organizations contact new arrivals in the community, offering all types of services, merchandise discounts, friendliness, and a pat format to introduce new people to each other and to the community.

Usually each organization has a monthly luncheon featuring a guest speaker. See if you can't arrange to be the speaker one or more times during the calendar year. There are from 25 to 100 or more attendees at the typical luncheon. Many of them are potential investors or have spouses that invest. This nest of prospects is certainly one of the most lucrative to work, as the newcomers to the area normally establish new insurance and brokerage relationships. The first salesperson on the scene usually has an inside track to their business.

In addition to the monthly luncheon, the organizations can supply a short biographical sketch on area newcomers for a fee. This list is usually supplied on a weekly basis to subscribers and is well worth the money.

A great starting point is to contact the hostess(es) in your area personally. Meet with them and try to win some small part of their investment business. If they do business with you, they are most likely going to tell countless numbers of newcomers your name. Successful efforts here can bring a steady stream of prospects your way.

Prospect Source 9:
Inactive Firm Accounts and Prospect Lists

Many firms have a large number of inactive accounts as well as a supply of old leads that never became accounts. These names can be contacted with a fresh idea or a different approach and converted into

Goethe really understood security salespeople, as evidenced by his observation: "One of the greatest things in this world lies not so much in finding out where we are, but in what direction we are moving." Which way is your production heading?

excellent clients. I acquired at least six large accounts from the branch dead file! Send a letter to each name, *followed up by an order-asking phone call* on a specific timely investment.

Gregg C., San Antonio, Texas, less than six months out of my sales course, obtained a supply of old leads (not accounts) to work on for a municipal bond offering. One such contact resulted in an immediate order for municipal securities large enough to provide a net commission to Gregg of $1200. A subsequent order the following month yielded a net commission to Gregg of $7200! Not bad for a 24-year-old just starting up the ladder to success.

Free leads like those above are many times available just for the asking.

Prospect Source 10:
Club Members

Country clubs, swim clubs, social clubs of all types exist in every community throughout this land. Their membership lists are usually available through an existing member, or they can often be obtained simply by asking. Social club members are excellent prospects for investment and for insurance business.

The more elite and exclusive the club, the more likely it is that the investment and insurance business available through the individual members is large. A direct pursuit of the members by a mail campaign with phone follow-up can reward you with substantial business plus high-quality referrals.

It is not necessary to go to the expense of joining a club solely for the potential business that exists from the members. If your ideas are good and well presented, the prospects will buy whether or not you are a club member. The same applies to civic clubs. It is not necessary to join to be able to obtain business from members.

Even if you are the joiner type, just being a member does not entitle you to any business from fellow members. *It is your sales efforts and sales ideas that bring in the commission dollars.*

Prospect Source 11:
Noncompetitive Salespeople

One of my most treasured prospect sources was any salesperson who sold products or services that did not compete directly with my own products. Salespeople, particularly commission-based salespeople, are normally outgoing, garrulous folks, who feel a kinship with their brethren who are trying to earn a living through selling. The feeling of kinship is naturally strongest toward noncompetitors.

Whenever salespeople get together, they often exchange stories about prospecting methods, closing techniques, and earnings potentials. Sharing successful ideas can benefit the participants in many ways. One great benefit I found was to exchange prospects. New, quality names to call and see are constantly needed if sales are to expand. The old saying "the more the merrier" is an absolute truism when it comes to clients and prospects.

Learn who the outstanding salespeople are in noncompetitive fields in your area. Make it a point to call them and meet them for breakfast (lower cost!) or lunch. Concentrate on the high earners in real-estate, Cadillac, Continental, or foreign car sales; yacht brokers, and the like, and you will find people who know the people you would like to have as accounts. Make a friend, be a friend to successful salespeople, and they will frequently either give or make available the names of dozens of top-drawer prospects.

General Motors annually furnishes Cadillac dealers with a list of late-model Cadillac owners in the immediate area. This list is, of course, a primary tool for the salespeople at Cadillac dealerships to use in trying to sell more cars. This list can be extremely valuable to you. Usually the people who own late-model Cadillacs are in upper income brackets and investment-oriented. Make an effort to get a list copy, either from a salesperson or from a secretary you befriend.

One of the men who went through my sales course was from Minneapolis. This prospect source fired his imagination, and upon returning to his home he went to the leading Cadillac dealer and was given a demonstration ride (what else would you expect?) and an excellent sales pitch. He told the salesman that some day soon he hoped to buy a top-of-the-line model and that he would encourage clients to use stock-market profits to buy Cadillacs. Sugarplums danced in front of the car salesman's eyes about the future car sales possible through this young man. A second meeting was all that it took for my young salesman to get a copy of 2800 names and addresses of late-model Cadillac owners. This one source produced over 100 new accounts for him and started him on the road to sales success.

Ford also supplies Lincoln Continental dealers with lists of late-model Continental owners. That list's power is just as good as the Cadillac list, and every effort should be made to get it.

In my view, the noncompetitive salesperson is one of the greatest sources of quality prospects around. Carefully explore the potential for good business that these colleagues provide.

A great truth can be learned from top security sales-people in the Confucian age: "He who loses his temper, loses the order."

TWO THINGS YOU CAN DO TODAY TO MAKE YOUR BUSINESS GROW!

1. *Turn your focus on tax-deferred annuities for the entire day. (I assume you are licensed—if not—start today the procedure for getting licensed). Call every client and prospect you can and point out the dynamite features in TDAs that make them needed in every portfolio: no principal risk, high untaxed interest earned (until later withdrawn), ready access to all or part of your money just as if it were in a bank. Set up an appointment for every day next week.*

2. *Learn the features of a particular tax-deferred annuity available for sale in your state. Choose a no-load, disappearing withdrawal charge for easier sales. Be sure you have plenty of brochures to enclose in all outgoing mail for the coming 2 weeks. Each brochure must be accompanied by a return card to be completed by the prospect.*

The prospect sources listed in this chapter by no means exhaust the possibilities. Many others are available to you, as a seeker of names, including purchased lists from list brokers. The main thing to understand is this: the bigger your pool of high-level prospects, the more likely it is that you can extract commissions with a consistent contact approach.

Build a good prospect file. Keep adding to it. Make order-asking contacts with the people in your file. You will be a success!

The Real Key to Success: Organized Consistent Prospecting

The road to success in selling investment products is traveled almost exclusively by those who have learned how to organize their prospecting efforts. Consistency, as well as organization, in prospecting is necessary if you are to reach and maintain a high level of earnings.

People selling investment products should strive to *be prospect-conscious every waking hour!* Prospects abound in every area of this country. Casual acquaintances and close friends alike are prospects, and you should be asking for their business. Even if the people you know do not buy, they might refer others to you.

If you are a churchgoer or a member of civic clubs, you will always find the opportunity to meet new people and let them know that you specialize in the careful handling of money. You must continually make a special effort to widen the circle of people who know your name well enough to call you in the event that investment dollars become available to them.

Outgoing, would-be sales stars look for prospects whenever they eat out in fine restaurants or bars! They start conversations with the owner or manager or with prosperous-looking patrons. Always they try to steer the conversation to the ever-absorbing topic of making money.

When you go on vacation, seek prospects among fellow vacationers. Many salespeople have found their best clients to be people met on vacations. The pressure-free environment often provides more time for a prospect to think about investing.

Prospects are also to be found where you spend money for goods or services. Doctors, dentists, lawyers, accountants, and other business people are not only potential clients of yours but are centers of influence that could lead other clients to you.

Organizing for a consistent prospecting effort involves completing the following tasks.

Building a Prospect File

Many salespeople do not understand how to construct a prospect file that is clear and easy to use. Without this invaluable tool, they handicap themselves in the struggle to earn more dollars. A good prospect file should contain *no less than 1000 names, addresses, and phone numbers*. Each prospect must be carefully selected for *"buy-ability."* Initially, buy-ability is based on what prospects do, where they work, or where they live. Each detail must be legibly recorded on a heavyweight, lined, good-sized card that will stand up to hard use. The file of cards should be prominently displayed on top of the desk to serve as a daily reminder that there are calls to be made. Bad markets, inclement weather, feeling disinclined—*nothing* is acceptable as an excuse for failing to make prospecting calls.

Top security salespeople stay tops because: (1) they welcome responsibility and (2) seek help when they need it. Are you working at becoming a top security salesperson?

TWO THINGS YOU CAN DO TODAY TO MAKE YOUR BUSINESS GROW!

1. *Check the broad tape for any news causing sharp ups or downs in stock positions recorded in your cross reference. If quickly communicated, the news might produce more business—either add-on buys or sells.*

2. *See that your cross reference is up to date! This is a gold mine; don't fail to keep it current.*

Maintaining the Prospect File

Once established, the prospect file should grow through the daily and weekly addition of names of people met "cold," obtained through referrals, or encountered at various kinds of functions. Each quarter, the file should be *purged* to remove the prospects who are obviously time-wasters or whom you have determined have little or no investment potential.

Maintaining a Daily Regimen of Prospect Contacts

Each working day (no exceptions!), a number of the names in the file should be called, seen, or contacted by mail (a common "do-able" number is 20). Each must be asked for an order on a specific attractive item. (Yes, you can ask for orders by mail!)

Maintaining an Inventory of Current Direct-Mail Pieces

In order to take advantage of timely investment opportunities with prospects who can't be contacted by phone or in person, a supply of attractive mail pieces with appropriate customer inquiry cards should be constantly available in good supply. Any items mailed out should be logged on the calendar for phone follow-up a week after the mailing.

The biggest sales successes I have met and taught say the major factor in their success is the effort made in prospecting. I have yet to meet a person who prospected diligently over a long period of time and was not successful. A strong prospecting effort alone can make you successful! A skilled, trained effort simply shortens the time and heightens the financial payoff.

Daily prospecting produces results just like a daily body building or daily diet control. Consistency of effort produces winning results only if orders are always asked for from a reasonable number (20 or more) of qualified persons.

Cold Calling Successfully

The phone is the single greatest asset for any seller of intangibles, yet many salespeople never learn how to use it effectively. Thousands of potentially good salespeople fail in their profession because of their lack of skill in handling that perplexing plastic piece of electronic equipment.

Selling to prospects by phone is much different from, and more difficult than, selling to established clients by phone. Let's focus on the process of making cold calls to total strangers.

When you call strangers it is important to keep in mind that prospects can only judge by what they hear. Except by the still-rare use of a picture phone, prospects cannot see your natural, beautiful appearance; the immaculate clothes; the positive, reassuring manner. Nor can they view any exhibits, charts, or statistical data that normally might be used as evidence in a face-to-face meeting.

The recipient of a cold call can make judgments based only on your voice and tone inflection, the clarity of your logic, and the facts you outline. Prospects quickly form an impression of the caller. Normally, sellers making a first cold call to a prospect have about 20 seconds to make themselves and their products attractive enough for the prospect to be interested in hearing more. Those first few seconds on the phone are vital, and they should be carefully rehearsed so that you know how to grab and hold the prospect's attention.

In making *absolute cold calls* (neither a referring source nor a direct-mail warm up), paying attention to several key points can help you gain a higher degree of productivity from the effort you expend. They include the following:

1. *Pronounce the prospect's name correctly.* People love to hear the sound of their names, but *only* if correctly pronounced. This is especially true of individuals who have surnames that are difficult to pronounce. If you are unsure how to pronounce the prospect's name correctly, *ask!* Make every effort to learn the correct pronunciation *before* the sales call. You can usually accomplish this by asking the secretary or receptionist who answers the phone to say the prospect's name.

2. *Introduce yourself distinctly.* Be sure to pronounce your *own* name clearly and distinctly, without racing through it or mumbling, in your effort to get to your sales pitch.

3. *Use the prospect's name again.* When you make your opening statement, repeat the prospect's name. Whenever possible, if permission has been granted, get on a first-name basis. This reduces tension and breaks a social barrier.

4. *State a valid reason for calling.* Too many sellers barge into the cold-calling fray without thinking of plausible reasons for interrupting the prospect at work (daytime) or at home (usually nighttime). Without a valid reason for calling, the conversation limps along or the prospect severely shortens it. The lack of validity in the call causes a low score, in terms of orders or appointments obtained, whereas presenting the prospect with reasons for why you are calling now creates an atmosphere of credibility.

5. *Make the conversation two-way.* To be successful in cold calling, it is important for you to involve the prospect in the conversation. You can normally accomplish this by asking the prospect questions, zeroing in on what the prospect needs or wants. A one-way, uninterrupted sales pitch is not only boring to both parties but is generally unproductive. Being a good question-asker is a key part of becoming a good sales-producer.

6. *Try to exude confidence, enthusiasm, product knowledge, and warmth.* Of the six key points for cold calling, far and away the most important is the selection of a *valid reason* for calling. Before you pick up the phone to dial a stranger, you *must* carefully select one or more good reasons for intruding on that person's time and privacy. Otherwise, your batting average will be low enough to discourage you completely, perhaps to the point of leaving the business of selling intangibles.

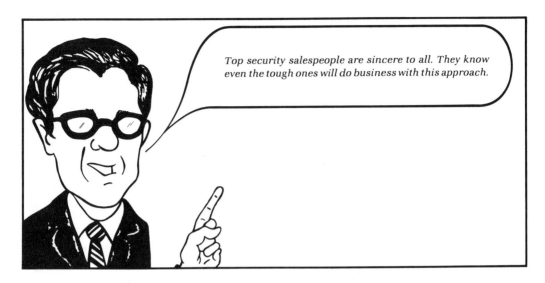

Top security salespeople are sincere to all. They know even the tough ones will do business with this approach.

Many salespeople have the mistaken impression that the number of calls they complete is the only goal and measure of cold calling. They stress the quantity (which *is* important) but give too little emphasis to the quality of the call.

Faulty Technique—No Valid Reason. Following is an example of a phone approach used (most ineffectually) by thousands of salespeople in the securities industry. It is an approach I have observed and absolutely deplore, because it proceeds in a bland and innocuous style and has been a primary cause of the low productivity or even failure of its practitioners.

Joe Salesman: "Mr. Prospect, my name is Joe Salesman with QRX Company, a member firm of the New York Stock Exchange. I am calling you today to introduce myself and my firm. I would like to compete for some of your business and have an opportunity to meet you and tell you about all the fine services and products my firm has to offer. Could I meet with you this afternoon or tomorrow morning?"

John Prospect: "Sorry, but I'm tied up, and besides I already have a broker. I'm not interested in any other. Thanks for calling."

On the surface, the contents of the call certainly seem all right. An appointment is requested after the introduction has taken place; the tone is pleasant. *But there is no punch, no specific product offered, no urgency implied. There is no valid reason for the call,* at least valid and plausible from the prospect's point of view. And in order to get past the initial hurdle of a cold call, the prospect's viewpoint is the only one that matters!

Despite my negative assessment of this approach, some small degree of success may be had with it, simply because the user is making some contact with a prospect. An occasional prospect may be looking for a broker. This is where the quantity of calls can sometimes make up for their lack of quality. Some prospects will agree to an appointment or they will volunteer information or ask questions that could lead to an account and an order. But prospects *that* ripe are rare.

Superior Technique—The Valid-Reason Approach. When you apply skill in selecting a valid reason for the call, the number of accounts opened per 100 cold calls made can zoom, often astronomically.

Listen in on a different approach—a *valid-reason approach.*

Again assume that our mythical Joe Salesman has gotten through to John Prospect:

Joe Salesman: "Mr. Prospect, this is Joe Salesman with XYZ Firm. You don't know me, but I am calling you today for a very special reason."

John Prospect: "What is it?"

Joe Salesman: "Mr. Prospect [repeating the name], my firm is underwriting a new issue of common stock of Pacific Gas & Electric. The new shares are coming out tomorrow at $22 per share [specific product and specific time]. *Buyers tomorrow will not have to pay any commission cost whatsoever!* All costs will be paid by the seller. The shares yield 11.3 percent and are rated at the highest possible rating by Standard & Poor's. Normally, these free-of-buyer-commission shares are offered and taken by our existing clients. However, *my manager has allocated me some shares for new accounts*, and that is why I am calling you today [valid reason for calling, one that is plausible to the prospect]."

John Prospect: "What did you say the price and yield were?"

Joe Salesman: "The price *tomorrow* will be $22 per share. The yield will be 11.3 percent from a dividend that has never been reduced in over 100 years. If you are interested in high quality and high income and in avoiding direct commission cost to you, I will try to get you up to 500 or 1000 shares.

(Place a scarcity value, if possible, to help stimulate the prospect's desire.) If I can get shares for you at that special price, how many would you be interested in?"

I have trained thousands of salespeople to use this phone approach effectively, and with a much higher degree of success than they have achieved with any other phone contact.

The key points to remember in constructing a valid-reason phone approach are these:

1. Offer a specific product, preferably a high-quality, well-known name.
2. State a specific time within which an answer is needed.
3. Present a specific value strong enough to induce the prospect to agree to the order or the appointment.
4. If possible, present a product that has the appeal of scarcity.

What to Use as Valid Reasons

Here are some examples of valid reasons sellers of intangibles can use in their approaches to strangers:

1. *New issues of common stocks or bonds.* As in the Pacific Gas & Electric illustration, there is something magnetic about the words "new issue" that attracts buy orders from strangers. The feeling is that they are getting in on the ground floor, and at a price that is the same to all buyers, large or small. The absence of a direct commission is another inspiration to buy.
2. *New issues of unit trust with a specific yield.* A powerful valid reason for a call, with size *always limited* by the issuer, these have a scarcity value easy to get across. New issues also carry an urgent message: "Act now or miss out on the opportunity." That message is one of the most powerful during cold calling.
3. *Common stock.* Many top brokers select a common stock with *special news* that might affect the next day's (or week's) market price. The news might be a research wire or report that the firm would like to communicate to investors as rapidly as possible so that an informed decision can be made. Or it might be some other important item like an oil discovery or merger announcement.

4. *Invitation to a "free lunch."* Sandwich and drink lecture lunches held at the office at noon for a select few prominent people (for scarcity value) is an excellent valid reason for calling. Most people find it difficult to be rude and hang up abruptly after having been invited to lunch.

5. *Invitation to a special evening seminar.* A talk featuring ways to save on income taxes is an excellent valid reason for calling: "You do want to save on income taxes don't you?" Can you imagine anyone saying "no" to that question?

Questions to Make Progress When Cold Calling by Phone

Asking questions of a prospect is a powerful way to extract information that might be helpful in determining what products to emphasize or what the potential size order may be. Here is a list of questions that have been effective in getting prospects to talk and disclose information about themselves and what they want or need. You will, no doubt, think of others that will be effective, too:

1. Can you use high, tax-free income?"

2. "Do you feel that investing in low-risk, high-potential-profit stocks fits in with your investment objectives?"

3. "Would you like to earn high interest, pay no current federal or state income tax, yet not risk losing any money?"

4. "What was the best investment you ever made?"

5. "Do you still have it [the 'best' investment]?" Or "Why did you sell it?"

6. "What is your tax bracket?"

7. "Would you like to save on income taxes this year?"

8. "Would you like to have brand new Standard & Poor's sheets on every stock you own?"

9. "Would you like me to get a research opinion for every stock you now own that worries you?"

10. "Would you like to have all your bonds reviewed as to quality ratings, current prices, and current yield?"

11. "Would you like a free copy of our weekly market letter each week for the next three weeks?"

12. "Would you like to have all your life insurance policies professionally reviewed and evaluated as to current worth, costs, and coverage?"

13. "Would you like to be on our select mailing list of people who are notified when new issues of common stocks and bonds are available for purchase without direct commission?"

14. "Would you like some information on how to create a tax shelter for current income?"

15. "Are you satisfied with how your money is working for you? In stock? In fixed income?"

16. "What service do you wish you were getting from your broker that you're not getting?"

17. "What do you think a good broker should do for you?"

18. "What do you think a good insurance person should do for you?"

19. "Do you believe what you are doing with your assets is good enough considering our current inflation rate?"

The objective in asking questions is to get answers that provide clues as to what and how that prospect can be sold. Be sure to listen intently to the prospect's replies so that you can be deciding what is most suitable based on the comments.

Benefits of Cold Calling

Cold calls are very beneficial whether you are a new or an experienced seller of intangibles. One of the big benefits is that they force you to keep up to date on the products you are offering, on world

Good security salespeople are well aware that the adage "Buy low—sell high" is the secret to stock-market success. Never in recent market history has it been so easy to aid clients and prospects in achieving the first half of the success formula.

TWO THINGS YOU CAN DO TODAY TO MAKE YOUR BUSINESS GROW!

1. *Assess your personal appearance. Is your hair neat? Are clothes cleaned and pressed, not frayed or badly worn? Do you look conservative?*

2. *Get the current tax table. Ask each client or prospect their tax bracket; tell them that this info can be of help in deciding to transfer to muni investments or from mini investments.*

103

events, and on economic happenings. News communication today is almost instant and can quickly cause a change in price of bonds, stocks, commodities, options, mutual funds, and even interest rates on tax-deferred annuities. If you cold call, you must stay current with such changes, and the changes give you valid reasons.

Another benefit in making cold calls is that they help you to hone your selling skills. The constant practice of trying to overcome objections and of learning to respond quickly to a prospect's questions, anticipated or not, develops sales toughness and expertise. Making cold calls keeps you alert, like a well-trained boxer.

The third benefit from consistently making cold calls is the financial reward obtained as a result of new client business.

Excuses for Cold-Call Failures

Despite the benefits that can be gotten from a disciplined, daily cold-call routine, many sellers of intangibles don't and won't make them. Here are some of the reasons they give for not cold calling strangers:

1. *"Tried it and failed.* I just wasn't getting anywhere with prospects." Translation: the ones who use this excuse never mastered the cold-call selling skill.
2. *"Don't like my own self-image."* Many salespeople feel it undignified to call strangers. They feel somewhat like peddlers and believe that cold calling is beneath them. Translation: ones who use this excuse have a misconception about what it means to be a professional salesperson.
3. *"Afraid of rejection."* Many salespeople are super-sensitive, and their egos are easily bruised and damaged. They can't tolerate hearing the word *no*, and the occasional rudeness they encounter devastates them to the extent that they cannot get up the nerve to continue to cold call.

In actual practice, cold calls make a lot of sense and dollars for the salesperson who understands and believes in the selling game. It is necessary only to harden yourself against a certain number of failures that are certain to happen and to be cheered on by your successes.

Out of 100 cold phone calls, a good seller might open two or three accounts plus line up four or five appointments. That would be a good result! It would also mean that 90 percent or so of the calls met failure. Selling is often said to be partially a numbers game. To a great extent that is true. But the development of selling skill makes it easier to turn the numbers to your advantage.

How to Be Successful at Cold Calling

Success in cold calling lies principally in three characteristics:

1. *Sticktuity.* The dogged determination to complete a prescribed number of calls each working day is essential.
2. *Product knowledge.* In-depth knowledge of a product helps develop confidence and breed enthusiasm, important qualities that can be transmitted to a prospect.
3. *Enhancement of selling skills.* The constant learning and practice of selling skills makes for a higher percentage of closes.

Reasons for Failure at Cold Calling

Factors that cause failure in cold calling, even in those who doggedly complete a quota of daily calls, are these:

1. *Lack of enthusiasm.* Presenting a product in a monotone or a phlegmatic manner almost insures a turn-down.
2. *Lack of confidence.* Salespeople with only a flimsy knowledge of their products are quickly detected by prospects. Displaying a lack of knowledge of the facts and details of the product lowers the seller's confidence level and forces the prospect to reject the offer.
3. *Lack of product belief.* Many salespeople know their product but don't really believe in it or its value to a prospect. Therefore, they can only make half-hearted attempts to sell it. Here is another LeRoy maxim: *You have to believe—truly and strongly—in what you are selling if you are to do consistent good work in cold calling by phone. Your belief comes through the phone with great clarity; so does your lack of conviction.*

Cold Calling: 3 Objectives

A telephone call to a total stranger—the cold call—can be exhilarating, challenging, and often the source of a mind-boggling financial reward. Skilled cold callers know that the first step in undertaking this prospecting method successfully is to select with great care a valid, plausible-sounding reason for making the contact. Once the seller selects a valid reason and initiates the cold call, he or she carries the objectives for the call as armor during the joust with the prospect.

Although cold calling is a numbers game in the sense that a high enough number of completed calls will get some orders even for sellers with mediocre skills, acquiring a high level of phone selling skill can substantially increase the size and numbers of orders eventually obtained.

A skill that can up the cold-call batting average lies in this: Keep in mind the three cold-call objectives and progress from one to another until one or more of the objectives has been accomplished.

Let's look at the objectives that you should strive for on each cold call:

Objective 1:
Get an Order

When you call a stranger, what you want is an order—an order that converts the prospect into an actual, bona fide client. You want

Top security salespeople have learned to be concerned about clients rather than competitors. Competitors don't give orders, clients do!

TWO THINGS YOU CAN DO TODAY TO MAKE YOUR BUSINESS GROW!

1. *Review all of your month-end statements for accuracy of positions.*
2. *Call everyone who has an odd-lot position to round out if possible, or sell to consolidate. Upgrade holdings to higher quality and to those recommended by research.*

an order that will provide commissions that pay your bills and maintain your standard of living. You want an order that will boost your morale, expand your ego, and produce the high that you can't match with the most powerful stimulants. So the first objective is to *ask for the order!*

Objective 2:
Get an Appointment

The facts of selling life are such that a diligent, hardworking salesperson might complete 50, 100, or more order-asking calls in a single day and not get a single order! With that possibility (some might say "probability") in mind, and after being told "no" to the order-asking question, it's time to pursue the second objective.

If you fail to get an order when you ask on a first-time cold call, try to get an appointment. Try to get the prospect to agree to see you, even for just a few minutes, at the prospect's convenience. Present the prospect with a choice of alternate times.

Face-to-face meetings usually result in more substantial orders than are granted on a cold phone call. Face to face, you have a chance to make your sincerity, honesty, and product knowledge more visible to the prospect. "Belly-to-belly" selling provides you with the opportunity to use visual aids of all types, the chance to break down social barriers, to create a deeper rapport, and to discover more about the prospect's assets and investment objectives.

Many financial products cannot easily be sold over the phone. The appointment and the more personal encounter make it easier to get larger orders for products like tax shelters, tax-deferred annuities, mutual funds, insurance, and the like.

Here is another LeRoy maxim: *The appointment must be "sold" just like any other product.* Prospects must perceive some personal benefit in giving *any* salesperson time in their schedule. If you ask for just a few minutes or the opportunity simply to "drop off" some special information, the prospect is more likely to grant permission.

Objective 3:
Provide a Free Service

Certainly it isn't difficult for anyone to grasp the basic objectives of cold calling strangers and asking them for an order, failing to get one, and then requesting an appointment. Certainly it isn't difficult to imagine that the great majority of cold calls will result in a turn-down for objectives 1 and 2.

What's next? Defeat? Should you just quit and go on to the next prospect? No! the next step is to try to accomplish objective 3, perhaps the most important secret to being successful at opening accounts by phone: offering a free service.

Although you must keep all three objectives in mind while you make cold calls, bring objective 3 into play only after getting turned down for an order *and* turned down for an appointment. Properly handled, the offer of a free service will be accepted more than 50 percent of the time. That batting average should satisfy almost anyone, and the success factor helps to take the boredom and potential trauma out of cold calling.

The service you proffer should be so attractive that it is extremely difficult for any prospect to reject it. If possible, the service should also help to extract financial information from the prospect in order to pinpoint specifics to use later in follow-up sales contacts.

What kind of free services can you offer strangers during a first-time phone call? Here are some good items that many investors want and that most investors find difficult to refuse—items that, if accepted, *can lead to the order or the appointment you want.*

Free Offers

1. *Free* Standard & Poor's sheet on every single stock the prospect owns.

2. *Free* research opinion on any "worry" stock the prospect owns, an opinion that might resolve a dilemma as to whether to sell, buy more, or simply hold on.

3. *Free* valuation of a prospect's portfolio detailing current prices and yields on all stocks and bonds held, as well as gains and losses yet unrealized.

4. *Free* bond ratings on every bond issue held. Many bonds are up-graded or downgraded each month by the various rating services. These grade changes affect bond values. Large bondholders value this service.

5. *Free* subscription to the biweekly (monthly) market letter for a four-week period.

6. *Free* invitation to lunch (sandwich and drink) and/or to attend a special timely seminar on tax-saving ideas.

7. *Free* analysis of all life-insurance policies.

8. *Free* booklet on tax-saving ideas.

The best free offers are items 1 through 4, because in order to get these "something-for-nothing" offers the prospect has to disclose significant personal financial information. This information can later lead to the order you are seeking.

Illustration of the 3-Objective Cold Call

Examine carefully the following typical cold call scenario to see how you can use the three-objective approach in your cold-calling program.

John Prospect: "This is John Prospect."

Joe Salesman: "This is Joe Salesman with XYZ Firm, members of the NYSE. My firm is underwriting a new issue of common stock of American Telephone at $51 per share. It is coming out tomorrow, and the people who buy it tomorrow will not have to pay any direct commissions. The shares are rated A+ by Standard & Poor's and currently yield 9.9 percent. Normally these shares are taken by our own clients, but my manager has allocated me some shares for new accounts. That is why I am calling you today [valid reason]."

John Prospect: "That sounds pretty good."

Successful, experienced account executives learn from others' mistakes. They know that they will never live long enough to make all the errors themselves!

Joe Salesman: "We think it is an outstanding opportunity to buy high-quality shares and not pay direct commissions. If you would like to reserve up to 500 shares I will try to get them for you. How many would you be interested in if I could get them [objective 1: asking for the order]?"

John Prospect: "Hold on, I didn't say I was interested in buying right now. All my money is tied up in other investments."

Joe Salesman: "I can understand how you might feel reluctant to place an order with someone you have never met, even though the stock is an attractively priced, blue chip like American Telephone. Look, I am going to be in your area tomorrow and again the next day. I would like to come by and drop off a copy of the prospectus on American Telephone. Even if you decided not to take advantage of this special offering where you can save on commission, you might want to read about it and the potential we believe it offers. What time would be best for you? Late tomorrow afternoon? Early the following morning? I can only spare a few minutes [objective 2: asking for an appointment]."

John Prospect: "I'm pretty well tied up both times, and it's really not necessary for you to come by."

Joe Salesman: "You sound like a very nice guy. You haven't been rude or hung up abruptly like many people [*this statement is a winner!*]. Because you have been nice enough to listen to me, I want to do something special just for you! I would like to *send you a brand new* [pause right there to give the prospect a chance to dream momentarily of a Mercedes or Jaguar] Standard & Poor's sheet on every single stock you now own [objective 3: providing a free service]." (Maybe his current broker hasn't done that for him. It sure isn't likely.)

In order to get that "free" offer what must John Prospect do? You got it! He must disclose his entire stock portfolio. With that ammunition, Joe Salesman might later get an appointment or order. If the offer is accepted, the S&P's must be sent promptly (better yet, hand delivered!). Each S&P's should have a note attached: "Our research currently recommends purchase [or sale]." The prospect should be called again, after the sheets arrive, to review each holding, or to discuss quantities of any uneven lots to round up or round down, or to discuss eliminating small, meaningless holdings.

Providing the free service frequently leads to the order or appointment that you so strongly want.

To sum up cold-calling objectives, if you don't get the order, ask for an appointment. If you don't get the appointment, give away a free something that is so good it is not likely to be refused. Free "somethings" are great account builders and make the cold-calling game not only productive but enjoyable.

Any experienced advertising expert can attest to the fact that "free" is the most powerful advertising weapon ever devised. Salespeople who make legal and judicious use of the word, backed up with the delivery of available services or items, will see their appointments and orders grow.

Mining the Cold-Call Gold

Gold has been a much desired commodity for thousands of years because of its wondrous qualities of durability, malleability and ductility, as well as its density and beauty. It has no peer, worldwide, for retention of value and for ease of convertibility into whatever passes for coin of the realm. Gold, however, is a very scarce commodity. The primary sources of supply are South Africa, Russia, Canada, and the United States. Nations and individuals ceaselessly hunt and dig the earth in the search for a few grains of this precious metal.

In this age of modern communications, the seller of intangibles has, as the equivalent of gold, prospects. The endless supply of unknown people comprise for sellers of intangibles a veritable gold mine. Properly mining the gold of prospects can bring the riches of Midas to hard workers who actively work their "claims" by using all their selling skills.

Here are some key points to focus on in tapping the mother-lode of prospects: the daily regimen of making cold calls to total strangers. These points, if mastered, can produce nuggets of gold as valuable as those dug out of a mine or panned from a river.

Enthusiasm Sells and Convinces

Cold telephone calls permit a prospect to judge the seller, the product, and the value of the contact based *only* on what is heard.

Enthusiasm is contagious. If you are to make a success out of telephone cold calling, you must force yourself to be enthusiastic.

Use inflection to convey your confidence; avoid a monotonous delivery. In order for your enthusiasm to be assessed as real, not phony, you must be offering a product that (1) you truly believe is good for the prospect and (2) presents a good value at the time of the offer. A strong belief in what you are selling is one of the most powerful gold-mining tools.

Product Knowledge Sells and Convinces

Salespeople who have in-depth knowledge of the product under discussion make more sales and make them more easily. Knowledge makes it easier to overcome objections, too. Real, rather than superficial, knowledge can be perceived by a cold-call recipient very easily; and so can lack of knowledge.

If you really want to succeed in mining the cold-call gold, you must study and thoroughly master all the information, benefits, features, advantages, and disadvantages of any product you are trying to sell to strangers. Your presentation will gain strength because you have retained a superior store of facts. Objections will not surprise or throw you; you will simply be able to counter them by relating the proper features and key sales points.

Persistence Makes Sales

Plenty of good salespeople are knowledgeable about their product and radiate enthusiasm when discussing it; yet some of them earn very little because they lack the gumption to discipline themselves to "go to the mine" every day.

To mine the cold-call gold effectively, you must dig for prospects every day. A good way to do this is to call enough prospects (*not* clients) to get at least 20 or more "no's" from orders asked for. If you daily make enough presentations enthusiastically rendered to get you 20 "no's" from products in which you believe, inevitably some golden "yeses" will creep in.

Selecting High "Buy-Ability" Prospects Makes Sales

To mine the cold-call gold, the effort must be made to call only those prospects with the financial wherewithal to purchase the prod-

Top security salespeople reach the pinnacle of success because they make the effort to see that each recommended security fits into their clients' overall picture. Make sure that your suggestions suit the clients' needs and you will reach the top!

TWO THINGS YOU CAN DO TODAY TO MAKE YOUR BUSINESS GROW!

1. *Don't speak too rapidly; slow down your speaking rate and increase your inflection. You will be better understood and make more sales. Be fact-sure, and confidence will radiate.*

2. *Don't use broker jargon, like "P/E ratio" or "break out from a long base." Concentrate on the following 3 things and you will get more sales.*
   —profit potential (be clear about your expectation)
   —time frame (state the expected time to earn)
   —risk (point out the risk, if any)

The simpler the language, the greater the number of orders you will get.

uct you are offering. Nothing discourages a seller more than going through a presentation to what turns out to be an unqualified buyer. Cull and restrict your prospect list to high-income people and you will naturally strike more gold, more often. Avoid calling numbers randomly selected from the white pages. There are too many unqualified buyers to make that strategy highly effective.

In-Person Cold Calls

Cold calls made face to face rather than by phone can often produce substantial clients. Most prospects feel more at ease about dealing with someone they can see. They are more likely to disclose details about their financial circumstances.

Here are some gold-mining tips to enhance your selling skills. Whenever you leave your office to go see prospects (or clients) on a scheduled appointment, adhere to the following:

1. *Bring a story book.* Visual aids are powerful persuaders to use as evidence in convincing a prospect to buy. Use them whenever possible.

2. *Reconfirm the appointment time.* The day of the scheduled appointment (or day before, if it is an early morning appointment), call the prospect and confirm the meeting time and meeting place.

3. *Ask for referrals when you reconfirm.* When reconfirming the ap-

pointment make a statement like this: "I have to be in your area about 30 minutes before I see you. Whom do you think I might call on before I meet with you?" You may get a referred preappointment lead that turns out to have much larger potential than the prospect. *Remember: If you don't ask you won't get!*

4. *Ask for referrals when you leave.* After concluding your visit with the prospect, whether or not an order has been obtained, say: "As long as I am in this area, whom do you think I should see before I go back to my office?" Many prospects who are reluctant to grant a preappointment request for a referral will grant a postappointment referral request. You may have done so well conveying your sincerity, honesty, and product knowledge during your presentation that prospects who reject your proposal may soften the blow with one or more referrals. And those who have agreed to buy your proffered product may want to get someone else into the same "hot water" they've just stepped into. Frequently, you can obtain several good leads from a prospect simply by asking directly for them. What have you got to lose? Do it!

5. *If you leave the office to make a cold call, make several.* Even if you don't get a referral on the pre- or postappointment request, just drop in cold on a prospect in the same area and start a conversation by any means you can, then work the conversation around to your specialty and special story-book product. *There is an unlimited supply of gold in prospecting strangers.* All you have to do is meet new people every day, show them what you have to offer, convince them that they need it, and you will do business. Don't make the common mistake of leaving your office to call on one person, completing the presentation, and then returning to the office having made only one pitch. Make the time out of the office more effective by arranging to see new prospects and your business will grow bigger.

Special Tips for Special Prospects

Here are a few more sales-building thoughts that may help you in mining the cold-call gold. Certain groups of people are excellent potential prospects for hard-working, aggressive sellers of intangibles, yet these people are often difficult to reach or just unreachable. Getting through to these choice prospects is a challenge, and often worth the extra effort.

Dentists

One high-earning, hot-potential group is dentists. The demand for their service is high, as is their earning and investment ability. Calls to the dentist during the typical nine-to-five workday are carefully screened by the receptionist to weed out sellers of all types. What can be done to reach the target?

I have found that many dentists get to the office prior to the first appointments (usually scheduled at 8:30 to 9:00, depending on the area of the country). They arrive early in order to do some preliminary work or simply catch up on mail, pay bills, or take care of other mundane details of a practice. An early morning phone call, at 8:15 or 8:30, frequently is answered by the dentist (as hired hands normally try to show up a minute or two before the scheduled workday begins). Once you have gotten through, you have the opportunity to sell yourself and your product. No guarantees that it always works, but it is certainly worth the small amount of early morning time that it takes to try. Besides, who else of substance would you have the opportunity of reaching at 8:15 A.M.?

Doctors

Doctors represent another high-earning, high-potential group of prospects for cold-call gold mining. Getting through to doctors is a very difficult task. Normally they make hospital rounds in the morning and see patients in the afternoon. As with dentists, their receptionists have been carefully coached to screen out salespeople. "Leave word" most often goes unreturned. There is no sure method that works to get through to doctors, but for those of you who want to prospect doctors within a close enough radius to meet with them if the opportunity is given, I have a nifty, gutsy way to try. (If you don't have nerve and a strong desire to reach the target, skip the next few paragraphs and go to the next chapter.)

For those of you who *do* have prospecting nerve and a desire for some medical gold, here is a ploy that frequently is effective. If you want to reach the doctor, simply call the doctor's office. The secretary/receptionist will answer: "Dr. John Prospect's office." After hearing this cheery greeting, just deliver the following message and hang up before any questions can be asked: "Tell John that Joe will pick him up for lunch at 12:15 Thursday. [The call is made on Monday or Tuesday.] He can reach me if necessary at 558-6000." Read the message again. There is no request to speak to the doctor. You do *not* identify your firm or your profession. You do not leave your last name. When the message is delivered, here is what frequently takes place. The doctor starts thinking, "Was I drunk recently and made this lunch date? Who is this Joe? Is my mind not functioning? Nurse, did you have me down for lunch with a Joe at 12:15 on Thursday?"

"No, doctor!"

Finally, after ruminating and questioning his memory the doctor calls the number and asks for Joe.

You got through to the target! Now you had better take advantage of the moment. Your nerve got you this far.

Joe Salesman: "This is Joe Salesman with ZXY, members of the NYSE, and even though we haven't met, I thought you might have lunch with me Thursday at 12:15. I was going to be in your area anyway, and you might want to hear some very new legal ways to save on income taxes."

Dr. John Prospect: "Well, it's nice of you to ask, but really I can't make it then."

Joe Salesman: "Look, you're human, you have to eat [said with humor]! When *do* you have lunch? I'll adjust my time and you may learn some tax-saving ideas that will be very worthwhile to you. You would like to save on income taxes, wouldn't you?" (The last question is most assuredly a "hot button.")

Dr. John Prospect: "Okay, you got me. How about picking me up at 12:15?"

Joe Salesman: "Okay, I'll be there."

Certainly it doesn't work every time, but at least it gives the opportunity to reach a high-income person who might not normally respond to other tactics.

Here's what I found as a result of the "yeses" I received to the luncheon invitation. The doctors I met were, in all cases, nice, intelligent, and conscious of having been conned into the appointment. They politely, intently listened to me pitch my product of the moment. If they liked it and bought from me, of course they let me pick up the tab. Strangely enough, if they decided not to buy, they usually grabbed the check and insisted upon paying so that they would not be obligated.

Not a bad outcome. Free lunch if you "lose," in the sense of not getting an order, or a new client at the cost of a lunch. Certainly worthwhile in either case.

Lawyers and CPAs

How about lawyers or CPAs? Can the same ploy be used? Certainly! If you can't get through any other way, and you are sure your target is a genuine prospect for your products, try the method outlined for doctors.

All About Secretaries

Whether you are using the phone or the face-to-face approach, most of the time you will find your pathway blocked by secretaries—secretaries whose duty it is to defend their bosses from solicitations.

Secretaries for the most part are wonderful people who can help you in your desire to get through to prospects. You should never lie to or mislead a secretary. You should do your dead level best to make her like you and to get her to understand your product and the good it might do for her boss. Make a secretary your ally and not only will she help you get through to her boss, often she will help sell her boss.

Secretaries are also frequently capital pools themselves. They may have money available for investment. They may know family members who are investment-minded.

Yes, make every effort to treat secretaries with the utmost respect and it will pay off for you as it frequently did for me. Learn the secretary's name. Pronounce it correctly and record it for future use.

One of the best clients I ever had was secretary to the owner of a

Good security salespeople understand that history teaches that life is competition. Compete with your own sales records, or those of other brokers, and you will spur yourself on to higher goals.

textile mill. To get to him I had to go through her. She was an extremely smart woman who knew as much about her boss's business as he did himself. I told her that I wanted to talk to her boss about a deeply undervalued textile stock uncovered by our research department. She asked me questions about it, intelligent ones, and then I walked her through my story book on the stock. It turned out that she had $500,000 in securities and cash, and was actually a bigger, more active investor than her boss! She had built up an inheritance through prudent, careful investing. She bought my idea herself and then sold it for me to her boss and a dozen other family members and friends. Yes, secretaries can be tremendous allies for cold callers who seek prospecting gold.

PREVENTIVE MEASURES AGAINST SALES "BLUES"

Immunizing Against Stockbroker Diseases

I have had the privilege of helping to train thousands of salespeople for their work in the securities industry. Additionally, I have had the chance to closely observe many thousands of other account executives at work in their natural habitat, the branch office. Of the thousands who enter the securities selling field with high hopes of success, a great number fail during the first 12 months of actual action on the firing line. The dropout rate in the securities industry is estimated at 25 percent during the first year. Another large percentage fall by the wayside in year two, and attrition continues, although to a lesser degree, each successive year.

Phone Shock

One of the great causes of failure is the contracting of a broker's deadly disease that I call *phone shock*. This disease can be readily observed by focusing a trained eye on the activities of brokers as they perform their daily tasks. Many brokers who start out their career actively calling strangers and soliciting orders or appointments meet so much rejection that their egos become badly deflated. They dread making the prescribed number of "cold" calls (their own or a manager's quota), and they begin to rely heavily on direct mail. They fervently hope that what they send out will waft back to them in orders

by the prospects being convinced merely by reading the
rful written material enclosed.

Such brokers seem to have developed a fear that the phone will electrocute them if they pick it up to make an out-going call. They live each day in hope that some acquaintance will call them and place a fantastic unsolicited order.

In order to seem to be working hard, both to the manager and to themselves, they surround themselves with mountains of paper and envelopes and mailing lists. They always look industrious as they are addressing and stuffing envelopes, recording information on prospect cards, and getting additional supplies of printed materials. They busy themselves with the careful reading (page by page, slowly) of prospectuses, research material, *Barron's,* the *Wall Street Journal*, and any kind of other financial material.

Brokers who have contracted phone shock will do anything rather than force themselves to call strangers to seek orders or appointments. Many brokers suffering from phone shock become enthusiastic about technical analysis. The world of bar and point and figure charts and their daily maintenance absorbs them. These brokers kid themselves (and others, if they can) that they are making a tremendous effort in trying to select timely, "right" investment ideas, and that once their research is complete (somehow, it never is complete) they will use the phone to aggressively recommend the chosen beauty.

The only known cure for phone shock is the recognition and acceptance of its presence (a manager or an interested friend or relative may be able to point it out—tactfully) and the implementation of a daily discipline for the completion of some minimum number of order-asking, appointment-requesting phone calls.

Curing Phone Shock

If you recognize a case of phone shock and yet can't regularly force yourself into the daily discipline of making out-going calls, sit down with your manager and ask him or her to be more of a taskmaster. Prepare daily call sheets detailing the names and phone numbers of the prospects you solicit, and turn them in to your manager or sales manager. (The taskmaster should occasionally spot check a few prospects to get a feel for the prospect's reaction.)

The extra burden of the daily supervision of a failing account executive is not a chore managers love, and many let salespeople who need this type of push—who are not self starters or motivated enough on their own to go out and seek business—fail.

Top security salespeople who develop business through lectures have learned: "Nothing can be said after 40 minutes that means anything."

TWO THINGS YOU CAN DO TODAY TO MAKE YOUR BUSINESS GROW!

1. *Call every client with a losing position. Discuss the situation. Add on, if favorable; transfer to something else, if not. You must talk to "losers" or you will lose them.*
2. *Ask 10 clients for 3 referrals to be placed on your mailing list for 4 weeks (no charge).*

The realization must eventually dawn on phone shocked salespeople that if they are to make it up the ladder of success, it has to be as a result of out-going, order-asking calls, whether made by phone or face to face. Hiding under the mantle of paperwork and reading is a plot that just won't work for any length of time; and to behave thus certainly will not bring the desired degree of success.

100-Share Syndrome

The other disease that afflicts brokers is the *100-share syndrome*. This disease is transmittable. I have visited offices where everyone had it! It is insidious, and it saps the seller's strength and enthusiasm.

The 100-share syndrome is often employed as a closing technique. It may frequently follow an excellent presentation of facts and benefits. Check the following scenario and you will spot the disease:

Joe Salesman: "Hi, John! This is Joe Salesman. I'm calling you this morning to tell you about a stock just recommended by our drug analyst. I have read the report carefully and it looks like a terrific value right now. The shares are priced at $28. The yield is 5 percent from a dividend that has been raised every single year for 15 consecutive years."

John Prospect: "That sounds pretty good."

Joe Salesman: "What's even better is that the earnings have gone up every single year for 15 consecutive years, and the stock is selling at the lowest price times earnings in its history."

John Prospect: "What has been the price range for this past year?"

Joe Salesman: "The shares have sold above $35 each and every year for the last 10 years at some time during the year, and the past 12 months have been between 27 to 38. By the way, it has the highest quality rating by Standard & Poor's: A+."

John Prospect: "How about sending me the report?"

Joe Salesman: "I will do that, *but how about buying 100 shares today?*"

Many times, a salesperson will make a good presentation about a well-chosen common stock and wind up with a weak closing question: "How about buying 100 shares?" Of course, any order-asking attempt is better than none, but what if the prospect says yes? An order for 200, 300, 500, 1000, or more might have been obtained, only to be lost because of the 100-share syndrome. Skilled brokers know to ask for large orders. It is always easier to work downward from a 1000-share request than it is to move upward from a 100-share, a small order to request!

Curing the 100-Share Syndrome

The cure for this disease lies in monitoring your phone calls with a cassette tape or asking a colleague or your manager to monitor your phone calls. Once you become conscious of the presence of the 100-share syndrome, you are on your way to licking it. The cure lies in forcing yourself to ask for large orders (remember the alternate close?).

Handling "No Sales"

One of the most frustrating moments any seller of intangibles is likely to experience comes when the prospect declines to buy when asked for an order. This rejection may send salespeople into a tailspin. Their heads reel and they ask themselves over and over again where the sales pitch failed. *Missed key points . . . omitted sales features . . . pertinent client benefits . . .* march through their brains as they try to pick up the pieces and perhaps get back on the sales track.

A "no sale" is particularly galling to the salesperson who has taken the time to carefully qualify the prospect, arrange a face-to-face interview, align all the facts in a beautifully sequenced presentation that finally zeroes in on a particularly client-stated need.

Failure to obtain an order must be an accepted fact of life in selling intangibles. No matter how logical and eloquent the sales presentation, there will be many "no sales" in an average selling week. How should a "no sale" be handled?

Sellers of intangibles must learn to control their emotions much like a skilled poker player, who cannot allow his facial expressions to be a dead give-away for his holdings. When they are told "no" by a prospect to whom they have devoted a lot of their time, energy, and thought, many salespeople show irritation and anger.

This anger, once it surfaces and the prospect or client sees it, even for an instant, is enough to destroy the possibility of a sale at a later date or of a referral. The seller's dissatisfaction can be seen in an impatient gesture, a fleeting facial grimace, or a quickly stifled word of exasperation.

Selling skills involves learning to control your outward emotions while inside anger rages or disappointment reigns. When a closing fails, make every effort to maintain an aura of calmness and to summon up a smile as you ask why the prospect did not buy.

Many times, there is a valid reason why a perfectly prequalified prospect, properly "pitched," doesn't yield and grant an order. A death, a job change, some unexpected event might have legitimately caused a change in the prospect's investment approach. That is why it is important always to ask the prospect's reasons for not committing.

1. *Listen carefully to the prospect's response.* Perhaps an opportunity to sell at a future date will arise. Try to leave such prospects with the impression that you value their having listened to your sales presentation and that you will always be willing to help them in any possible way.
2. *Impress on the prospect that service is the key point of your business.*
3. *Leave the prospect feeling that you are a "good guy" and so the prospect "owes" you a shot at any future business.*

One of my most enjoyable and memorable sales occurred through the proper handling of a "no sale."

I had just given a lecture to some employees in the aircraft industry. After the lecture, while coffee was being served, one employee

Good stockbrokers have learned that the market is the best teacher of humility. They know to weigh each profit potential carefully while keeping a wary eye focused on the risk.

began discussing with me his personal financial situation. During the fact-finding he disclosed that he had $25,000 available for investment, and would like to meet with me to investigate various investment possibilities relevant to his particular needs. We agreed to meet at my office the following Saturday morning.

Saturday morning arrived, and my prospect showed up promptly as scheduled. Prior to the meeting I had prepared an investment proposal for putting the $25,000 into a common stock mutual fund. I positioned my chair next to the prospect and carefully explained the benefits of professional selection and management on a continuous basis. Carefully I pointed out the advantages of diversification and the powerful compounding impact over time through automatic reinvestment of dividends and capital gains.

I waxed eloquent! Never was I more explicit, precise, and understanding of a prospect's needs and desires. The presentation was capped with a graphic illustration as to what his $25,000 could amount to in 10 years if the future results duplicated or approximated the previous 10 years. The anticipated results were just short of breathtaking! How could anyone not buy after so cogent and logical a presentation?

When I asked for the order, my prospect did not buy! My mind raced, reviewed the presentation, searching for any flaws, missed facts, or benefits. None popped to the surface. My perception was that I had made an almost flawless presentation.

Keeping my smile I asked, "John, I don't really understand why you aren't putting your money to work in this fine fund. The track record is excellent, the management prudent and highly regarded. It suits your needs and objectives. Do you mind telling me your reason for not investing at this time?"

John replied: "LeRoy, in between the time we talked, after your lecture and this appointment I received a transfer notice from my company. I am going to have to move to Burbank, California, soon. Housing in California is priced much higher than in North Carolina, and I will probably need most of that $25,000 for the difference in cost of houses."

John had a very valid reason for not investing. I could not be angry at him. The job transfer had been a sudden occurrence, and he was naturally reluctant to invest in securities before meeting his housing needs for his family.

I wished John good luck in his new job and location. I informed him that I would always be as close to him as a telephone, and that should he ever have funds to invest he could call me collect. The interview was graciously terminated. No sale was effected, *no commission earned, end of story . . . almost!*

Six months after my "no sale" I got a phone call from a Joe B. He introduced himself and asked if he could meet with me. We arranged to get together on a Saturday morning in my office.

I arrived a little early for the appointment to set the stage. I arranged the chairs at my desk next to each other. I cleared up all unnecessary clutter to provide the aura of neatness and efficiency. A mutual fund graph illustration was placed on my desk for easy viewing.

Joe showed up on time and we chatted to get familiar with each other and ease the strangeness common to first meetings between salesmen and prospects.

I asked Joe, "How did you get my name?"

Joe replied, "I was working in the aircraft industry in Burbank, California, when I got notified that I was being transferred to Charlotte, North Carolina. A buddy, John D., who used to live in Charlotte, filled me in on a lot of things I needed to know about the area. He told me that if I needed a broker you were the one to call!"

I said, "That was very nice of John to refer you to me. What is your particular investment situation that requires my help?"

Joe continued, "Well, I sold my house in Burbank and bought one here. Housing here is much less costly than in California, and I have about $25,000 left over to invest. What do you think I should do with the money?"

As you readers might already have guessed, I sold Joe B. $25,000 worth of the mutual fund that I had tried to sell to his friend John!

The selling-skill moral of this story is to handle a "no sale" with the utmost aplomb!

1. Smile.
2. See that no anger or irritation shows, even for an instant.
3. Ask why the prospect did not buy.
4. Show that you appreciate the prospect's having given you a chance to make your sales presentation.

If you adhere to these points, you will be laying the groundwork for turning the "no sale" into a future "go sale"—either with this prospect or with someone this prospect refers to you.

Acting When
Potential Profits Become Losses

Every seller of securities who makes recommendations to prospects about a potential profit in a stock, convertible bond, commodity, mutual fund, warrant, or option recognizes that an unforeseen adverse factor could turn the potential money gainer into a disastrous loss.

Having obtained an order in an investment that later underperforms, many salespeople are so upset, and assume that their clients are equally disturbed, that consciously or unconsciously they avoid contacting the clients who hold the loss position. Brokers feel ashamed that their judgment of the situation or their market timing was widely off the mark. They generally do not want to face the clients or even talk to them.

The unspoken hope is that maybe time will right the situation. If not, maybe the customer. irked by the lack of contact, will drift off to another broker at some other firm, so that the broker whose judgment was wrong will never have to confront this self-created problem.

Failure to contact losing clients shuts off the commission flow. It creates ego damage through the realization that the unwillingness to admit faulty judgment is simply an act of cowardice.

Sellers of securities are certainly aware that risk exists in almost everything they sell. They must accept the fact that losses inevitably will occur and prepare themselves mentally to deal with clients whose investments are losing money.

Good security salespeople realize that success comes from hard work involving (1) good record-keeping; (2) daily prospecting; (3) order-asking conversations; and (4) increased product knowledge. "Prepare yourself the night before for the coming day and you will do business—bigger and better."

TWO THINGS YOU CAN DO TODAY TO MAKE YOUR BUSINESS GROW!

1. **Set aside a two-hour period every week (same time) to scan ValueLine, Wall Street Transcript, Barrons. You may get an idea that will enthuse you.**
2. **Visit your local library. Skim a book listed under "Sales." to sell more, you constantly have to work on improving your selling skills.**

The consistently best approach to handling clients experiencing losses is to *stay in touch! Don't let losing customers feel that they are alone.* Call, console, write, send information about the loss situations. Ignoring a loser only creates bitterness, dries up referrals, and often results in lawsuits.

Before contacting a client holding a loss, reinvestigate the situation. Be prepared to render a well thought-out current opinion backed up by all the most recently available facts so that the client, even though hurt, will feel that the salesperson is still deeply interested in the client's welfare.

If "hold" is the opinion, be sure the client understands the potential for further risk and all the pertinent reasons for an expected price recovery.

If "sell" is the opinion, make every effort to get the client to accept the loss and seek recovery and profit through a different investment.

Often, I have found that a drop in price occurs without rhyme or reason and affords an excellent opportunity to invest additional dollars at an even more attractive price. "Averaging down" is a very appealing strategy to many investors, and with a little encouragement from the salesperson they will follow the original commitment with equal dollars. Only encourage this tactic when you truly believe the situation merits a larger total investment. Care should be taken that clients who are averaging down do not invest too large a portion of their total assets into a single situation.

Losing clients must be contacted as consistently as if they were winning. *Many investors get more upset by the lack of information and contact than by the loss itself.*

Never assume that clients are so angry over losses that they do not want further contact.

Never assume that clients have no more money to invest and therefore should not be contacted.

Never assume that losing clients will be unwilling to listen to a transfer idea that might regain the losses.

The proper action to take when a client is sitting with a loss is to call or see the client. Present all the facts. Offer recovery hope through holding, purchasing more, or selling and repositioning the money.

Losses are emotionally draining. When losses are maintained too long, they cause inertia. My experience is to eradicate losing situations when they can be offset with realized capital gains. People just naturally feel better about a loss when it is ameliorated by a gain.

Where no capital gains are available for offset purposes, attempt to get the client to accept the loss before it becomes long term so that the maximum tax benefit will be available. Deductions against highest taxed income lessen the bite of the loss and free up the client's capital for other investment opportunities. Recommendations to accept the loss should be made only when you truly believe an equal or better opportunity exists.

LOCATING PROSPECTS THROUGH THE MAIL AND SEMINARS

Making Research Reports
Produce Orders from Prospects

As I write, there are over 44,000 registered representatives of New York Stock Exchange Member Firms. To this army add thousands of National Association of Security Dealers (NASD) licensed salespeople who work for over-the-counter firms.

One of the prime commission-generating products for this large selling group is common stock. Shares of common stock are bought and sold annually at a total value that exceeded $7 billion in 1979. An awesome amount to be sure and each seller of intangibles struggles to get a share of the luscious commission pie associated with $7 billion in share sales by telling the merits of current stock favorites to friends, relatives, and other prospects. Most stock solicitations are made by phone for many valid reasons, including the opportunity for dialogue, the sense of urgency that can be generated by the seller, the ease of contact, and the potential for making a large number of contacts.

Despite the attractions of making stock sales by phone, many brokers use mailing of research reports, either to back up verbal presentations or to try to initiate interest in prospects.

In my opinion, *much of the mailing is a waste of money, time, and effort.*

The average target for mailings of stock reports is inundated with unsolicited mail of all types, including investment ideas. Affluent prospects deal with the influx of "buy-me" mail by "round filing" it (tossing it in the wastebasket) after a quick glance.

Despite the low return (in terms of orders obtained) of direct mail, brokers collectively pour millions of dollars into it, hoping for a positive result. Many individual account executives find it easier to lick envelopes, stuff them with research material, and mail them (at company expense) than to go through the pain of calling or seeing people and risking rejection.

Plan the Research-Report Mailing

Uncontrolled, unplanned mailing of research reports is a drag on profits for the firm and a time-eater for the salesperson, yet its use continues to grow year after year. The mail *can* be an effective tool to open accounts and create orders for common stock, however. The trick is to plan mail strategy. When you zero in on a stock recommended by your research department as one you would like to build a strong position in for your clients, go through the following steps:

1. Prepare a story book for use in selling prospects face to face. Learn the information cold.
2. Order a supply of the reports (generally not over 200). See that the reports are original-print copies rather than photo copies.
3. Select two response cards to enclose with the report.
4. See that your name, address, and phone number are clearly marked on each report. Use a rubber stamp, a label, or attach your business card.

Top security salespeople merchandise one product or idea each month in quantity to clients and prospects. They learn the product or idea thoroughly and then present it with enthusiasm, confidence, and sincerity.

TWO THINGS YOU CAN DO TODAY TO MAKE YOUR BUSINESS GROW!
1. Schedule 2 to 4 appointments for Saturday morning at your office.
2. Pray for rain on Saturday so that appointments will not cancel out to do more entertaining things.

5. Personalize each copy with a handwritten note, preferably block-printed in red ink.

After completing these preparations, you have set the stage to get maximum mileage out of the mailing.

Alert: When you select the research report for the mailing, pick a one-page write-up. People normally do not read multi-page reports with any degree of enthusiasm or dedication. They most often want a capsule that is easy to digest rather than a heavy outpouring of technical data.

Personalizing each report with a handwritten message is a laborious task, but highly productive. It gets a much higher degree of readership than mailings without a personal inclusion. Take great care with the personalized note. Any statement that can be considered inflammatory, nonfactual, or misleading may later come back to haunt you—in the form of a lawsuit.

The note I favor, time-tested and trouble-free, simply says, "Dear Joe: Call me right away, as soon as you have read this." I then sign it and write out my phone number.

That simple message, "Call me right away after you have read this," is good enough to make the recipient read the report, or at least look at it and think twice before discarding it. And many times that message accomplishes the goal: a call from the prospect to the broker. If you follow the personalized report up with a phone call a few days later, the imprinted message tends to encourage the prospect to grant you an appointment or even give you an order.

The New York Stock Exchange frowns on the underlining of research reports, so that practice should be avoided. (The NYSE naturally believes that, left to their own inclinations, salespeople might be tempted to underline only the good aspects, failing to give equal attention to any negative parts.)

Target the Mailing

To get better results from a nonclient list, include in the mailing potential investors likely to be familiar with the spotlighted company or its products, either as suppliers to the company or as distributors or consumers of its products. Let's assume, for example, that the stock in the report is for a drug company with interests in proprietary and ethical drugs. Candidates for the mailing include:

There are three basic requirements for success in selling securities—Intelligence, product knowledge and persistence. Any one of them can make you successful as long as it is persistence!

TWO THINGS YOU CAN DO TODAY TO MAKE YOUR BUSINESS GROW!

1. *Set up a file of approved prospecting letters—for tax shelters, muni bonds, tax-deferred annuities, DWR individual account management, referral, unit trusts, U.S. government securities.*

2. *Test one letter today by mailing to at least 10 prospects and following up with a phone call. Log the results when you know them.*

1. All doctors (listed in the Yellow Pages)
2. All wholesale druggists
3. All pharmacists
4. All drugstore owners and managers

If the chosen stock is a photo industry stock, such as Eastman Kodak or Polaroid, the nonclient mailing list should include all listings in the Yellow Pages that start with the word "Photo." The listings can run from under 50 into the thousands, depending on the geographic area of solicitation. It is always much easier to sell prospects on the stock of a company they are familiar with because of some regular contact with the company's employees, products, or services.

The positive results of a mailing of a research report are more influenced by the personalization and follow-up phone call than by what is actually contained in the report itself. *Don't mail more than you will actually follow up by phone.* That good rule makes for more effective results.

Never mail a report to a business, even though it's one with a connection to the featured company. Take the time to call the company and find out the correct name of the manager, the president, and/or key officer(s), and address the report to their attention.

Finally, let research reports remind you to pinpoint prospects who are not already in your prospect file.

Using the Mail Effectively

As I mentioned in the preceding chapter, millions of dollars each year are spent on direct mailings by insurance salespeople, stockbrokers, commodity agents, and other sellers of intangible investment products. And shockingly, most of this money goes down the drain because the salesperson who is the main beneficiary has no follow-up phone plan or undertakes a scattered, haphazard mailing of untimely or out-of-date material.

Dollars by the millions are also wasted on individualized letter writing both to existing clients and to prospects. As shocking as the money wasted in mailings is the fact that a great many college graduates escaped from their alma maters unable to construct even the simplest business letter. I have witnessed great numbers of salespeople agonizing over writing a letter, devoting hours to writing, editing, rewriting, in order to suggest a minor portfolio change or to answer a request for particular information.

Precious selling hours have been and are currently being wasted on the preparation of rather simple messages to be sent to relatively few people. You can stop this waste of time and money supply by learning the basic strategy in making the mail work for you.

Here is a typical scenario, one that is played and replayed almost daily in every sizable sales office.

Jill Saleswoman has to furnish an opinion on three stocks at a prospect's request, or perhaps she wants to compose a letter to a prospect who has just moved into an expensive house.

During prime selling time, Jill sits at her desk thoughtfully gazing out into space, pencil in hand, hand posed over a yellow pad. She jots down a couple of sentences, pauses, scratches out a couple of words, and writes another sentence. The phone rings, and Jill talks to a client for ten minutes. Hangs up the phone, picks up yellow pad, stares at it again. Makes a few more corrections. The manager calls Jill in to discuss a problem. Thirty minutes later, Jill returns to her desk. The phone rings. She talks to another client. A colleague comes over to talk about supper and Saturday night plans. Two other brokers involve Jill in a conversation about gold and interest rates. Time for lunch. The three go out for lunch. Service is slow, and they don't get back for an hour and a half. Two phone calls to return.

After those are completed the yellow pad is again picked up, stared at, and a few more scarcely legible notes made. Finally, at day's end, the note is handed to a secretary to type. Obviously, the letter won't be typed today. Besides, the secretary is overloaded, and the typing of the letter takes its place behind the others she has to do. At the end of day two, the secretary gets to Jill's letter but can't read the chicken-scratchings. She tries to locate Jill, who is out on a sales call. Note is held over until day three. Day three finds Jill screaming, "Where's my letter?"

Pointing to some hieroglyphics, the secretary snaps, "I can't read your lousy writing. What is this supposed to mean?"

Jill can't decipher it herself, makes a guess, and tosses out a few extra sentences for the secretary to remember to add. A typed copy is available on day four. Jill doesn't like the way it sounds, so she corrects the draft. This really annoys the secretary, who now has to redo it. She drags her feet, puts the letter at the bottom of the pile, and finally gets a corrected copy for Jill's signature by the next day.

The manager, whose duty it is to review all correspondence, gets a carbon copy to initial before the original goes out. He reads it and yells, "Hey, this isn't right!" Jill is called in and shown the error. The manager also corrects some of the English, and a new draft is given to the secretary to type. The secretary is fed up with Jill by this time, and she waits another day before completing what should have been a simple business letter.

Scenes like this are quite common and extremely frustrating to all parties: the salesperson, the secretary, the manager, and the prospect, who did not get answered promptly.

The way to use selling time for real selling, take care of the normal out-going correspondence, and still use the mail to prospect is to develop what I call the *ticket-factory concept.*

I believe sellers of intangibles should think of themselves as "fac-

Calvin Coolidge should have been a sales trainer for stockbrokers. Following his immortal words could make every AE an outstanding success:

"Nothing in the world can take the place of persistence. Talent will not. There are many unsuccessful men with talent. Genius will not. Unrewarded genius is prevalent. Education will not. The world is full of educated derelicts. Persistence and determination are omnipotent."

TWO THINGS YOU CAN DO TODAY TO MAKE YOUR BUSINESS GROW!

1. ***Check out the costs of leasing (new or used) a computer typewriter. The memory unit could hold all names of prospects and approved letters in a variety of topics. This tool, properly used, can double a good producer's income.***

2. ***Learn all the various applications of this immensely helpful tool. The salesperson may also become your client and a referral source.***

   If the cost per month is too much for you to bear, test your sales ability. Try to get the manager or other aggressive AEs to split costs and share in use.

tories" whose purpose is to manufacture executed tickets each day. In order to maximize output, any good factory tries to automate as much as possible. Salespeople should also try to automate letter writing and mail prospecting. One way to do this is to create letters covering every key product you sell and applying to every recurring problem you dealt with in your client relationships.

Establish a sample letter file containing typed samples of letters covering every conceivable situation. Give each letter a number. Note which enclosures go with each letter. And be sure to avoid problems by having your manager approve each letter before you use it.

Once these steps are completed, have each letter typed on the typewriter your secretary uses. Most of the letters then will need only a typed-in name and address to make them personal. Others may call for the insertion of special information on appropriate lines. All of them can be printed in quantity (100 to 500, depending on estimated use) at a local print shop. When a letter has to go out, all that is required is to type in the name (and blanks as/if required) with the same typewriter. The type style will then match the printed letter, although its darkness may vary depending on the state of the typewriter ribbon.

If you are featuring a certain product, such as a tax shelter or a tax-deferred annuity, you can simply instruct a secretary to "Send letter 4 to these 10 people," and give the secretary the prospect cards for names and addresses. The secretary then notes on the cards, *Letter 4, 11/12/88* and then types the names and encloses the designated material. All this takes place without any hassle or wasted time on the secretary's part, or, for that matter, on yours.

You will be able to review your prospect cards and easily determine what has been sent and when. Follow-up phone calls to each prospect in the mailing should be logged for a week after mailing.

A lot more sales are likely with this organized approach to direct mail, for you will virtually have automated one process for bringing a lot of orders into your factory to execute. The intent is to create a steady stream of prospects making incoming calls as a result of the regular mail solicitations they receive.

Each letter going out must be hand signed (*no printed signatures,* PLEASE). The envelope should also carry a handwritten message in red ink along the lines of the following:

1. Free SEMINAR TICKETS ENCLOSED
2. CONFIDENTIAL
3. PERSONAL
4. TAX-SAVING IDEAS
5. EARN 14% [or what currently is attractively available in high-yield investments]

Each letter must also have a handwritten postscript (P.S.), again, preferably in red, the attention-getting color. The P.S. should be a message similar to this:

> *P.S.*
> *Call me right away (555-6000) after carefully reading the enclosed.*
> *LeRoy Gross*

People are funny creatures. On the whole, almost everyone reads a short P.S. *before* reading the body of the letter. The P.S. does the real work of the letter because it calls for a specific, immediate action based on apparently urgent information.

Some branch offices have a computer typewriter with a memory unit that can store thousands of names and sample letters. This piece of equipment is worth many times its cost in terms of the time and money it saves and the accuracy it provides.

If the branch cannot afford to lease a unit, you might want to consider chipping in with several colleagues to split the monthly charge for leasing a new unit or perhaps a lower-priced used machine. (The cost qualifies as a tax deduction!)

With the help of the computer, a regular mail contact program can be efficiently operated, and that will help to make the automated ticket factory a reality.

Direct Mail Minus the Postal System

Direct mail does not always have to go through the U.S. Postal system!

Here are some sales-building ideas for getting prospecting material into the hands of prospects at a low cost per piece:

1. Look into getting the newspaper delivery boy or girl to deliver a prospecting piece (complete with return card) with each paper. This method of distribution costs a fraction of the mailing costs. The benefits are in shortening the distribution time lines and the possibility of effecting geographic concentration in affluent areas.

2. Look into hiring a teenager to distribute the selected material under each door of a high-rise apartment or condominium. The benefits here are the same as those in item 1. Just be sure to choose a high-tariff building.

Send mail in bulk to zip code areas whenever possible; doing so avoids the expense of first-class mail. *It is better to make more contacts than to spend more of the mail money on postage per each.*

Here are some tips that will be helpful in building the master set of letters or in writing any letter:

1. Make sure the prospect's name is spelled correctly. Why alienate a potential client by failing to take the time to learn how to spell both first and last names?

2. Make sure that any title is correct. Addressing a vice president as "assistant vice president" is just asking to have the content of your letter ignored.

3. Create a headline, an attention grabbing opening statement, if you want the body of the letter to be read.

4. Be careful in your word choice. Technical language can be a sales killer rather than a sales maker. The simpler you can make your words, the better understood your message will be.

5. Try to keep letters to one page. Long-winded, preachy letters don't sell as well as briefer messages.

6. End the letter by asking for an order or an appointment or an immediate phone call from the prospect.

Making Direct Mail Produce
High-Quality Appointments
and Tax-Free Municipal Accounts

Almost every securities salesperson would love to have a clientele comprised of very affluent investors whose taxable annual income at present—as well as that expected for the future—would lead them to be repeat buyers of tax-free municipal bonds.

Tax-free municipal bonds can be big generators of commission income to the salesperson when sold in a "portfolio" environment such as:

1. Municipal bond trusts, or

2. Municipal bond mutual funds

Municipal bond portfolio unit investments come in a variety wide enough to suit almost any investor's desire. Some of the more popular varieties follow, to give the reader an eye-opening look at the possibilities available to reach a large segment of the high-income populace:

1. *Short-term municipal investment trust units.* Average life: 3 years.

2. *Intermediate-term municipal investment trust units.* Average life: 10 years.

3. *Long-term municipal investment trust units.* Average life: 20–30 years.

4. *Floating rate municipal investment trust units.* The rate of tax-free interest normally fluctuates up and down in step with the prime

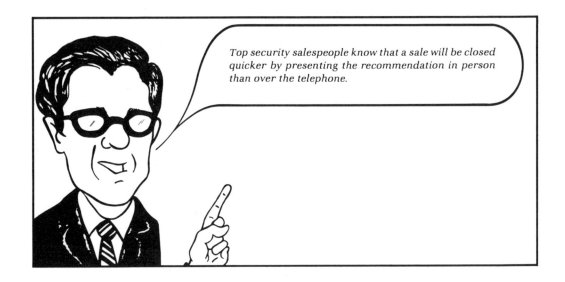

Top security salespeople know that a sale will be closed quicker by presenting the recommendation in person than over the telephone.

rate. This fluctuation is designed to keep the principal value relatively stable to avoid major loss in the event of redemption prior to maturity.

5. *Insured municipal investment trust units*. These trusts—short-, intermediate-, and long-term—are designed for the "worried" municipal buyer who is fearful of issuer defaults. All municipal bonds within the trusts are rated AAA and are insured as to principal and the timely payment of interest.

6. *"Zero" coupon municipal investment trust units*. These pay no annual interest but are designed to provide a large federal tax-free gain at maturity.

7. *Low-quality municipal bond funds*. These are designed to provide *high* federal tax-free income from lower-rated bonds that are professionally selected and managed.

8. *High-quality municipal bond funds*. These funds consist of issues selected from highly rated bonds; they are managed by bond experts.

In addition to "packaged" municipal bonds, the individual municipal bond market offers an incredible array of commission opportunities for the knowledgeable salesperson.

Some of the super-attractive features available in the individual municipal bond market lend themselves to aggressive marketing because of the great selling *words* that can be used to create business.

Here are just a few of the types of municipal bonds that have enormous appeal to the purchaser interested in tax-free income:

1. *"Put" Bonds.* This type of bond carries a provision that allows the purchaser to "put," that is, sell the bond back to the issuer at par value. This assurance alleviates the worries about a rise in interest rates that would make non-puttable bonds drop in value.
2. *Insured Bonds.* These bonds are not only guaranteed by the issuer as to prompt payment of principal and interest but additionally guaranteed by one or more insurance companies.
3. *Discount Bonds.* One of the most marketable and marketed types of municipal bonds, the discount bond, is bought for *less than its face value* on or before maturity date.

Once a salesperson is knowledgeable about municipal bonds, the problem becomes one of marketing this knowledge to a great number of qualified investors.

Getting enough qualified people to listen to a tax-free investment proposal each week seems to be an arduous task for most securities salespeople. Getting strangers to *regularly initiate calls to the salesperson* about a municipal bond investment seems a task that borders on the impossible.

Despite the seeming difficulties expressed in the preceding paragraphs, both goals can often be accomplished by using a special direct-mail/phone-call approach that has been developed. It has been field tested and effectively used by hundreds of brokers.

A special municipal bond prospecting form has been designed so that, if it is diligently used and followed-up as outlined, it should produce tax-free municipal bond appointments, accounts, and commission dollars. (See Exhibit 1.)

Every working day before you leave the office, take the time to complete *ten* (10) of these forms using a *red thick-writing felt-tip pen.* Be sure to *print all letters and numbers clearly enough and large enough* that even a weak-eyed, wealthy investor would have no trouble reading your message.

Be sure these handwritten (not typed) messages are sent to wealthy prospects assumed to be municipal investors, judging by where they live or what they do for a living.

After filling in the date and the prospect's name, list *only one municipal bond* that you really believe to be a good value at the time. Be careful that your selection issue is "thick" in supply—that is, in

How Much is Tax-Free Interest Income Worth to You?

This table shows investors in various Federal tax brackets what an effect of tax-exempt interest yields from municipal bonds

For example if you are in the $45,800-60,000 taxable income bracket across the chart, this means, that for a tax-exempt yield of 7%, you after taxes.

Under the Revenue Act of 1978, if taxable income is ($000's)

		$23.5 to $28.8
Single Return	($000)	
	$29.9 to	$35
Joint Return	($000) $35.2	$45
Tax Bracket	28% 30%	33

Tax Exempt Yields

(%)			
	6.0	8.3	8.5	8
	7.0	9.7	10.0	10
	7.5	10.4	10.7	11
	8.0	11.1	11.4	11
	8.5	11.8	12.1	12
	9.0	12.5	12.9	13
	9.5	13.2	13.6	14
	10.0	13.9	14.3	14
	10.5	14.6	15.0	15
	11.0	15.3	15.7	16
	11.5	16.0	16.4	17
	12.0	16.7	17.1	17
	12.5	17.4	17.9	18
	13.0	18.1	18.6	19
	13.5	18.8	19.3	20
	14.0	19.4	20.0	20
	14.5	20.1	20.7	21
	15.0	20.8	21.4	22

1984 Tax Year

Yield figures are app

The information contained herein was obtained from sou
basis of federal taxes enacted subsequent to the publication

PaineWebber

Federal Tax Free Municipal Bonds   PaineWebber

Date _____

We suggest for the portfolio of _____ the following Federal tax free municipal bonds subject to prior sale and/or change in price.*

Moody's Rating	S & P Rating	Amount	Security Description	General Obligation	Revenue or Other	Coupon Rate	Maturity	Yield to Maturity	Approx. Price % of 1000.	Current Yield

*Municipal bonds are exempt from federal income taxes. Most are also exempt from state and local income taxes in the state of issue.

Account Executive _____

State _____

City _____

PLEASE CALL RIGHT AWAY WHILE THE ABOVE BONDS ARE AVAILABLE _____ (Collect if Out of Town)

EXHIBIT 1

terms of your firm's inventory or in terms of "Blue List" availability. It becomes self-defeating to create an interest in an investment that you are unable to obtain.

After this information is properly written on your form, it should look like the one in Exhibit 2. *You are now ready to make this form into one of the hardest hitting municipal bond prospecting pieces in the securities industry.*

In the space remaining under your one bond listing, write a personal letter (print legibly) using the prospect's first name and signing off with your first name. The use of both first names creates in the prospect's mind the possibility of a prior acquaintance that helps get your message read and digested.

The personal letter that you write should be just like the one in Exhibit 2. This illustrates a message that is compliance-safe and that could produce for you that "most wanted" call—an *"incoming"* call from a stranger seeking an appointment with you or giving you an order. Expect to write fifty of these carefully handwritten notes each week to generate some incoming orders and accounts for municipal bonds.

But what if *no one* calls? The stage has been set for the most important "follow-up" call. If your letter was sent to an executive or professional at the office address, you wait a week after mailing and then call the office. Most of the time the phone will be answered by a secretary who normally will ask, "Who's calling?" When questioned, respond with your first name only and with a little urgency in your voice, as follows:

Federal Tax Free Municipal Bonds

PaineWebber

Date _10/18/84_

We suggest for the portfolio of _____ the following Federal tax free municipal bonds subject to prior sale and/or change in price:*

Moody's Rating	S & P Rating	Amount	Security Description	General Obligation	Revenue or Other	Coupon Rate	Maturity	Yield to Maturity	Approx. Price % of 1000.	Current Yield
AA		100M	NYS Med.		✓	10%	10-1-04	10%	100%	10%
			Care							
			Montefiore							
			Hosp. Revenue							

*Municipal bonds are exempt from federal income taxes. Most are also exempt from state and local income taxes in the state of issue.

DEAR BOB,
CALL ME. RIGHT AWAY
WHILE THESE HIGH
QUALITY TAX-FREE BONDS
ARE AVAILABLE!
LeRoy
_(212) 432-7400_

LeRoy Gross
Account Executive
State _NY_
City _NY-140 Broadway_

PLEASE CALL RIGHT AWAY WHILE THE ABOVE BONDS ARE AVAILABLE _212 432-7400_ (Collect if Out of Town)
PHONE

EXHIBIT 2

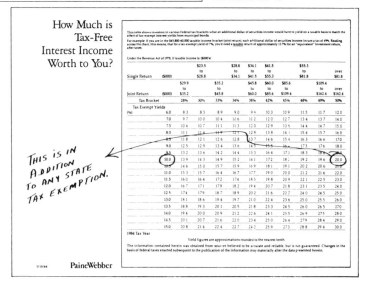

How Much is Tax-Free Interest Income Worth to You?

THIS IS IN ADDITION TO ANY STATE TAX EXEMPTION.

PaineWebber

Secretary: "Who's calling, please?"

Broker: "This is Ed. I would like to talk to him *right* now. It's about that letter he *failed to answer!*"

That informal hurried approach, suggesting a failure on the part of the boss, will normally get you through to the prospect. Once through, you discuss your special tax-free bond idea, the prospect's investment objective, and why he did not respond to your letter. The conversation should lead to an order or an appointment.

I have brought you this far. The rest is up to you.

Making Low-Cost/No-Cost
Seminars Produce Big Bucks

Holding public seminars as a means of obtaining prospects is gaining increasing favor with all types of firms that sell financial products. Firms like this forum-prospecting method because it provides a relatively cheap way to reach high-potential prospects in a manner that is meant to be significant and meaningful.

However, the proper promotion, set-up, and delivery of a sales-producing seminar is very difficult. One of its great proponents is Alan C. Snyder, President of Dean Witter Reynolds Insurance, who has given hundreds of effective seminars on a variety of financial topics. So have I. Our hard-won expertise is condensed in this discussion. We have used all the information related here to close sales totaling in the millions. Our success was not instant; success developed through application of good techniques characterized by hard work and good planning.

Even if you feel unsure of your ability to make effective presentations in public, try to force yourself to do it. You will improve with practice and if you follow our system, you will be positively reinforced with substantial sales.

Learn to Speak Effectively in Public

Public-speaking courses, given at night at community colleges or YMCAs, can help make your delivery better. Look for one and take it.

Toastmasters is an excellent nationwide organization to help improve speaking skills. Join your local chapter! You will also find Toastmasters members a fine group to prospect, as they usually include the up-and-coming people in the community.

Basics for the Presentation

In preparing your presentations, take into consideration the following suggestions:

1. *Prepare an attention-getting opening statement.* Example: "In every group of 100 people in the United States today reaching the age of 65, 87 of the 100 are trying to survive, attempting to get along on less than $5,000 a year *from all sources* including Social Security!"

2. *Cite a negative example.* Illustration: "Don't do as thousands of people are doing, letting their money earn low bank savings rates fully taxable at their highest brackets."

3. *Cite a positive example.* Illustration: "Do as many intelligent investors are now doing, placing their money [name specific products]."

4. *Prepare an order-creating closing statement.* Example: "Everyone in this room tonight should plan to take some of their money and put it to work in [name a product that you've highlighted in your presentation]."

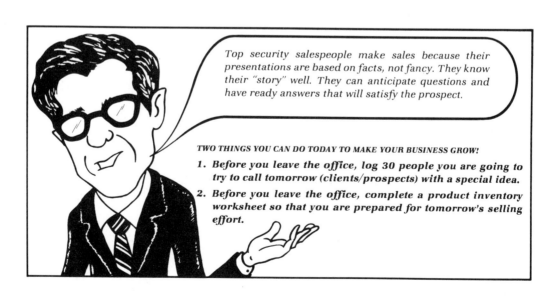

Top security salespeople make sales because their presentations are based on facts, not fancy. They know their "story" well. They can anticipate questions and have ready answers that will satisfy the prospect.

TWO THINGS YOU CAN DO TODAY TO MAKE YOUR BUSINESS GROW!

1. *Before you leave the office, log 30 people you are going to try to call tomorrow (clients/prospects) with a special idea.*
2. *Before you leave the office, complete a product inventory worksheet so that you are prepared for tomorrow's selling effort.*

As you rehearse your presentation to make it more effective, try to avoid the following common problems:

1. *Speaking too fast.* Racing through a presentation destroys a great part of its value. Allow time for emphasis and pauses as well as time for the audience to think and absorb what you are saying. If you want to imprint your message on their minds, slower is better!

2. *Poor enunciation.* Be sure of the correct pronunciation of any different words you intend to use. Be scrupulous about enunciating clearly so that the audience can easily understand exactly what you say and not confuse words with similar-sounding words.

3. *Weak ending* Don't let your voice die at the end of a sentence. Many speakers trail off and swallow sentence-ending words. That makes any listener strain to hear, and it destroys the impact of your remarks.

4. *Hesitation sounds.* Noises like "er," "um," and "uh" are destructive. They actually kill the effectiveness of even the best material. Substituting pauses for these unself-confident-sounding syllables will greatly improve the impression you make on the audience. To help rid yourself of the "uh" syndrome, simply tape-record your presentation. Listen to it with pad and pencil in hand, and mark down the number of times you hear "uh" and "er" and "um." This scoring procedure will make you conscious of the habit. Once you become conscious of it, you will be on your way to eliminating the unattractive, unself-confident sounds from your pattern of speech.

Organizing, Delivering, and Following Up Public Seminars

Public seminars have become a most effective stage from which sellers of intangibles can sell themselves, their firms, and specific products. Many of the best producers in the country developed their clientele primarily through effective and frequent seminar presentations. What holds true for them can become true for you.

Building a business and regularly providing a steady stream of new accounts through a seminar program is not an easy task, nor is the method effective for every seller of intangibles. However, for ambitious people who want to reach a high income level and who are willing to pay the price of hard work, the seminar approach can be one of the *most rewarding and consistent* of all prospecting methods.

This chapter is devoted to helping you learn the skills involved in conducting seminars and avoid the common mistakes.

Collecting existing clients or new prospects together in a forum environment gives you, as the sponsor, a great opportunity to make large sales and to sell yourself to a degree impossible by other means.

Existing clients are an excellent target market for more business. You should not be surprised that explaining new products and services or providing an investment overview strengthens your relationship with them. What more efficient, yet personal, way could there be to inform and sell? *You are controlling the presentation.* The content can be tailored to the most appropriate group in attendance in order to maximize results. New business can be gotten from the "bring-a-friend" opener. New business may come from reviving an otherwise dead account. New business may develop when good clients discover you provide a service they didn't know you sold. Seminars are one professional approach for new business that maximizes your time.

Prospects are the primary source from which new business will come. The seminar gives you an opportunity to explain something of interest to potential investors in an unthreatening environment. You whet prospects' appetites with an invitation describing the benefits that the new knowledge will provide.

Listen to Alan Snyder, President of Dean Witter Reynolds Insurance: "The seminar is the tour through the kitchen. You serve the meal at the close. The new client/prospect gets exposure to timely investment ideas that might greatly benefit him." Happily, outside experts with third-party power can be used when necessary or available (e.g., financial-product wholesalers, tax-shelter or insurance specialists).

Low-Cost Ways to Beef Up Seminar Attendance

Diligent, thoughtful salespeople seek various "sponsors" to get a group together. The attendees at sponsored seminars are just as good and valuable prospects as those obtained at high expense by direct mail or newspaper ads.

Typical of sponsored seminars are talks given to civic club groups such as Rotary, Lions, Kiwanis, Optimists, and like organizations. When given the opportunity to speak before groups like the above, don't make hard-sell specific recommendations. Instead, try to intrigue the audience with new concepts such as tax-deferred annuities, tax shelters, and trading strategies.

Usually, the time allotted for such talks is only 25 to 30 minutes. Make every effort to finish in time to allow for a few questions. Inform everyone that you have made material available to pick up on a special table. The material should have your card attached and a return card of some type that can be sent in to obtain more information. Remember to check the return card so that it is not mailed back to the home office. *Put your name and branch on it!* Where possible, try to obtain the membership list of the sponsoring group for a later mailing.

Public corporations can frequently be persuaded to let you give a seminar on "their" stock to the stock-holding employees. Seminars of this type can be most productive, and you can suggest one, two, or three sessions.

Prospect for corporate seminars by calling local corporation presidents, treasurers, or key officers to explain what you would like to do. In trying to sell them on sponsoring your seminar, you might wind up with an account. A contact made under such circumstances makes phone prospecting easier. Close with a brief description of several new products and services being offered "now" through your firm.

Finding Sponsors

Many types of sponsored seminars are available to put you in front of an audience *without your having to spend any (or many) funds*. These low-cost or no-cost seminars are every bit as valuable in producing prospects as the high-cost ones. The following list shows you possibilities for speaking engagements.

Public Libraries

Frequently, public libraries will furnish a room and advertising for an investment seminar. If the talk and attendance are good, you can probably arrange to hold a seminar quarterly.

Civic Clubs

The "emergency speaker" letter is a very effective tool in lining up talks to groups. Calling the presidents of civic clubs and offering to

Top security salespeople reach the top and stay on top because they adhere to the three primary rules for success in our business: (1) prospect; (2) prospect; (3) prospect!

TWO THINGS YOU CAN DO TODAY TO MAKE YOUR BUSINESS GROW!

1. **Contact the president of a community college or business college in your area and see if you can persuade him or her to let you conduct a series of night classes on investing, for adults.**
2. **Contact the president of the business and professional women's club. Meet her (get the account!) and see if you can speak at a breakfast meeting.**

conduct a program is also effective. (Get the list of presidents from your local Chamber of Commerce.)

Department Stores

Because they are always interested in building traffic in their stores, store managers are good prospects to whom you should try to sell the "sponsor" concept. One or two managers often will become your clients, too! Notification of the seminar can be put into their customers' statements (no extra mailing cost for them or you) or the stores' newspaper ads. Offer to pay half the cost and handle the reservation requests.

Publicly Held Corporations

Seminars based on preretirement counseling for retiring employees frequently can get you into a corporation and its executives. One-session seminars based on an analysis of the company's stock versus the market may also kindle interest.

Special-Interest Groups and Organizations

Accountants' societies or the medical and legal societies all need program speakers at their monthly meetings. Some sellers of intangibles regularly address the partners of major accounting firms, dispens-

Good security salespeople know that in the stock market the meek do not inherit the earth. Are you asking for three referrals each day?

TWO THINGS YOU CAN DO TODAY TO MAKE YOUR BUSINESS GROW!

1. *Call Boy Scout and Girl Scout leaders. Arrange to have a troop and parents visit your office one night to learn about the fascinating world of investments. Free coffee and cookies . . . and you might get some good accounts.*

2. *Clip two write-ups of business promotions from the newspaper. Send clippings and note. Follow up with phone call a week later.*

ing product information to them so that they can anticipate their clients' questions. Contacting these groups can sometimes put you in front of the wealthy, powerful people who represent the best prospects. Tax shelters and insurance, as part of an overall financial program including stocks and bonds, are good presentations for such groups. Small-business groups naturally respond to using pretax dollars to fund business insurance.

YMCAs/YMHAs/YWCAs

Frequently, "Y" associations sponsor classes on investments. Try to get yourself appointed as the instructor for a quarterly course. Many of the attendees will sooner or later make investments or buy insurance.

Community Colleges/Business Colleges

Teaching institutions often use, and pay, experienced people to teach an investment course to students, who pay for the privilege. Imagine your getting paid to prospect! It does happen, and it could happen to you if you contact your local educational institutions.

Condominium Associations

Many retirement communities have club rooms and seek out speakers to entertain and teach retirees. The associations usually furnish the facilities, equipment, and refreshments, without cost to you. This market is especially big in Florida and California.

Critical Choices

The Topic

The selection of a topic for a seminar is most crucial if your promotional material is to draw the attendance that you desire. In recent market environments, subjects such as "Estate Planning," "Ways to Save on Income Taxes," and "Learn How You Can Earn a Guaranteed Lifetime Income" have normally produced the largest turnouts. Often, lectures on specific products are too narrowly focused to draw well.

Three-session courses on learning about all facets of investing, but heavily slanted toward high-income investing, have consistently attracted attendees.

Whatever your topic selection, refresh your knowledge on the subject material so that you will increase your confidence. In presenting the material, you will want to present the image of the *helpful professional*. Your role will be to *sell yourself* to the group as a knowledgeable person, rather than to educate the group to a great degree.

Date Selection

Once you have selected your topic, you must choose a date for your seminar. You should consider checking for upcoming sporting, political, TV, or local events that might detract from the potential attendance at your lecture. Be aware of major religious, state, and national holidays. Night seminars usually draw best on Tuesdays, Wednesdays, or Thursdays. Middle or late December is usually a poor time for seminars; people are too busy with the holidays.

Time

After carefully selecting the date, choose a time that will allow potential prospects to arrive at your site after work and dinner. For some areas of the country, where many people commute, 8:00 P.M. is ideal. In other areas, 7:30 P.M. is the most suitable time. In retirement areas, such as Florida, people will come to lectures at 10:30 A.M., especially if coffee and juice are offered, and 4:00 P.M., so that they can be through in time for supper.

Consider offering two lecture times in your promotion. One might be a morning time for retired people and the other an evening time for workers, as well as retired people. One of the most successful account executives in the country ($750,000 gross) works in a major city and developed his business solely through same-day lectures using the morning and evening times.

Lunchtime seminars can be an especially effective means of developing prospects. The best time is 12:30 P.M. to 1:30 P.M. on Thursdays. The procedure is to call local business people, doctors, accountants, and lawyers to inform them that they are invited to a special seminar from 12:30 P.M. to 1:30 P.M. on a specific Thursday. Tell them that only a limited number of people can attend, as the seminar will be held in the conference room of your office. Say that sandwiches and coffee will be served. If they can't make it, tell them that you are repeating the seminar on the following Thursday. Make every effort to

Henry Ford said it, and he wasn't even a stockbroker! "Thinking is the hardest part of work, which is probably the reason so few engage in it."

try to pin them down into accepting for that day. This process gives you Monday, Tuesday, and Wednesday to make prospecting calls offering a "free lunch" and an interesting topic. If no one accepts or shows up, you have lost nothing. If two or three attend, you have a great chance to convert them into accounts. Lunchtime seminars make calling easier and provide a lot of prospect contact.

Most people have to eat lunch, and, if they can eat "free" and learn something interesting about tax savings, they may be inclined to attend, or at least to request the information. You also might draw prospects who would not go out at night to attend an investment seminar.

The Site

The site for your public lecture is one of the most critical choices; it will significantly affect your attendance. One key item is the availability of free parking. Local, well-known motels or restaurants solve the parking problem. Other popular lecture sites are schools, country clubs, and libraries. Choose a site, if possible, that is popular, perhaps a landmark, so that instructions for getting there are easy to follow.

You may be fortunate enough to have large and accessible office facilities that can accommodate from 10 to 30 people. Whenever an office can be used as the lecture site, "classes" are more effective because the surroundings are businesslike. Seminars in branches also make it easy to arrange future appointments: the prospect has already "been there."

How to Draw Attendance at Unsponsored Seminars

Direct Mail

You have several choices available to attract prospects to an investment seminar. The most popular, and generally most successful, is direct mail. Direct mail requires extensive thought, work, and preparation. Take these points into consideration.

1. You and the branch manager must determine the number of pieces to be mailed, due to the expense involved.
2. Select the area to be mailed carefully. You want to select affluent prospects for whom the lecture site will be easily accessible.
3. Assemble the names on cards or lists, and prepare mailing labels.
4. Decide with the manager whether to mail first class or bulk mail, by zip code area or addressed to "resident." By mailing bulk, you can realize substantial savings, reaching more people with the allocated dollars. An additional benefit to "occupant" mail is that such mail is *not* forwarded to people who have moved, so that new tenants, who would not have been on the address list, receive the "occupant" mail.

Sometimes, purchased lists are workable. However, they usually cover too broad a geographic area to be effective for an individual branch. These are best left to national lead programs, particularly when the lists are of magazine subscribers, tax-shelter purchasers, and stock owners.

Newspaper Advertising

Another way to publicize seminars is to place an ad in the local newspaper. Results in garnering attendees vary widely, and local experience with seminar ads is your best guide to whether to use this medium. Sometimes, direct mail combined with an ad is highly effective. The choice depends on costs and prior experience in your area.

Phone Contact

The third method for drawing attendance is to use the phone extensively to try to interest people in coming to the seminar. This way is a recommended *supplement* to any lecture, for it accomplishes two purposes. The primary goal is to try to build attendance. The secondary goal is to make contact with potential prospects for future appointments or for the sale of one of your products, *whether or not they attend the seminar*. Phone campaigns are particularly effective with existing clients. After you make the initial contact, follow up with the invitation detailing time and place.

Television

In a few areas, UHF television stations have pull power at low cost, and this route may be effective in gathering people to a lecture. The branch manager, in conjunction with the advertising department, can assess the efficacy of this approach.

Allow Enough Lead Time

Once you have chosen your promotional medium, be sure to allow adequate response time. If you promote too far in advance of the seminar, the number of attendees usually drops. The same holds true if you promote too close to the seminar date. Judging from experience, direct mail with an enclosed response card should be mailed approximately two to three weeks prior to the lecture. This allows time for the normally slow U.S. mail system both to deliver and to allow the return card to be received.

Newspaper ads should be run ten days to two weeks prior to the lecture, to allow coupon returns to be received and confirmed. One problem that can destroy a well-planned seminar is the failure to allow sufficient time for the direct mail pieces to be approved, printed, and received at your branch. Check this particular lead time through your manager when you are planning your seminar. Allowing time for delays is smart business practice.

Confirm Responses

Once a coupon response is received, immediately send a written confirmation on your stationery *relating the time, date, and place of the seminar.* Additionally, contact each responder by phone a day or two before the seminar to reconfirm attendance.

Important: *This phone contact should be made by you, not by your sales assistant!* In talking to the prospective attendee, you have an opportunity to build rapport and, possibly, provide investment help or even obtain an appointment prior to the seminar. Frequently, seminar attendance can be "built" by informing each attendee that he or she is allowed to bring one or more friends. By encouraging others to attend the seminar, attendees frequently lock themselves into coming, when they might otherwise simply change their minds and fail to attend. Encourage husbands and wives to come as a unit. If they are both exposed to the same information and to your personality as the lecturer, it is usually easier to get a closing appointment.

If a three-session seminar is being conducted, *confirm each session* by mail and phone to try to keep and increase attendance.

The people who answer the telephone at your branch office must have a reference sheet with all details of the time, date, and place of your lecture so that they can properly handle phone requests. Neglecting this detail can scale down the attendance that you have spent money and hard work to obtain.

Rehearse Your Seminar

The best speakers in the world freely admit to being on edge before delivering a talk. When giving a presentation to a public group, you should normally expect a case of butterflies. Here are several key

Every good security salesperson could become a star if he or she only understood that the job is not to devote the bulk of time to trying to peer into the dim future but to do the daily work that can be clearly seen.

points that will help you to deliver a good talk despite the inherent tension:

1. *Rehearse your presentation* with your spouse, manager, or colleagues. Doing so will help you sharpen up your talk and give you more self-confidence.
2. *Make an outline of your talk* on 3 × 5 cards or printed sheets.
3. *Write your notes legibly* so that when you refer to them, they are easy to read.
4. *Time the length of your talk* and allow about 15 minutes at the end for questions. Try to limit your talk to 45 minutes to an hour.
5. *Be conscious of audience comfort.* The seats may not be comfortable for the audience, or the room may be too hot or cold. Many people need a rest break along the way. It is better to leave them wanting more information than to give them too much.

You must remember that your *main objective is to sell yourself*. Try to create an image of trust. Do not be all knowing, but try instead to project the picture of a diligent, informative broker who will make every effort to help lessen the client's investment risk and increase the client's income.

Finally, *tape-record the actual lecture*, as well as a rehearsal, to serve as a guide to the parts you did well on and to help you correct those areas in which you were weak.

Visual Aids

People learn by what they hear *and* what they see. If they can hear and see, they tend to understand more easily. Selecting and using visual aids can measurably improve the impact of an investment presentation. Many types of visual aids can help improve your talk, ranging from flip charts, blackboards, 35-mm slides, and overhead projections to video-tapes.

Easel Pads

Use large easel pads only for small groups, where everyone in the group is close enough to read the material on the pad easily. *Don't write on the pad as you make your presentation.* The tendency to write fast and illegibly is normal, but by doing so you will destroy the effectiveness of the thought. Besides, your back would be toward the audience, and you would find yourself talking to the pad rather than to the prospects. The one exception is if you have asked the audience to tell you their goals or otherwise contribute information.

Prepare easel-pad visuals in advance so that you have simply to turn the pages and expand upon the points shown on the pad. Print large letters and use inks of different colors to focus the audience's attention. Once you have made several easel-pad presentations, you will be equipped to give others more easily, since the work of building the presentation has already been completed.

Blackboards

Generally, blackboards are not effective visual aids, even for small groups. Visibility can be bad due to the poor physical state of the board, the quality of chalk, the size of the board, and the lighting in the room. Using a blackboard requires much erasing and rewriting. As with easels, writing legibly and rapidly is a rare talent most people lack. Using the blackboard puts your back to the audience, and you end up talking to the board.

Blackboards can best be used to list your name and perhaps one or two main themes or points that remain constantly in view throughout the presentation.

35-mm Slides

Many speakers like to use 35-mm slide presentations. These clearly visible aids are very helpful to the audience. If you use slides, you can almost forego your notes and instead take your cues from the slides, expanding your talk from the key points in the slides.

One disadvantage of slide presentations is that the lights must be dimmed. The semidarkness may cause nodding heads, which may disconcert you, and your lecture will, unfortunately, fail to influence the sleepers. Another disadvantage of slides is the possibility of equipment failure or that the screen will be too small for the audience to view the slides well. Despite the potential disadvantages, however, the positive features of color, high visibility, and readability make 35-mm slides a most attractive visual aid at seminars.

Be sure to number your slides so that you or an assistant may easily and carefully place them in the carousel. Out-of-order slides can seriously affect the quality of your presentation, and the audience may miss key sales points.

Many lecturers maintain slides sets already mounted in their own carousels so they need simply place the carousel on the projector. Their talk is in order and ready for the beginning of the show, with no frantic, last-minute scrambling. Keep in mind that not all slides will fit in any carousel. Most Kodak carousels do fit the different Kodak projectors.

Overhead Transparencies

Overhead transparencies are very effective visual tools for adding power to a presentation. They can be shown in a more brightly lit room than can be used for 35-mm presentations. You can write on a prepared transparency in colored pencil to highlight a particular point; that involves the audience more deeply in the subject.

As with 35-mm presentations, the possible failure of equipment can cause a problem. A large screen is necessary for good visibility. Once a set of transparencies is made, they can be used for many presentations before they deteriorate from warping or scratches.

Do not type material on overhead transparencies. Typed copy is very difficult to read from a distance. Precise, large lettering (color is helpful) by a professional graphic artist is most effective. *Don't try to save money on slide preparation.* If the visuals are poorly done, the audience's impression of the speaker suffers.

A word of caution: when you are preparing visuals with easel pads, 35-mm slides, or transparencies, don't try to crowd too much information on one panel. It is better to have more slides or panels than to crowd a slide or picture.

Video-Tape

For small groups, video-tape provides a consistency of presentation and the magic of television, both of which can greatly aid the seminar. Two *caveats:* first, without multiple screens, video-tape is usable only for small groups, and second, the video presentation must be followed up with a strong summation.

Giving the Seminar: Final Preparations

1. Arrive at the site at least one hour before the seminar.
2. Have with you the list of reservations, your outline, and a kit of handout materials to give to each attendee. If the meeting is at a hotel, restaurant, or any other place where a marquee directs attendees to the proper room, see that the name and meeting directions are correctly displayed.
3. Your own portable meeting sign (Blank Company Seminar) is a valuable seminar aid for any site that does not have a marquee.
4. See that a check-in table is set up near the entrance and is run by your spouse, a friend, or a sales assistant. Each registrant should be given the handout material and instructions to fill out an information request and turn the form in at the end of the seminar.
5. Check with the manager of the facility to see that water is available, to find out at what time coffee or refreshments are to be served, and to confirm that all facility-provided equipment is in place and functioning.

The Meeting Room

The selection of a meeting room can often play a major role in determining the effectiveness of the seminar. When you have the opportunity to choose a room (local branch seminars or library seminars typically do not offer the luxury of choosing a setting), consider the following checklist:

1. Is the room large enough to hold comfortably the number of people who have reservations?
2. Are there enough chairs available to seat the expected attendees?
3. Is there a podium for the speaker?
4. Is the heating or air conditioning so noisy as to cause distraction? Is the temperature properly set? Cooler is better. Do you know where the heating or air conditioning controls are?
5. Is it a partitioned room? If so, will other parts contain a noisy gathering at the time of your lecture?
6. Is there a table for water pitchers and glasses and for coffee if it is to be served later?
7. Do you know where the light switches are located? Do you or an assistant know how to control the lights properly?
8. Can you arrange the chairs so that each has a clear view of the speaker and any visuals to be shown?
9. Can the most distant person easily hear you, or will you need a microphone? (Microphone use is encouraged to save the speaker's voice and to make it easy for everyone to hear.)
10. Are there sufficient ashtrays available?

Often, top security salespeople reach the top because they have learned to sell the interview before selling the product!

TWO THINGS YOU CAN DO TODAY TO MAKE YOUR BUSINESS GROW!
1. *Call prospects and clients until you have lined up a personal appointment for every day next week.*
2. *Call 10 strangers and ask them to buy a quality, high-yield, tax-free bond available from inventory or blue list.*

Equipment Checklist

Nothing can frustrate a speaker more than to have an equipment failure during a presentation. Despite all precautions, sometimes equipment conks out or never gets delivered to the room. In such cases, you must fall back on your own resources and rely on your rehearsal and your notes to carry through the seminar.

A little preparation and planning can help avoid the catastrophe of equipment failure. The checklist that follows will avoid problems that have plagued and embarrassed speakers in the past (including me!):

1. Bring an extra bulb if you are using a 35-mm slide projector or overhead projector.
2. Make sure you or a trusted helper know how to operate the equipment properly.
3. Retest the projector and the order of your slides.
4. Bring an extension cord long enough to reach the appropriate outlet.
5. Arrange for a large screen.
6. Learn how to raise the screen if it is a portable one.
7. Make arrangements for a microphone. Make sure it works properly.
8. Either arrange for a projectionist for any 16-mm sound film you intend to show, or make certain that you or a helper know how to thread and run the machine.

9. Preset the video machine to start in the right place. Avoid those agonizing minutes waiting for it to start.

Conducting the Seminar

Encourage early attendees to seat themselves at the front of the room. On their own, people will generally sit toward the rear. If attendance is small, it is discouraging to have everybody clustered at the back. Here are more hints that will help you to run a better seminar:

1. *Don't start on time.* Parking may be a problem for many people, and late arrivals may spoil the early part of your talk by creating some disturbance as they check in and get to their seats.
2. *Don't start too late.* Starting long after the scheduled time tends to irritate the punctual arrivals. Plan on starting 5 to 10 minutes after the scheduled time.
3. *Arrange for someone to tape your presentation* for later review.
4. *Try to relax the audience with your opening remarks.* Use humor if you can, but nothing ribald that might convey the wrong impression. The best humor pokes fun at the speaker.
5. *Encourage questions at the end of your talk,* as well as during your talk, to involve your audience. If you ask frequently for questions, you tend to liven the lecture with audience participation. Your answers become more meaningful because you assume the role of a teacher or a learned person.
6. *Don't be afraid to say, "I don't know, but I will get the answer for you."* This lends credibility to you as a person.
7. *Sum up the key points of your presentation* and create an open forum for questions. (If a second session is to be given, remind the audience of the time.)
8. *Coffee after a seminar is a great help in keeping people in your presence* and giving them a chance to ask individual questions. This gives you a chance to get appointments.

Seminar Follow-Up Procedures

You may do everything right in planning for and executing your seminar, but if you don't use good follow-up procedures, the effects of

171

your lecture and all your effort may go for naught. The following guidelines can show you how to maximize postseminar appointments and obtain clients:

1. *Send a letter the day after your seminar* thanking the prospect for attending. Personalize your response by mentioning some of the questions you feel you answered especially effectively. Enclose a portfolio review form or an information request card.

2. *Call each attendee within 48 hours.* The impression you gave attendees is most vivid in the first few days after the talk. As time passes, your image and what you discussed rapidly fades from their memory, as well as any impulses they may have had to invest with you. When you call, seek a critique of your talk. Exude friendliness and try to pinpoint any investment interest. You must seek an appointment to discuss investment matters that bother them, points not covered in your lecture, or points not made clear to them.

3. *Send a letter to those people who confirmed their attendance but did not show.* Invite them to your next seminar. Seek a personal appointment. Don't write them off too quickly, as they responded once before.

4. *Send a second letter within two weeks* and keep attendees on a regular mailing list for six months. Remember, most prospects become clients only after the fifth or sixth contact. Don't give up unless there is an obvious insurmountable personality conflict or unless they just aren't suitable prospects for any of your products.

5. *Call again after the second letter* and seek an appointment. Tell about a specific feature in a particular product. Sometimes you may open the account with a very small order and then get a personal appointment to review a client's entire financial situation.

GETTING PAST THE "NO!" AND CLOSING

Fighting the Word "No!"

Any commission-paid salesperson who makes a real effort *each day* to get orders or appointments from prospects (as well as clients) is going to get a lot of "no's." "No's" are part of a salesperson's life, and you should learn to expect that answer the majority of the time you ask for an order or an appointment.

Don't Take "No" as a Personal Rejection

Many sellers of intangibles quit because the "no's" get under their skin and become unbearable, almost painful. Rather than accept the pain, they tend to lessen their daily portion of "no's" by making fewer calls or trying to substitute other work (such as paperwork or reading) for the gut-wrenching effort involved in asking strangers to do business.

The seller of intangibles must fully understand that the wealthy prospect is a target, literally besieged with all kinds of sellers trying to get some of the prospect's dollars. Car dealers want the wealthy person to trade frequently, buy second or third cars, give a car as a present. Real-estate sellers always have a wonderful opportunity available, a self-liquidating, tax-saving apartment or shopping center, possibly requiring little or no money down if the prospect assumes all obligations. Sellers of all kinds are after the well-to-do individual, and especially anybody selling anything high in price is hot on the trail of the rich. The very well off are constantly under attack, badgered, and besieged from all sides by a myriad of sellers.

"No!" spoken harshly to those solicitors is a potent weapon to rid oneself of those unwanted, undesired sellers and their pitches. "No!" uttered forcefully, even snidely, does its job well in turning sellers away.

A good salesperson must understand this aspect of a prospect's psychology. The loudly spoken, positively uttered "no!" *is simply a prospect's capital defense.* Prospects who do not say no to over 90 percent of the sales pitches they receive will *soon have no money!*

If you are going to make your living selling intangibles, you have got to learn to deal with "no!" Understand that no-saying prospects are not rejecting you personally; they are simply putting a shield around their money. You, of course, will try to penetrate that shield. In order to make your goal attainable, learn to prepare a *counter* for the expected "no." Develop automatic strategy that gets you temporarily by the "no" and leaves you in the game of trying to make a sale.

You Can Fight a "No"

Program yourself to respond to the word "no" by asking a question. If you are convinced that the product or service that you offer is a good value, you can train yourself to respond something like this: "This value looks so attractive for you right now. What are your reasons for saying no?" Get the prospect to respond and disclose objec-

Top security salespeople try to make sure they do not overlook a single potential customer or sales opportunity. They stay ahead of competition by starting work earlier and planning tomorrow's calls tonight!

TWO THINGS YOU CAN DO TODAY TO MAKE YOUR BUSINESS GROW!

1. *Test your sales pitch on your favorite stock of the month with your manager. Let him test your knowledge, point out flaws, and help make your sales points harder hitting.*

2. *Do the same with some of the tougher brokers in your office. This will serve to sharpen your sales pitches and help you in making bigger sales (remembers to always ask for minimum orders of 1000 shares).*

tions. Once prospects get into the conversation and voice the reasons for not buying, you may learn what they *do* want (a different product or service) or what additional information you should present to convince them about the proposed transaction.

My premier sales training friend Lee DuBois (the Birmingham, Alabama, patriarch of good salespeople) has taught thousands of attendees at his training sessions to respond to the word "no" with a memorized phrase: "Obviously you have some reason for saying no. Do you mind if I ask what it is?" According to Lee, once the objections are voiced there is a good chance that you can whisk them away by using a couple of other "commit-to-memory" phrases (no one said gaining selling skill was going to be easy!). Sometimes, you can brush objections away with the help of this particular calming comment: "Suppose everything was just the way you want it, and you had money to invest right now."

That lovely phrase is then followed with Lee's trial closing favorite: "Then in your opinion do you feel you would buy this low-risk, high-gain-potential stock that pays a high dividend?" A "yes" to that question is a clear signal to try again for the order.

Persist Past the "No"

To succeed in selling intangibles, you must learn to sell past the first "no," the second "no," and even the third "no!" Stick it out through several "no's" and you'll wind up with orders that the less determined, less skilled sellers miss. You will get orders from strangers, who may develop into long-term, repeat-business clients. Continuing the selling process by *repetition of facts and benefits* after hearing "No!" makes for many a sale.

Ignore "No"

A second way many skilled salespeople fight the word "no" is to ignore it. They simply act as if they do not hear it. New features, facts, or benefits not given to the prospect initially are brought up as additional ammunition. Even repeated "no's" may be brushed aside by presenting additional evidence to make the prospect ready to buy. Never allow the talk to be one-sided. Continually involve the prospect deeply in the sale by asking questions, trying to elicit opinions from which you can glean an opening to drive home a key point that could lead to the order.

Closing: How and When

Salespeople who aren't doing as well as they believe they should from the number of sales calls they complete often tell us that they are uncertain about how to close and when to close. Many people selling intangibles really don't understand that to close you have to *ask the prospect to make a decision*. Their selling skill may enable them to outline all the features, give facts, and detail benefits; but unless they actually *ask for an order* they are unlikely to be rewarded by earning a commission.

How to Close

How do you close? Simply ask the prospect a question! Try to phrase the question so that the prospect is presented with a choice of two positive courses of action, either of which could well result in an order. Be sure *never* to ask a question that can be answered "no!"

1. Would you like to get $20,000 worth of these tax-free municipal bonds on the offering or $15,000? Which quantity is best for you?
2. While the stock is low do you want to enter an order for 1000 shares at $20 or 800 shares?
3. Do you want to place $25,000 in this tax-deferred annuity while we can get you a guaranteed *minimum* interest rate of 9 percent or $20,000? Which amount is best for you?

Really good producers know that no monopoly exists on good sales ideas. They "copy" ideas that work for others, gladly! They don't worry about being "unoriginal." If something works for someone else, they are willing to give it a try. How willing are you to try others' ideas?

TWO THINGS YOU CAN DO TODAY TO MAKE YOUR BUSINESS GROW!

1. *Plan how to better tomorrow's sales effort.*

2. *Write notes—"Call me right away"—and sign your name on 10 somethings (not prospectuses) that you really believe right for investors. Mail them before you leave the office today. List the names for follow-up phone calls next week. Be sure to enclose two somethings that can be completed and returned to you. Resolve to do this every day before you leave.*

You always want to make the prospect dwell on the choices you select and choose one.

Never give the prospect the choice between *buying and not buying!* As you can imagine, given that choice, quite often the prospect chooses not to buy. This is the wrong way to ask for a decision: "Do you want to buy 100 shares?" The way the question is phrased leads many prospects to say "no" almost automatically.

When to Close

When to ask for an order? Many sellers of intangibles worry constantly about when they should directly ask the prospect to buy. Should it be at the end of their sales presentation? Should they try to close near the end? In the middle?

Ask for an order as soon as you notice any buying signals. You may ask for the order early in the sales presentation, you may ask for the order in the middle, or you may ask at the *end*. As a matter of fact, in the world of skilled selling you may ask for the order *several times* during the sales presentation, not just once.

Just make sure you do ask for the order!

A good selling skill to develop is being smooth in asking "testing" questions that normally a prospect answers with a yes. Testing questions are what my good friend Lee DuBois (Birmingham, Alabama) calls trial closes. Lee is one of America's top sales trainers and one of its most skilled sellers, too. Trial closes, says Lee are "opinion-asking" questions so phrased that the answers help you determine whether the prospect is ready to be closed. Here are some closing questions to put in your sales arsenal:

1. "In *your opinion*, do you feel that investing in *low-risk, high-potential-gain* stocks is in line with your particular objectives?" (If you get anything but a yes answer I will be shocked.)
2. "In your opinion do you feel that investing *without risk* and earning high *untaxed current interest* is in line with your particular objectives?" (Tax-deferred annuities)
3. "In your opinion do you feel that earning *tax-free interest* at a *high rate* is *important to you?*"

When you get that yes answer to a trial close, then follow through and ask for an order. Remember to present the prospect with a choice—a decision to make between two attractive offers. Help the prospect arrive at a decision by repeating facts and benefits.

If the prospect fails to buy when asked to make the decision, just go back and try another trial close, reemphasizing your main sales points.

This process can be reiterated in the same sales presentation. Don't expect the miracle of getting an order every time. It just doesn't work that way in the selling world. What you want to do is improve your batting average by getting *more orders, bigger orders*.

Closing frequently, whether early or late, often will help make your paychecks grow.

Picking Up on "Close Now Signals"

All salespeople who seek to close orders and lock up a commission should constantly be on the watch for buying signals emanating from the prospective purchaser. Prospects being solicited either face to face or by phone often give clues that they are ready to buy. These buying clues come in two forms. One is a verbal signal and the other is a physical signal. Physical signals are helpful only if you are making a face-to-face presentation.

Sellers of securities who do most of their business over the phone have to train themselves to be good listeners in order to pick up quickly that a prospect has made a decision to buy.

Verbal Signals

Unskilled salespeople who concentrate only on what *they* are saying and really don't absorb the prospect's remarks often miss sales that should have been closed. Listening carefully is more productive than spewing out a constant flow of facts and figures.

The following brief scenarios depict typical vocal signals to search for in a prospect's remarks. Whenever vocal buying signals like these are received, end the flow of facts and benefits and ask for the order.

Joe Salesman: "This stock is selling below book value and yields 7 percent from a dividend that has been raised each of the last five years! That's not all. The earnings per share are in a significant up-trend and should come in 20 percent over last year—enough to warrant another dividend increase even larger than the last! You ought to buy 1000 shares."

John Prospect: "[Verbal buying signal] When would I have to pay?"

Scenario II

Joe Salesman: "This bond yields 8 percent free of all federal and state tax! In your tax bracket, that would be like earning more than 16 percent in a taxable investment. The bond is AA rated by Standard & Poor's, and the principal repayment comes due in 10 years, just when you expect to need your money. You ought to get 25 of these bonds while they are available."

John Prospect: "[Verbal buying signal] How long will it take to deliver the bonds?"

Scenario III

Joe Salesman: "This is an excellent income stock. The current yield is 9.5 percent from a dividend that has been increased each year for the past 18 consecutive years. The outlook for future raises looks good. The dividend is paid quarterly on the first day of the month."

John Prospect: "[Verbal buying signal] When does it go ex-dividend?"

Physical Signals

In face-to-face presentations, you must not only listen carefully for verbal signals that tell you the prospect is ready to buy; you must also keep your eyes focused on the prospect's face and body for physical signals that signify the close is ready to be accomplished.

Here are the most common physical signals that it's time to close:

In every selling office, salespeople can usually be divided into three groups.
1. Those who make things happen
2. Those who watch things happen
3. Those who wonder what happened
Which group are you in?

TWO THINGS YOU CAN DO TODAY TO MAKE YOUR BUSINESS GROW!

1. **Make a list of thinly traded OTC issues of local banks or insurance companies. See if your firm does or can make a market in those issues.**

2. **Contact members of the board of directors (phone or personal visit) to advise them of your interest in their stock and offer to help them buy (or sell) as their need or desire arises. Many brokers have developed substantial business following this method; you can, too! Get the directors' names from the annual reports.**

Change in Arms Folded Across Chest

The folded-arms position is a defensive position in which a prospect envelops his or her body and protects it by wrapping the arms about the self. As long as the arms remain locked around the body no sale will ensue. Carefully observe the prospect, who is listening to the salient features and benefits. If the prospect audibly exhales and limply drops arms to sides, that prospect has decided to buy. Ask for the order at that point! Enough facts and benefits have been presented to win the prospect's trust and gain the order.

Loosening of Clenched Fists

Many prospects listen intently to a presentation with fists clenched tightly, a resistant defensive posture. If, during the presentation, the prospect suddenly relaxes those fists, the decision has been made to buy. When you see those fists relax and the hands open, stop rendering features and benefits and ask for the order.

Rubbing the Chin

When prospects absorbed in listening to a presentation begin to rub their chins slowly, as if stroking a Van Dyke beard, that is a clear signal that the prospect is ready to buy. Upon observing the stroking motion, stop the flow of facts and ask for the order!

Stroking the Nose

When listening prospects begin to stroke their noses slowly with a forefinger, those prospects have carefully considered all aspects of the proposed investment and are ready to buy. The order should be asked for as soon as the buying signal is observed!

Touching or Examining a Document that Requires a Signature

A good face-to-face seller of intangibles pitching a product that needs a customer's signature in order to produce a bona fide sale normally keeps the document in view during the entire presentation to serve as a silent reinforcement during the interview. Documents completed except for needed signatures are much less threatening to prospects for their names have already been typed in. Only the places for signatures remain blank. (Whipping out a complicated form that has to be completed after a presentation may kill a sale. The prospect wonders about the traps lying in wait in the fine print.)

The filled-out document, conspicuously in view at all times, is easy for prospects to pick up and read. A prospect who does that is transmitting a clear buying signal that shouts, "If there are no real hooks in this document, I am going to buy!" When you notice this perusal of the document, ask for the order.

Being sensitive to buying signals is just one more way of increasing sales and commission income.

Closing: 9 Techniques That Work

"Sale closed!" That phrase brings a smile to any salesperson's face. The hard work of prospecting, presenting, and finally getting an order is over for the moment, a time of respite before beginning another sales attempt. A commission successfully earned is an inspiration to go out and seek more business.

Rarely do salespeople analyze how the close was obtained. For skilled salespeople, closes are similar to the physical reflex actions of well-trained athletes. Skilled sellers act and react to prospects' responses and objections, parrying, countering automatically, giving barely a conscious thought to following a specific procedure. Such professionals are fine tuned, thoroughly conditioned from the experience of giving thousands of sales presentations. They know what to do in various selling situations, but most would be unable to articulate their own closing techniques.

Unskilled salespeople, those who get orders occasionally, sufficient only to survive but not thrive, consider any closes to have been pure luck! The low producers don't accept that they use skill in getting the order. Most of them do not really believe that they can "get better" and really *acquire* selling skills. They, like many of their supervisors, believe good salespeople are born, not made.

The key to sales success is in developing the skills common to sellers. Such techniques may be acquired in classes taught by accomplished sales trainers. Such skills are whetted by role-playing with coworkers. Books, training tapes, slides, and movies devoted to the art of selling all can help make salespeople better at that crucial skill, closing—*getting the order!*

Nine ways a seller of intangibles can close are discussed in this chapter. These nine are simply the best known, commonly used closing techniques. Others exist, and still others will someday be invented. But the punch in these nine can enable you to earn an above-average living every working year.

Close Technique 1:
The Future Close

Face to face with a single prospect or a couple, the *future close* can be very effective, but it should be used only after you have gained substantial information from the prospect through a series of polite but probing questions. These questions must inform you not only about what the prospect hopes the money invested will do but what the prospect requires the money invested to do.

One of my favorite probing questions is phrased like this: "If I gave you an investment idea today about a low-risk, high-potential-gain situation and you made $20,000 after taxes by accepting my idea, what would you do with that lovely extra money?"

That question accomplishes several things. First, it plants the idea in the prospect's mind that the seller may possess some wonderful idea that just might make money. Second, it makes the prospect

Have you ever thought that the reason you don't get more big orders is that you don't ask for them? Many brokers rush to settle for a small or occasional order without making the extra effort to increase the size or frequency.

TWO THINGS YOU CAN DO TODAY TO MAKE YOUR BUSINESS GROW!

1. Call three of your clients to tell them their buying power. They may place an order with you once they realize that they do not have to put additional cash into the account in order to purchase more stock.

2. Prospect the owner of the restaurant at which you normally eat every day. A familiar face is always hard to turn down.

consider what luxuries or additional financial security might be attainable with profits earned from an investment.

The future close uses to advantage the answers a prospect gives. All you have to do is listen carefully to the response. Here are the steps in making a future close:

1. Get prospects to picture themselves in the future enjoying the results of an investment made under your guidance.
2. Point out to prospects their need or desire for the profit.
3. Close with a question such as, "Isn't that what you really want your money to do for you?"
4. Repeat key benefits.
5. Ask for an order.

The future close may come into better perspective for you as you read the following sales scenario. Assume that the prospect is a young businessman in his late thirties. Assume also that all the facts, benefits, and risks have been pointed out to the prospect and the seller is preparing to future close. The seller has asked what the prospect would do if the prospect made $20,000 after taxes from a low-risk, high-potential-gain stock that was being strongly recommended.

After an appropriate pause, the answer was, "I'd buy a late-model Mercedes, steel gray, with a sunroof and red leather interior." (In working the future close, it is important to let prospects describe fully and enthusiastically what they want profit dollars to buy.)

Broker: "I can just *see you* right now driving along the beach on a beautiful sunny day in your steel-gray Mercedes, with the sunroof open, saying to that beautiful lady by your side, 'Honey, did you know that I bought this car with the profit I made on 2000 shares of XYZ?' I can even see the admiration in her eyes as she leans back into the plush red leather upholstery and says, 'Wow!' "

Prospect: (dreamily) "Umm! That would sure be great!"

Broker: "Isn't that what you really want? A luxury car paid for with stock-market profits? Profits earned from a low-risk stock?"

Prospect: "That's what I want all right."

Broker: "I truly think there is a real possibility of your getting what you want if you get 2000 XYZ shares while they are at this low point and hold them for the potential gain that our analyst foresees. With the low risk we believe exists, you might want to get 3000 shares, especially considering the high dividend yield that you would be receiving while waiting for this potential gain. Which quantity do you think is right for you now, 2000 shares or 3000 shares?"

Prospect: "I'll take 3000 shares. I might want a stereo tape-deck, too!"

Of course, in the real world prospects don't just roll over and hand their money over to a seller. But prospects can be sold and are sold by salespeople who use various techniques. The future close is one of those techniques. Try it out on carefully chosen prospects and watch it work for you.

A future close might be employed with a product like a tax-deferred annuity. Assume that the salesperson is talking to a married couple about moving bank savings into a tax-deferred annuity to build a bigger retirement fund.

Salesperson: "I have pointed out to you the really great advantages of putting your money to work in a tax-deferred annuity. By your remarks I can tell that you understand clearly that you will not pay any current income tax on the interest your money earns for you each year. You also know that you can withdraw part or all of your money any time you want prior to beginning to receive lifetime monthly checks. While your money is working for you, your principal is guaranteed safe and will grow fast and untaxed until you take it out later."

Mrs. Green: "I really do like the features that we can take some money out if necessary, and not pay any tax until our original capital has been withdrawn. I just hate to pay the government taxes every year on the interest our money earns."

Salesperson: "That is an attractive feature. The real plus is that in 16 years when you are ready to retire, at the current rate of interest your money will be approximately four times what it is today. That's a big enough sum to let you draw a large monthly check each month for the rest of your lives!"

Mrs. Green: "That sounds pretty good. I like the thought of large monthly checks coming in forever."

Salesperson: "I can just see the two of you in sunny Florida in your beautiful condominium enjoying the good life. I can picture

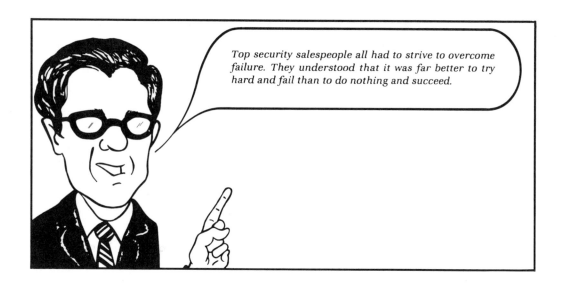

Top security salespeople all had to strive to overcome failure. They understood that it was far better to try hard and fail than to do nothing and succeed.

Mrs. Green going out to the mailbox the first of each month and coming back to the apartment with an envelope saying, 'Honey, our check has arrived from XYZ Life.' Isn't that what you both really want? A happy, carefree retirement in a warm climate, with a check each month the rest of your life. Money that you cannot outlive! Many people aren't worried about dying, but they *do* worry about living too long and not having enough money to get along on in this inflationary world."

Mr. Green: "*That is our goal:* retirement with an assured income to supplement our Social Security and pension benefit."

Salesperson: "Since there is *no initial sales cost* to buy this tax-deferred annuity, you might want to put $40,000 of the $50,000 you have, which is now earning you taxable interest, to work right away, earning untaxed interest at a high rate until you are ready to take it out. Or maybe you want to put it all in right now while the interest rate paid you is high. Which amount would be your choice, $40,000 or $50,000?"

In the foregoing scenario the seller tries to get the couple dreaming, picturing themselves in their ideal retirement spot, enjoying the results of the earnings on their money placed in the tax-deferred annuity.

The scenarios and variations are limitless. Carefully choose prospects who can visualize a future benefit; they are the most suited for a future close. Once having decided to close this way, make a strong effort to get them into a mood to dream.

Close Technique 2:
The Comparison Close

People are conditioned all their lives to compare things in order to determine values. Sellers of intangible investments should use this natural trait to help make sales.

The *comparison close* is quite simple in concept and in execution. Here are its key points:

1. State the facts and benefits of two different investment alternatives.
2. Weigh the risk versus the reward potential in each for the prospect.
3. Close with a question that gives the prospect a *choice between two positives where the choice of either results in an order.*

Let's suppose you are a broker trying to get a prospect to buy shares of common stock. The conversation might go like this:

Broker: "Our Research Department has come up with two excellent stock ideas that might make money for you."

Prospect: "What are they?"

Broker: "One is a high-technology company selling at about $25. They have a new product that should revolutionize the industry. The earnings could double in the next two years, and we believe the shares could go from 25 to possibly 50 or higher. The risk always exists that the product may not function as well or sell as well as expected. The dividend yield is only 2 percent. It's what we call high risk, high potential. Right for aggressive investors."

Prospect: "That sounds interesting to me. What's the other stock they like?"

Broker: "The other company is a special situation. The shares are selling 25 percent below book value, now about $20 per share. The current yield is 8 percent from a well-covered dividend, and we think the earnings will rise substantially because they have a big backlog of orders and because of the improving economy. It's also stock in the kind of corporation that is often referred to as a "takeover" candidate. Only 5 million shares are outstanding. This appears to be a low-risk, high-potential-gain situation that also provides good current income. Many conservative clients like this type of stock. The risk is that the economy may slacken and their backlog of orders get reduced due to cancellations."

Prospect: "That sounds good also. Which do you like better of the two?"

Broker: "You know your situation, your makeup, and how much risk you can take, as well as how you handle losses. Comparing the two, the high-technology company has greater gain potential *if* the investing public becomes enamored of their product and the potential for great growth. It also has greater risk. The dividend is low, and so is the book value. The second company should hold its value better in a slowing economy. It offers good upside gain potential, and the high dividend should be a help in slowing any price drop due to a general market decline. Based on your knowledge of yourself, which do *you* think is best for you right now? The high-potential, high-risk technology company, or the low-risk, high-gain-potential, high-yield special situation? They both look good right now."

Prospect: "I like the special situation stock."

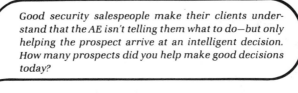

Good security salespeople make their clients understand that the AE isn't telling them what to do—but only helping the prospect arrive at an intelligent decision. How many prospects did you help make good decisions today?

TWO THINGS YOU CAN DO TODAY TO MAKE YOUR BUSINESS GROW!

1. **Keep your own troubles, problems, and complaints to yourself.**

2. **Be cheerful, look cheerful! Nobody really wants to do business with a pessimist who has a hang-dog, beaten appearance and outlook. Look carefully at yourself in the mirror before you come to work. Clothes may not "make the man" but they can sure influence your mood and others who see you.**

Broker: "Do you want me to try to buy you 1000 shares at 20 or 800? Which quantity do you think is right for you now?"

Prospect: "Get me 800 shares for now."

When you are building for a comparison close, provide a *choice between different degrees of risk* and between different estimated gain potentials. Although you might think the more conservative alternative is more frequently chosen with the comparison close, that's not necessarily the case. The ultimate choice depends on the state of the market (bull markets create a speculative impulse in even the most conservative investor) and the prospect's personal attitude toward risk.

The attraction of the comparison close is that you present a choice to prospects and let them determine the degree of risk they want to assume.

Close Technique 3:
The Small-Matter Close

The *small-matter close* is a simple close. The seller focuses the prospect's attention on some small matter, easy for the prospect to understand and use as a basis for choosing the investment. The small-matter close differs from the comparison close in that only a single investment selection is presented. The prospect is still offered a

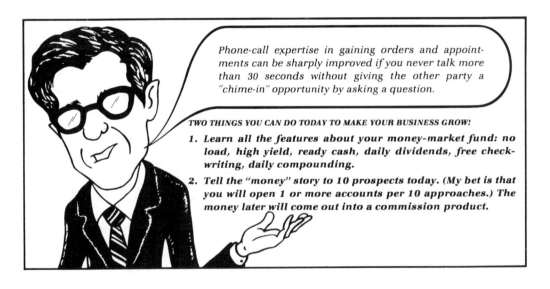

Phone-call expertise in gaining orders and appointments can be sharply improved if you never talk more than 30 seconds without giving the other party a "chime-in" opportunity by asking a question.

TWO THINGS YOU CAN DO TODAY TO MAKE YOUR BUSINESS GROW!

1. **Learn all the features about your money-market fund: no load, high yield, ready cash, daily dividends, free check-writing, daily compounding.**

2. **Tell the "money" story to 10 prospects today. (My bet is that you will open 1 or more accounts per 10 approaches.) The money later will come out into a commission product.**

choice, but the choice centers on some not too significant detail of the sale. The key to the small-matter close is to divert the prospect's attention from the big decision of whether or not to purchase by focusing the decision process on the handling of some little matter.

To make this close effective in a high percentage of attempts, assume an attitude that conveys the message, "I know you are going to say yes. You know you are going to say yes. What we must resolve is this small matter concerning the delivery." The prospect will pick up on your confident attitude about the worthiness of the recommendation, and the emotions of fear and doubt will be dispelled, attention placed where *you* want it.

The small-matter close involves these steps:

1. Focusing the prospect's attention on some simple part of the transaction
2. Presenting the prospect with a choice of ways to handle the simple detail
3. Formulating a question whose answer provides an order

Assume the following situation. The broker is trying to get a middle-aged prospect to buy 1000 shares of a low-risk, high-quality common stock that provides a high income from a well-covered dividend. The facts and benefits have been presented and reiterated so that the prospect clearly understands all aspects of this proposal.

Broker: "I am sure, like you are, that your investments should be in low-risk, high-quality, high-income stocks like American Telephone, stocks that offer gain potential and some prospect of increased income. Buying 1000 shares now while the market price is low seems prudent for a conservative investor like you."

Prospect: "I am conservative, all right. Safety and high income now, and more in the future is what I need."

Broker: "What you need to do is decide how you would want that 1000 shares registered. Would you want them in your name? Or would you prefer to register them jointly with your wife?"

Prospect: "I hadn't really thought about that. You better make it joint like our other stocks. Otherwise she [wink!] might really get angry at me."

Good security salespeople wanting to do better understand that they are not getting the maximum income out of the talents they have—to improve. They study what they have done and force themselves to do more!

TWO THINGS YOU CAN DO TODAY TO MAKE YOUR BUSINESS GROW!

1. *Make a list of all the affluent (real or suspected) you personally know but never have asked for an order.*

2. *Call them and ask for an order! (You can bet they are investing through someone. It might as well be you.)*

Broker: "Okay, would you want us to keep the stock here or send it to you?"

Prospect: "Send it to me and I'll put it in the box with my other certificates."

Broker: "I'll do that, and I'm really glad you chose the high-quality, high-income recommendations. At this point, investing conservatively is the right approach for you."

There are a number of other small-matter closing questions you can use. The main point is to have them prepared ahead of time and use them! Keep prospects' attention away from the big decision—to buy or not to buy—by having them concentrate on settling some small matter, and you'll be on your way to more closes.

Close Technique 4:
The Balancing Close

Many times when a salesperson is in hot pursuit of a prospect, the prospect manages to wriggle away from the pressure being applied by employing a time-tested defensive weapon: "I'd like to think it over." Typically, when sellers hear this oft-uttered phrase, they ease up and back off. Sellers tend to fear that if they continue to apply pressure, the "I'd like to think it over" will turn into a definite, resounding "no!" The salesperson all too often thinks, "I'll ease off and call next week!"

The prospect escapes for the moment and may devise a way to prevent the salesperson from making contact again. Of course the possibility exists that "I would like to think it over" is the simple truth; the prospect may just want more time. But more often than not, "I would like to think it over" is a device to put off the seller for the moment *and* for good.

The *balancing close* (often called the Ben Franklin close) is meant for those times when you hear those words of postponement, "I want to think it over." The balancing close can help you convert a "I-want-to-think-it-over" postponement into a sale right now. Here are the key points of the technique:

1. State any reasons the prospect has given for wanting to delay making the investment.
2. List several reasons that warrant the prospect's making a decision immediately.
3. Carefully restate the facts and benefits of the proposed investment.
4. Close with a question like the following: "Which is more likely to make you money [or save a cost], buying now while the price is low and attractive, or delaying and possibly missing out on this opportunity?"

The balancing close is a very difficult close to master. Even the most skilled sellers find it tough to change an "I want to think it over" into an immediate sale. Although it is tough to effectuate a close in this situation, don't stop trying! Think of the balancing close as simply another tool to use when the occasion arises. The more tools you have and the more practiced you become at selling skills, the higher your income will be.

Assume that a broker is trying to get a prospect to purchase 500 shares of a new issue of an A+ electric utility. The shares yield 10 percent at the offering price of $18. The buyer of the new issue shares will not have to pay a direct commission as the cost is borne by the share seller. Tune in on the conversation.

Broker: "This is an excellent opportunity for you to buy A+-rated (and that's the highest possible rating Standard & Poor's gives!) ZYX shares and not pay any direct commission. The dividend has been raised every year for the past 10 years, and future prospects for more increases look good. Considering the fact that your annual yield will be 10 percent, plus a capital-gain potential, you ought to be considering not 500 shares but 1000 shares."

Prospect: "That does sound good, but I want to think it over. The market looks weak and interest rates may move higher."

Broker: "I understand how you feel in wanting to think it over before investing your money. Before you do, let's review your reasons for wanting to take more time. First, the market looks weak now and, second, the possibility of higher interest rates concerns you. Against the concerns let's look at the reasons for buying right now. First, you can avoid paying a direct commission. Second, you are buying shares near the lowest price of the past 10 years. Third, interest rates could go down, forcing your shares up in price. And fourth, the market always fluctuates; it can be weak one day and strong the next. Determining the future won't be any easier later on."

"The important considerations are that you are buying high quality at a low price and you do not have to pay a commission directly. When you balance your reasons for delaying against the opportunity available right now, you might want me to try to get you more than 500 shares at the commission-free price of $20."

"You might think it over until next week, and then decide to buy and have to pay a commission, plus possibly a

Good security salespeople quickly learn that the greatest good-will builder (and referral getter) is to take more than their share of the blame for any loss and less than their share of the credit for any gain. Maybe you can take a cue from what the good and the great do!

TWO THINGS YOU CAN DO TODAY TO MAKE YOUR BUSINESS GROW!

1. *Call nonclient CPAs until you can entice one to have lunch with you today.*

2. *Topic: His view of tax shelters from his vantage point of return preparation—which to avoid, which have been most rewarding, which he might have a future interest in for his client. Build good-will with him and you create a referral center.*

higher price per share. What really makes better sense—buying now and avoiding commission costs or trying to guess what may happen to the market or interest rates next week and having to pay the sales cost and maybe a higher price for the shares as well?"

Prospect: "Okay, get me 500 shares at 18, but no commission better be charged!"

No guarantee of success comes with a balancing close (nor with any close, for that matter), but the balancing close does give you a second chance to go after an order that is slipping at least temporarily out of reach with "I want to think it over."

Practice, practice, and more practice is what it takes to increase your selling skills. Just knowing and being able to differentiate between the types of closes improves selling skills. Try them time after time with different prospects. You will quickly realize the benefits of knowing closing techniques.

When you hear the sentence "I want to think it over," picture a scale in your mind and imagine yourself placing two reasons for postponing the purchase on one side of the scale and three or more "buy now" reasons on the other side of the scale. Naturally, this creates an imbalance favoring "buy now." And that is exactly what you want to do, to try to create more closes from reluctant buyers!

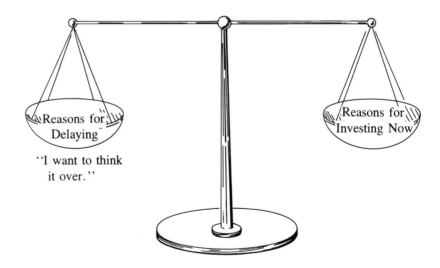

Close Technique 5:
The Authority Close

The *authority close* is perhaps the easiest close to understand and implement. It is a powerful close and one that is often appropriate to use. It works particularly well with first-time buyers.

The perceptive salesperson is cued to use the authority close when the prospect makes positive remarks about the proposed investment but, after being presented all the facts and benefits in a well-thought-out, logical sequence, fails to buy. When *asked* for the order, the prospect utters remarks like "That sounds pretty good" or "Gee, I didn't know that" or "That's great!" Every word the prospect says is positive, except that the words giving an order don't come forth.

In my opinion, based on years of experience, prospects fail to accept the proposal and place the order in such situations because *nobody orders them to buy!* These prospects require an authority figure to issue instructions to make the money commitment. Lacking that instruction, prospects of this type go unsold time after time, even though they always appear to be on the verge of granting an order. This is truly a frustrating situation for the unskilled salesperson who doesn't know the authority close.

Many people wealthy enough to be investing money now were raised in strict environments. They may have been told by parents exactly what to do at every point in their lives. They may have gone to military schools or other closely controlled educational institutions where they did as told. Other prospective investors will have served many years in military service, carrying out instructions issued by authority figures. People who have life experiences like these tend, as investors, to act only when told what to do in a very authoritarian manner that carries with it confidence and the assumption that the order will be carried out as directed.

As with all other closes the prospect's behavior and responses to your presentation will alert you to use the authority close. Here are the salient points in making an authority close:

1. Point out all the key facts and valuable benefits.
2. Make an authoritative statement. Do not ask a question as you would in most other types of closes.

Fortunately, there are many powerful authoritative statements that produce orders from prospects who don't say no but don't freely commit to an order, either. My favorites, ones that have worked time after time, are the following.

For Mutual-Fund Sales

"Endorse this form and your dividends, as well as capital gains, will be reinvested for you automatically without any sales charge!" This statement, clearly and forcefully presented along with the document properly completed except for the signature, has a high degree of success in obtaining the order.

For Stock or Bond Purchases

"Make out a check to ZYX Company for [state the amount] and I will see that you get sent your certificate as soon as possible." This positive statement authoritatively issued, with the focus and reassurance on the delivery rather than the purchase, often wins the order.

For Tax-Deferred Annuities

"Make out a check for [state the amount] to ZYX Insurance Company and we can put your money to work right away earning you high interest, untaxed currently, and all without risking even one dollar of your principal." This instructive close reemphasizes the key sales points and reassures the prospect while the order is being demanded.

For Tax Shelters

"Make out a check for [state the amount] to ZYX Company and you will get [again, state the amount] in tax deductions this year, plus

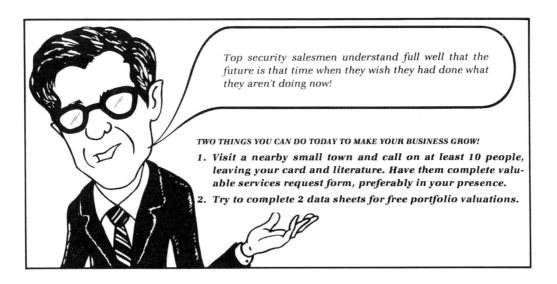

Top security salesmen understand full well that the future is that time when they wish they had done what they aren't doing now!

TWO THINGS YOU CAN DO TODAY TO MAKE YOUR BUSINESS GROW!

1. *Visit a nearby small town and call on at least 10 people, leaving your card and literature. Have them complete valuable services request form, preferably in your presence.*
2. *Try to complete 2 data sheets for free portfolio valuations.*

having your money work for you in [state the type of shelter, such as real estate or oil]." This strong statement focuses attention on the tax benefit as well as a possible future benefit from the dollars at work in the investment. Such statements are particularly effective in November and December when people are extremely tax-conscious.

To work really effectively, you must execute the authority close with an air of complete certainty that the prospect will acquiesce. The prospect must perceive that you *expect* your instructions to be followed.

Close Technique 6:
The Positive-Alternate Close

Among the most ancient of all closes and common to sellers of all types of goods, tangible or intangible, the *positive-alternate close* is highly effective. It will be one of the strongest tools in your collection of selling techniques. The positive-alternate close works well with old clients as well as new. And surprise! It can be used repeatedly, year-in, year-out, with the same client!

Here are the steps in the positive-alternate close:

1. Present all the pertinent facts and benefits to the prospect.

2. Present the prospect a choice of two courses of action (two positive alternates), each of which results in an order for you.

3. Close with a question that asks the prospect to choose between the two positive alternates.

That which makes the difference between one man and another—between the weak and powerful—the great and insignificant—is effort.

One great weakness that seems to afflict a large number of sellers of intangibles is the reluctance to ask for a large order. Many sales-people with excellent product knowledge and the ability to make fine presentations fail to earn sums commensurate with their talent solely because they are timid in requesting "size" orders. They are strong in presenting the facts and benefits and proficient at responding to tech-nical questions. Yet they fail miserably because they ask for small orders. I can't count the times I have listened to stockbrokers making a presentation in a very persuasive, coherent manner to a prospect, only to conclude with, "Why don't you buy 100 shares?" The distress-ing thing is that often the prospect says yes. If that same prospect had been asked for an order for 500, 1000, or more, the answer might well still have been yes!

The other upsetting aspect of the closing question, "Why don't you buy 100 shares?" is that the prospect might say no. The positive-alternate close makes it easy to ask for a large order and also makes it easy for the prospect to give an order, be it large, medium, or small. Instead of the potentially losing proposition inherent in buy/no buy choices, the positive-alternate close presents the prospect with a choice of buying *"some"* or *"some more!"*

The positive-alternate close focuses the prospect's attention on investing a large amount of money or a smaller amount, rather than on investing or not investing. Here are some sample positive-alternate closes.

For Unit Trusts

"Which would be best for you right now, 20 units of this high-yield unit trust free from federal taxation, or 15?"

For Stock Shares

"How many shares can you afford of this low-risk, high-potential stock? One thousand? Eight hundred? You tell me." It is much easier to work down from 1000 shares then it is to work up from 100 shares. Furthermore, many prospects are flattered that you consider them financially able to buy a large amount, and they respond with larger orders. Prospects often feel, too, that brokers wouldn't ask for a large order if they really didn't believe a recommendation was solidly based. There is a message for you in that fact: *Don't sell something if you don't really believe in it!* If you believe in your product, ask for big orders, even if you are talking to a small potential buyer.

Give a prospect the choice between two positives, and you will be on your way to higher earnings.

I witnessed a slight variation of the choice between two positive alternates in the office of Bill W., a top-producing broker. I overheard a conversation between Bill and a client whom Bill was trying to persuade to buy 1000 shares of a high-quality growth stock, then priced about $250 per share. You read it right: $250 per share! Bill was attempting to persuade this client to put a quarter of a million dollars into this stock! Tune in on the conversation:

Bill: "I have been following this stock for years. Technically it appears poised for a break-out above the $250-per-share level. The fundamentals look great, earnings per share are growing at 20 percent a year, dividends have been increasing each year, and a stock split is expected. The volume of trading is high and increasing. If the stock does what our fundamental research analyst and I believe, it might well sell for $400 per share this time next year. With 1000 shares you might make $150,000 as a long-term capital gain. However, if our Technical Department is right, it might have a quick run-up, to $300, in the next 30 days, and I might advise you to get out with a quick $50,000 short-term gain."

Client: "Go ahead, buy me 1000 shares!"

Bill just presented that prospect with the choice of a possible $50,000 short-term gain or a possible $150,000 long-term gain. He got the order! So will you if you use the positive-alternate close.

Close Technique 7:
The Sense-of-Loss Close

Sellers of intangibles invariably find themselves particularly effective with two or three closes. Trial and error and personality factors will just naturally lead the individual salesperson to regularly use the two or three closing styles effective on the greatest number of prospects. The *sense-of-loss close* is probably the most universally accepted of all closes as well as the *most powerful* close for any seller of intangibles to use on any prospect.

This particular close is easy to learn and remember, and is repeatedly effective, in various forms, with the same client. The features that characterize the sense-of-loss close are as follows:

Good security salespeople who produce consistently and earn high incomes year after year have learned that hard work, not brilliance, is truly the secret of success!

TWO THINGS YOU CAN DO TODAY TO MAKE YOUR BUSINESS GROW!

1. **Be resistant to the word "no." More sales are "not made" because the salesperson gives up than for any other reason.**

2. **See that you survive at least 20 no's today. See that every phone call incoming or outgoing, is an order-asking call. If you do that, you will get some yeses. Most salespeople miss their potential simply because they don't daily ask for enough orders.**

1. Carefully outline all the facts, risks, and reward potential to the prospect.

2. Impress on the prospect the benefit of acting right away.

3. Point out to the prospect a *possible loss* that a delay might cause.

4. Close with a question.

The sense-of-loss close requires you to build the urgency of acting now into your presentation. Allow your voice to rise and fall (avoid a monotone presentation) and make your enthusiasm for the proposal obvious even to the most phlegmatic prospect. A time for action must be absolutely specified (usually next day or next week). The potential loss to the prospect for not acting by the specified time must be highlighted and accentuated, and of course truthfully presented.

This close is adaptable to the sale of common stocks, new-issue securities of all types, bonds, tax shelters, tax-deferred annuities, commodities, options, and other financial products. Here are some examples of sense-of-loss closing questions for various investment products. Assume that all the facts and benefits have been made clear to the prospect.

Broker: "Tomorrow we're underwriting a new issue of common stock of Pacific Gas & Electric. The shares will be priced at $22 each. The yield from the current dividend is 11.3 percent. It is an excellent high-income stock with good capital-gain potential as well. The risk at this level looks low compared to the long-term profit possibility. It just fits in with your conservative nature and portfolio. A really exciting feature is that buyers tomorrow, at the $22 price, *will not have to pay any direct commission.*"

Prospect: "No commission?"

Broker: "You heard me right. The company pays all commision costs. There will be only a *limited number of shares available* of this high-quality issue and I will try to get you up to 500 or 1000 shares. I have to know today what quantity you want me to try to get for you. If you want more than 1000 shares I will do my best to get my manager to try to increase our allotment. The *sooner you let me know* the better chance we have of getting part or all of what you might want."

Prospect: "That sounds pretty good."

Broker: "Not only does it sound good, it *is* a good investment. *No commission directly paid by you.* High income and high quality. I don't want you to miss out on this opportunity and later have to pay a commission and maybe a higher price per share. While we have shares available you ought to reserve some. How many do you want? One thousand? Eight hundred? *I have to know today if you are to save commission costs.*"

When you have special values to offer, such as limited shares of a new issue of common stock at a fixed price, or a limited number of new-issue bonds at an attractive yield, you will find the sense-of-loss close effective with cold prospects as well as existing clients.

The sense-of-loss close is one of the great devices available when you're opening a new account. One of the best (and nicest) clients I had was obtained through a cold call and a sense-of-loss close. Here's the story:

My firm was underwriting a new issue of stock, Culligan, Inc., a manufacturer of water softeners. The price was set at $12.50 per share. A thousand shares (commission free to the buyer) was available, so I turned to the yellow pages (a marvelously helpful prospecting manual, by the way) and looked under water softeners. There were eight listings.

I tried calling the first three but was unable to get through secretaries who were properly defending their bosses from unwanted solicitations. (Secretaries who do their job well screen callers by asking, "Who's calling please?" "Does he know you?" and "What do you wish to talk with him about?" After receiving answers to these questions, the secretary most frequently takes the caller's number and lets the boss determine whether or not to return the call. Most often the decision is not to return the call and get exposed to a sales pitch.) By the time I made the fourth phone call, my anger and frustration were at a high point, and that caused me to take a different tack to try to get through to the prospect. On that fourth call I learned the following sales technique, one that you, too, can master if you have nerve!

The conversation went like this. Remember my emotional state: angry and frustrated, and I sounded it!

Secretary: "XYZ Water Pump Company."

LeRoy Gross: "Let me speak to the president. Right away, please!"

Secretary: "Who's calling, please?"

LeRoy Gross: "You tell him that LeRoy Gross [no firm name given] is on the phone, and that I *want to speak to him right now! Not later!*" [All this was said in an icy cold, angry manner.]

Secretary: "Just a minute, please. [She wanted to get away from this nasty caller! I then heard her on an intercom.] There's a Mr. Gross on the phone. He sounds angry and upset. I believe you better talk to him."

Mr. B.: "This is Mr. B."

LeRoy Gross: "This is LeRoy Gross. I am with XYZ Firm and I had to talk to you right away. My firm is underwriting a new issue

What a terrific stockbroker Dr. Joyce Brothers could be! Just listen to some of her philosophy, "I know what I want. I am not afraid to ask: I'll try asking for 10 things. If I am refused on 9, I'll simply dwell on the delight about the one yes."

TWO THINGS YOU CAN DO TODAY TO MAKE YOUR BUSINESS GROW!

1. **Place a high value on your time for selling. Don't fritter the day's prime selling hours away reading the WSJ, the broad tape, Business Week, company research reports, prospectuses, or posting trades and cross references.**

2. **Ask at least 20 different clients and prospects for an order today on a quality product.**

of Culligan, Inc., at $12.50 per share. The issue is coming out tomorrow. People who buy shares on the offering will not have to pay any direct commission. Before I sold shares to people in this area *I wanted the opinion of an expert like you!* Someone familiar with the company and its products. Since you distribute the product locally I thought you might give me your impressions."

At this point what emotions do you believe were being experienced by Mr. B.?

If you said "flattered" you were right. He was flattered that a representative of an NYSE member firm was *seeking his opinion about a common stock.*

Secondly, he was *relieved* that it wasn't an angry, upset customer on the phone, as he had been led to believe by his secretary.

Mr. B. proceeded to tell me in no uncertain terms what he thought about Culligan, Inc. He also told me he wouldn't buy it (what a mistake that later proved to be), and neither, in his opinion, should anyone else.

Those informational gems deflated me pretty well, but in the course of the conversation the following exchange took place:

Mr. B.: "By the way, what's the market doing?"

LeRoy Gross: "Up about 3 points."

Mr. B.: "What do you know about Mississippi River Corporation?"

I wasn't about to say "nothing"! I hurriedly looked it up in my trusty desk-top Standard & Poor's stock guide.

LeRoy Gross: "It looks like an income stock to me. It pays $1 in dividends annually. Last price is 16."

Mr. B.: "I have been watching that stock for a few months and I like it. If you can get me 300 at 16 I'll take 'em."

A bona fide order from a local company president! I hung up after getting the necessary information concerning bank references, social security number, and so on, and then got an okay from the manager to execute the order. That first order led to subsequent orders and the eventual transfer of $500,000 worth of securities from another firm, and annual commission income of approximately $10,000 per year! All that came from a cold call to a total stranger with the intent of using the sense-of-loss close (buy Culligan tomorrow and avoid direct commission costs).

Hopefully, you too will find the sense-of-loss close one of your most powerful sales-generating devices. Remember the following pointers for getting through to a decision maker:

1. Create a sense of urgency in your voice and manner.
2. Sound confident, as though there is no doubt that you will be immediately put through to the person you want to reach.
3. Create the impression that you know the prospect by giving only your name without identifying your firm or business.
4. Sound angry, dissatisfied, and upset.

Remember, if you don't get through you don't make sales!

Close Technique 8:
The Involvement Close

The *involvement close* is a very special close that is used only in face-to-face selling situations. It is a planned close that is brought into play only when all oral arguments and visual displays have failed to produce the desired order.

Like several other closing techniques, this specialized close requires a high degree of nerve (it's certainly not for timid sellers), and it

Top stockbrokers have two common characteristics. First, they are convinced beyond a doubt of the upside potential in specially chosen stock. Second, their very conviction gives them the power to persuade others.

TWO THINGS YOU CAN DO TODAY TO MAKE YOUR BUSINESS GROW!

1. *Focus on a single stock for the day and ask 50 different people—prospects or clients—to buy some. Incoming or outgoing calls? Ask for an order on each.*
2. *Try to get 20 or more executed buy orders on your focus stock today.*

has to be carefully rehearsed so that when it is put to actual use it is perceived in the correct light.

The typical involvement close situation arises when the prospect's signature is needed to consummate an order. Many purchases of intangible products necessitate the signing of at least one document before the seller can register a bona fide order. Here are some fairly common financial products where no commission can be earned unless the prospect signs a required paper:

Tax Shelters

The prospect must sign an agreement attesting to some specified minimum income or net worth.

Option Agreement

In order to be permitted to buy and sell listed option contracts, a fairly standard form must be signed attesting as to experience, income, net worth, and age.

Margin Agreement

In order to borrow monies/or securities through a securities firm (margin) to increase leverage, a standardized form must be completed giving the firm the power to liquidate the client's position, if need be, to protect the lender firm.

Top security salesmen understand that having a high IQ is a great asset but not nearly as effective and powerful as having a high "I will."

TWO THINGS YOU CAN DO TODAY TO MAKE YOUR BUSINESS GROW!

1. **Pick a local OTC stock priced under $10 per share with good EPS prospects. Learn the facts about it; build a story book on it.**
2. **Try to "give away" 1000 or more shares each week "free." How? By approaching prospects who have existing portfolios and showing them how, by agreeing to sell some of their shares, they might generate enough premium income to fully pay for some of the OTC shares—all accomplished without drawing on their savings or checking accounts.**

Tax-Deferred Annuity

This particular investment has an insurance company contract that the client has to sign in order to get the benefit of money earning current interest untaxed until later withdrawn.

Insurance Policies

An application must always be signed before any policy can be issued.

Mutual Funds

In order to reinvest dividends and/or capital gains, a signature is needed. To buy shares under a letter of intention at a reduced sales cost, a signed agreement is necessary.

Commodity Trading

In order to gain the leverage inherent in commodity transactions, a form must be signed authorizing the account liquidation if necessary, to protect the commodity firm's capital.

Investment Advisor Services

Prospects who wish others to choose investments discretionarily must sign an authorization permitting the activity.

Many prospects facing an enthusiastic salesperson who logically, efficiently builds an excellent case for a particular product still balk when it comes to the big decision of putting their mark on the dotted line.

After all objections have been overcome by the careful presentation of facts and benefits, after all questions have been answered and an order asked for several different times in different ways, all with no beneficial result, the time has come to use the involvement close.

Here are the steps in the involvement close:

1. Place the partially completed document with the prospect's name, address, and social security number already typed in, in full view, facing the prospect all during the sales presentation. Make the signature slot highly visible by placing a large red check mark by the space where the endorsement is needed.

2. Hand the form to the prospect to check the spelling and other information before signing.
3. Hand the prospect a pen and carefully indicate the signature line.
4. Make a closing statement: "This will help get your money to work for you as soon as possible."

The skilled seller of intangibles fully understands the prospect's fears about signing documents that become positive proof of their money commitment. Most agreements are scary things. They have been drafted by attorneys who are primarily looking out for and protecting the vendor's interest. The old cry of *caveat emptor* (let the buyer beware) still rings alarm bells in all prospects' minds when they are asked to sign a legal document. Fear exists that the document is an entrapment device, full of fine print and incomprehensible clauses that could turn out to be financially harmful if the seller's verbal picture turns out *not* to come true.

This one-on-one situation often becomes an insurmountable problem for the untrained seller. When all the ammunition has been fired and still no signature obtained, the involvement close can be used.

Let's assume that our hero, Joe Salesman, is down to the wire with John Prospect. Joe is trying his best to get John to sign a tax-deferred annuity contract. All the main sales points and features have been repeated and reviewed.

The scene is the prospect's office. The tax-deferred annuity form was all filled out, except for the signature, prior to the meeting, and it was placed on John's desk all during the presentation to serve as a silent salesman. Every time John looked down at the document, he could read his name. The subtle suggestion that he was an owner emanated from the document.

Joe, being a good face-to-face salesman, reiterates the key sales points. All the time he keeps his eyes focused on those of John Prospect. (Eyes that don't wander but radiate honesty and sincerity are one of the most helpful characteristics in convincing a prospect to buy.)

Joe: "What seems to appeal to you, and thousands like you, is the complete avoidance of income taxes (state or federal) on the money your money earns while it is growing."

John: "I like that. In fact, I love it! But even more I like the fact I can get all or part of my money any time, just about like money in the bank."

Good security salespeople soon find out that the way to get ahead is to do more than is necessary for clients, and keep on doing it!

TWO THINGS YOU CAN DO TODAY TO MAKE YOUR BUSINESS GROW!

1. **Take a nice low-commission-producer client to lunch—he or she will love the special attention.**

2. **Let the person know that you will pay close attention to the account no matter how small. Also, let that person know that referrals really help you. Many of the best "bird dogs" are small investors!**

Joe: "Yes, that is important and reassuring, but just as important is the guarantee that *you cannot lose even a single principal dollar*—very different from buying stocks, commodities, or even bonds. Since you don't have to pay any initial sales cost and you can earn a high rate of interest free of current income taxes, why don't you just transfer $40,000 from your savings account now? Just *okay* this form and I can get your money to work right away."

The foregoing situation is frequent in one form or another. The prospect says all the right things, agrees with you, understands the product, but simply freezes when it comes to the signing. When you reach this point, *try to gently force the signature* by removing your eyes from the prospect's face, and *stare at the form*, right at the spot where the signature is needed. Like a magnet, the prospect's eyes will be drawn to the signature spot. Seeing the name already typed or printed on the document makes it less threatening and carries with it the sense of ownership. With both sets of eyes on the signature the message is quite clear. Frequently this little extra pressure is enough to gain the endorsement.

However, if that doesn't work the next step is to involve the prospect in the action. Take a fountain pen (a good investment if you don't have one) from your pocket. Take off the cap and hand the pen to the prospect. Say something like this: "Okay this, and your money can start earning you 10 percent in annual untaxed current income without risking a single dollar!" The handing of the pen and its acceptance by the prospect is a powerful closing action, and many times, after all else has failed that will do the trick.

However, selling, like true love, seems never to run smoothly. If the handing of the pen, cap removed, does not immediately cause the prospect to bend over and sign, then get up your nerve and snatch the pen back from the prospect. This action of suddenly taking away a pen that has been offered in a friendly but businesslike manner will normally create an instant flare-up of anger. After all, who likes being graciously handed something and then having it abruptly removed?

After having snatched the pen away, simply make a half-turn away from the prospect, shake the pen as if to start the ink flowing, and turn back to the prospect again, handing the pen back with this statement: "I have been having trouble with this pen all day! Try it now, please."

I know you won't believe it until you have done it yourself, but this really works. When a fountain pen is snatched away and then reoffered after having been vigorously shaken to make the ink flow, the natural action is for the person now holding the pen (the prospect) to test it to see if it works. The natural way to do that is to make a mark with it. The piece of paper most handy is the document with the red, check-marked space for a signature. The normal test is to write one's name!

John Prospect: "This works fine now."

Top security salespeople are always new-account conscious. They seek new accounts each month from referrals and from their prospecting methods. They know full well that without a continuous supply of new accounts their account base (and thus income) will shrink due to the normal attrition of customers who die, others who relocate, and others who grow disenchanted with the market.

TWO THINGS YOU CAN DO TODAY TO MAKE YOUR BUSINESS GROW!

1. **Select a quality, research-recommended stock in which to try to build a position of more than 10,000 shares in 30 days.**
2. **Build a book of information about that stock for instant reference and to furnish you with the kind of knowledge that helps kindle enthusiasm.**
   ASK FOR THE ORDER!

Joe Salesman: "You really made a smart decision by putting your money to work to earn you high current untaxed interest, and without ever risking a single dollar of your principal."

After gaining a signature with the involvement close, cement the sale by telling the prospect how smart a decision giving the order is. It really pays big dividends to have a prospect leave feeling good about having made an intelligent decision and remembering your last few words as to why the decision is smart. (The "why" is simply a reiteration of the key sales points and benefits.)

Hopefully, the prospect will tell the next several friends about this wonderful, intelligent decision. The natural inclination of investors is to bring others into the fold, hopefully to share the future reward.

The involvement close (so named because the salesman actually involves the prospect in the closing procedure) can convert sales that seem doomed to slip away. It can also create some immediate referrals through the prospect's circle of acquaintances.

Close Technique 9:
The Ultimate Close

When you cannot call to mind any of the eight different closes discussed in the preceding pages, use the *ultimate close: Ask for an order!* This close certainly does simplify the selling process when memory or technique fails. Ask for an order!

Don't expect prospects to be so overwhelmed by your presentation of facts, features, and benefits that they will buy from you without having you directly, clearly *ask for an order!*

Telling Stock Buyers
What They Want to Know

Salespeople working for brokerage firms should, after careful study and approval from research and compliance departments, try to build positions in favored stocks. Too often I have seen account executives spin their wheels, wasting time researching and recommending stocks that for one reason or another were not suitable for developing into a large position. This brings me to LeRoy's maxim: *"If it isn't good enough to build a big position, it isn't good enough."*

With proper guidance and a good understanding of investor desires, stock-oriented salespeople can become tremendous producers with a reservoir of repeat commission clients.

In order to sell as much as you can, as quickly as you can, to as many people as you can—that is every salesman's objective—it is important to understand what turns people on to a common stock. You must know what investors everywhere want to know before purchasing a stock.

Beware of Common Turn-Offs

Many would-be big producers never make it because they sell the wrong features of the investment. They may correctly judge the value in the stock, but they fail in getting enough people to go along with their opinion. Some account executives are so steeped in knowledge about their chosen company that they flood the prospect with trivial information, but instead of making the sale, they *lose it*.

Others use brokerage jargon that confuses uninformed investors and bores sophisticated ones. By jargon I mean terms like *debt/equity ratio, P/E ratio, capital structure, outstanding shares, fully diluted earnings,* and so on. All pompous terms designed to impress rather than sell.

Still other brokers try the ouiji board approach, featuring the technical position of the shares. They try to overwhelm prospects with words like *pennant formation, rounding bottom, head and shoulders, resistance level, support level,* and *long base.*

Once in a board room I overheard a broker talking excitedly to a prospect. The conversation went like this:

Broker: "Mr. Jones, you really ought to buy some shares now, at the market! It's just had a break-out from a long base!"
Prospect: "Huh?"

Read the broker's pitch again. Do the words, no matter how enthusiastically uttered, make much sense to the average investor? Are they a turn-on to anyone, except perhaps a limited few who will risk their capital without knowing or caring about fundamental things like earnings and dividends? The broker may have selected a winner, but the chances of using that selection to make this sale were nil. He completely failed to understand certain selling techniques that would have enabled him to build a following for his idea.

How big a producer Elmer Letterman could have been in our industry by practicing his credo: when the outlook *isn't good, try the* uplook!

TWO THINGS YOU CAN DO TODAY TO MAKE YOUR BUSINESS GROW!

1. **Set a specific $ commission goal for today. Work to beat it before 1:00 New York time!**
2. **Get one new account today: cold phone call, in-person cold call, or asked-for referral. Just concentrate each day on getting those new account(s)! Your business will really grow!**

I observed that broker as he breathed his excitement over the phone. He extended one arm horizontally outward and upward in a swoop, to help clarify his exclamation, "It's just had a break-out from a long base!" The only problem with that emphatic gesture was that there was no picture phone, and the prospect *didn't* get the message. Are you sending out messages neither seen nor understood by your prospects?

Focus on the Desired Facets

Investors everywhere want to know three simple, basic things before buying a common stock. Let's examine them one by one.

Profit Potential

What's in it for the investor? *That's* what an investor wants to know most of all. The broker earns an immediate commission from the share purchase, but the client wants to have a target profit possibility pinpointed. The temptation offered the prospect of having more money later gets investors in the state of mind to spend dollars now on a recommended stock. If you want to make more sales to more people, zero in on the profit potential to them (estimated from analysts' projected targets).

Don't overstate the potential, for that can lead to lawsuits and compliance problems. But within prudent guidelines, ensure that prospects understand the earnings potential of the capital they are thinking about investing.

Time Period for Expected Profit

Setting a time period for the expected profit is important to encouraging the investment. The profit prospect may look good for doubling a client's money, but if the time period for the estimated doubling is 50 years, no sale is going to result! If the estimated time period for the potential value increase is one, two, or three years, the prospect can imagine its happening and can anticipate being around to collect if the payoff is realized. When pitching a common stock to a prospect, be sure to set a target price and a target time frame. You will sell more to more.

Ben Feldman, the number-1 salesman for New York Life every year for over 20 consecutive years, is a great believer in goal setting—with time limits—and within reach if every effort is made. He says, Salespeople who have no place to go aren't going anywhere!

Risk Estimate

One sure way to lose the clients that your hard work has obtained is to fail to point out the risk being undertaken. Clients can accept losses and still be clients—commission givers—as long as they have been properly alerted to any and all risk *prior to entering into the investment*.

Good salespeople seeking to build long-term relationships make an appeal to the profit motive, of course. But just as surely, they adequately alert clients to the risk undertaken. The opportunity then exists for the client to compare the risk estimate against the hoped-for profit. After comparing and relating to the time period recommended as the holding period, the client can fairly quickly form a judgment on the investment.

Think about these three things I've said clients want to know, and ask yourself if those aren't really the important things that *you* would want to know before investing your money in a common stock.

If you zero in on these three fundamental desires, you will make more sales and make them quicker. Your stock position building will grow, and so will your income.

The following illustration of a typical stock solicitation between broker and existing client can easily be modified to a broker/prospect scenario. Note carefully the absence of trivial information and the accent on the three things all stock buyers want to know.

Broker: "Let me speak to Ann Client right away, please."

Client: "Ann Client speaking."

Broker: "Ann, this is Joe Salesman. We have just now received a research report on ZXY Company, a company that I am really excited about. The stock is rated A+. Our analyst believes if you buy now there is an excellent opportunity for you to make 50 percent or more from the current level of about 17."

Client: "That sounds good."

Broker: "Not only does the potential profit look great but the analyst thinks a price rise could take place within 18 months. The shares are depressed, along with the market, and are selling below book value."

Client: "Does it pay any dividends?"

Broker: "Not only does it pay dividends, but it has raised its dividend every year for the last ten. The current yield is 7.2 percent. In addition to getting a good return on your money while waiting for a profit, we believe if you buy now at the 17 level you won't be running a great risk. The lowest price the shares have sold in the last ten years is 15½, and that low was reached at the bottom of a bear market when the earnings and dividends were lower than they are today."

Client: "That sounds like my kind of stock. Send me the report."

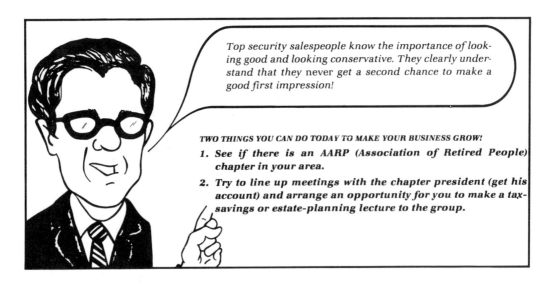

Top security salespeople know the importance of looking good and looking conservative. They clearly understand that they never get a second chance to make a good first impression!

TWO THINGS YOU CAN DO TODAY TO MAKE YOUR BUSINESS GROW!

1. *See if there is an AARP (Association of Retired People) chapter in your area.*
2. *Try to line up meetings with the chapter president (get his account) and arrange an opportunity for you to make a tax-savings or estate-planning lecture to the group.*

Broker: "I'll put the report in the mail today. The problem is that opportunities sometimes get away from you, as others quickly recognize the bargain value. This looks so attractive that you ought to get some today while the price is low. After you receive the report and read it, you might want to buy more if it is still available near today's price."

Client: "You really think it might move that quickly?"

Broker: "Look, Ann, this report is just out. A lot of brokers like me are going to recommend it. Other firms may also be attracted on their own or because our analyst has spotlighted the value. Maybe it will be the same price when you get the report, and maybe it won't. There are no guarantees in common stocks. Why don't you try to buy 500 or 1000 shares at the last price? I don't want you to miss out completely on this opportunity while you're waiting for the mail. Which quantity is right for you now, 500 or 1000?"

Client: "Okay, see if you can buy me 500 at the last price. If it starts to move or pick up volume just buy at the market."

TIPS ON SELLING PRODUCTS

Selecting Common Stocks
to Help Sell More Shares
to More People More Quickly: 8 Criteria

Every salesperson who works on commission for a brokerage firm should certainly be aware of the risks inherent in investing in common stock as well as the rewards. The risk of loss through stock trading creates such great fear in many sellers of securities (as well as in their clients) that they try to build and maintain business that concentrates on low-risk investments. These anxious souls push treasury bills, short-term bonds (government, municipal, and corporate) and no-risk products like tax-deferred annuities or insurance (which don't lose value except for inflation, a risk that cannot be avoided).

In order to make a living, though, the majority of security salespeople must face the loss of clients and clients' capital because they offer investments associated with risk, such as stocks, long-term bonds, convertible bonds, and listed options. A few are hardy enough to tackle the magnified risk of commodity trading.

I learned early in my career that if I was to protect my clients and their capital in stock or stock-related investments, I had better learn to protect myself against the suggestions of research departments and syndicate departments. Those departments do the best they can to make what they believe to be appropriate recommendations, but chaff inevitably gets mixed with their wheat. Another LeRoy maxim: *Carefully screen all research and syndicate suggestions.* Often I was encouraged to merchandise inventory stocks to keep the firm from losing on a position or to earn a profit for the firm. The problem there, though, is

Top security salespeople have learned that if they want more money to keep track of, they'd better keep track of their selling time.

TWO THINGS YOU CAN DO TODAY TO MAKE YOUR BUSINESS GROW!

1. **Send an interest-rate fact sheet (various rates of interest available on many different products from TDAs, U.S. notes, bonds, to municipals) to different CPAs or attorneys.**
2. **Call each and tell them to look for it in the mail and let you know if they would like to have this information on a regular basis. (You are almost certain to get some referrals or accounts.)**

that the firm isn't weighing the profit potential of the inventory item versus other investment alternatives for the client in respect to the client's objectives and the risk.

NYSE firms work continually to upgrade and improve research. I found it far better to make stock choices from their approved lists than to choose from other sources. Even with NYSE lists, I had to stay wary, realizing that lemons could still creep in.

During the learning process I suffered many a hard knock (in the form of lost clients) when I encouraged clients to make investments I didn't believe in deeply or to purchase financial products about which my knowledge wasn't broad enough. *The broker's "book" of clients is his or her single most valuable possession.* It is a possession that can provide a high level of income year after year if it is most carefully watched over. Constant care must be exercised to control clients' risk of loss to as modest and reasonable a level as possible under even the most adverse circumstances.

It was my experience (shared by thousands of stockbrokers) that every client for whom I made a lot of money stayed with me. After all, who would want to risk change during a winning streak? And I kept almost all the clients for whom I made a little money. Oh, they grumbled and mumbled about not having the current takeover candidate or the hot stock of the moment, but they stayed with me—traded with me—remained loyal to me. I found that I was able to keep most of the clients for whom I lost a little money. They too, would complain about the lack of winners, the aggravation, my commissions, and their losses, but they stayed as clients, attracted by the service I gave them, the hand-holding, and my sincere effort to make money for them.

I lost almost every client for whom I lost a lot of money. They naturally became bitter about their losses and sought a different broker to get a fresh start, a new viewpoint, in an effort to regain their lost capital.

That range of experiences convinced me to choose and weigh the risk when I was dealing in common stocks. I learned to estimate the risk before suggesting a purchase. My focus was on *not losing large amounts* of clients' money.

The perplexing problem lay in the initial selection of a common stock. Brokers are simply inundated with volumes of information. The large wire houses, in particular, produce so many research reports that it is beyond the ability of any broker to read and comprehend the total output. Many of the reports, although well researched and perhaps well thought out, are written in an incomprehensible manner. Some appear to be written to show off the writer's erudition rather than to inform the reader, simply and explicitly.

This is the problem you face. In addition to being deluged with your own firm's research, you are likely to be knee-deep in stock suggestions coming from a myriad of investment services, such as Value Line, Standard & Poor's, other brokerage firms, *Barron's* and *Business Week*, just to name a few. On top of the blizzard of printed material, tips and rumors abound. Hot tips can influence you to make hasty recommendations without having determined the real value, and without having recognized the true risk. Frustrating and aggravating are the mildest descriptions of this dilemma you face: trying to choose a stock to recommend from all of the thousands of candidates.

In order to simplify the procedure so that my selling time would be maximized, I devised a system for selecting common stocks. This system is workable in all types of markets. This system takes careful recognition of risk, and it allowed me the opportunity to *sell as much as I could, to as many as I could, as quickly as I could.* The system I devised for picking common stocks is not perfect; no system yet designed is fail-safe. But the system I designed is easy to understand, to adopt, and to use. Over time, my system has worked successfully for thousands to whom I taught it. It can be a factor in *your* building and keeping a book of clients.

The eight points you will learn to use are meant solely to help you with the initial choice of a stock to recommend. I believe it is necessary to develop a large position in several stocks, each stock carefully chosen, rather than to maintain client portfolios dotted with dozens and dozens of different stocks accumulated willy-nilly over the years. You cannot carefully monitor portfolios laden with too many different stocks.

In my opinion, establishing large positions in a few select stocks is a better route to follow, and actually less dangerous over the course of time. There is no more satisfying, thrilling experience in a broker's life than to build a large position (50,000–1,000,000 shares) in a stock, watch it rise to a sell point, and then advise clients to sell the profitable shares and reinvest the proceeds.

In choosing a common stock to recommend, you want a selection that will enable you to sell as much as you can, as quickly as you can, to as many as you can. Compliance department requirements must be kept in mind at all times to permit the maximizing of the sales effort. My eight criteria for stock selecting *almost assure broker freedom from compliance department restrictions.*

Stock Selection Criterion 1: Seek High-Gain Potential

If you are going to devote time to building a substantial stock position in your clients' portfolios, and if you are going to have clients exposed to the financial risks of stock ownership, you should have an anticipated, hoped-for, minimum profit target of at least 50 percent. This target is hopefully to be achieved in 12 to 24 months. Nothing creates referrals or retains clients and encourages client activity so much as the attainment of a large percentage gain in a holding period just long enough so that the gain qualifies for a low-taxed, long-term tax treatment. If you aim for too low a gain, you never get that profit-satisfied client who is the core of repeat business.

Aim for big wins and you aim for bigger, longer-lasting clients.

Stock Selection Criterion 2: Choose High-Quality Issues

As you seek to establish a brokerage business in your community, concentrate on recommending high-quality issues consistently. The more "unknown" you are, the more necessary it is to stress quality. The rationale is really quite simple. Strangers find it easier to say "yes" to a purchase if the offered product is high-grade. High quality in the investment adds assurance that transcends the salesperson. By constantly stressing high quality, you build an aura—create an image—about yourself and about your firm. The quality image, mirrored by your product recommendations, makes it easier for strangers to recommend their friends and family to you as potential clients.

In addition to making it easier to get "yeses," a focus on quality makes for larger orders. Big orders help propel you toward what must be your constant goal: selling as much as you can, to as many as you can, as quickly as you can.

Only Quality-Rated Stocks

When selecting a stock to merchandise in a big way to many people, one of my essential requirements is that the stock be rated A−, A, or A+ by Standard & Poor's. These ratings are based on an assessment of a company's financial strength. The quality rating has no bearing whatsoever on the direction the price may take in the future. There is great misunderstanding in the financial selling community about the S&P ratings. This misunderstanding tends to reassure the under-informed and uninitiated about the security of the current price or the potential for price recovery of a particular stock.

The Power of the "A"

Here are my reasons for suggesting that each stock chosen for position building be quality rated A−, A, or A+. All of us have been

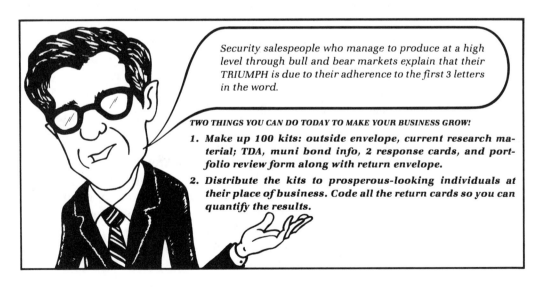

Security salespeople who manage to produce at a high level through bull and bear markets explain that their TRIUMPH is due to their adherence to the first 3 letters in the word.

TWO THINGS YOU CAN DO TODAY TO MAKE YOUR BUSINESS GROW!

1. Make up 100 kits: outside envelope, current research material; TDA, muni bond info, 2 response cards, and portfolio review form along with return envelope.

2. Distribute the kits to prosperous-looking individuals at their place of business. Code all the return cards so you can quantify the results.

brainwashed since the day we entered grade school that the letter A is good. All As on our report cards gained praise and recognition (and maybe a dollar or two). When you enthusiastically suggest a common stock rated A, the prospect receives the message, "This is a good stock." This thought makes it much easier for the prospect to buy.

Furthermore, when investors first make their entry into investing in corporate or municipal debt issues they are taught that the rating A is good, AA very good, and AAA excellent. Therefore, A linked to a common-stock recommendation makes the stock seem more acceptable, respectable, prudent, and desirable, all of which encourage the prospect to go along with your advice.

When a potential investor delays purchase, many times it is to allow time to seek the opinion of a third party. People most often sought out for stock opinions are other brokers, bankers, lawyers, and CPAs. If the stock is of recognized high quality, it is hard to knock or denigrate the recommendation. Frequently the high quality of a recommended issue brings about an affirmation from the third party. This agreement helps cement or create the sale.

When your living, your financial survival, depends on the commissions you earn, why jeopardize even one sale through accepting low quality? Just as many potentially good situations exist with high-quality stocks as with lower-quality stocks. At least at the recommending stage, the high-quality stock will create the better impression.

A-rated stocks provide more restful nights for investors. When stocks fall in price either because of circumstances at the individual company or because of a general market decline, holders of high-quality issues are generally less likely to panic. They are more likely to "average down" with additional purchases. High quality makes it easier for your clients to believe that the company will survive in an adverse economy and that price recovery is likely to occur, profits eventually to increase.

The Perils of Low Quality

Holders of low-quality issues become very uneasy in falling markets. They worry about company bankruptcy or the dearth of analysts advocating their positions. All the analysts seem to seek safety in bad markets by concentrating on recommendations for the purchase of high-quality stocks. Owners of low-quality stock very easily get panicked into selling into a steepening decline as they begin to doubt more and more seriously the company's ability to weather bad times. The flight from low-quality stocks magnifies losses. There is often a

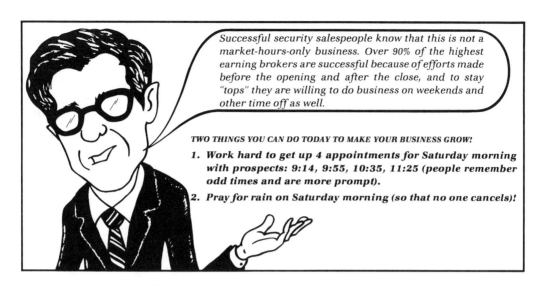

Successful security salespeople know that this is not a market-hours-only business. Over 90% of the highest earning brokers are successful because of efforts made before the opening and after the close, and to stay "tops" they are willing to do business on weekends and other time off as well.

TWO THINGS YOU CAN DO TODAY TO MAKE YOUR BUSINESS GROW!

1. **Work hard to get up 4 appointments for Saturday morning with prospects: 9:14, 9:55, 10:35, 11:25 (people remember odd times and are more prompt).**

2. **Pray for rain on Saturday morning (so that no one cancels)!**

massive rush to liquidate but only a few takers. Quality stocks certainly are not immune to severe price drops in market declines, but generally they enjoy a thicker market, a market more willing to absorb quantities at fairer prices, than is the case with low-rated issues.

High Quality Helps with Compliance

A-rated stocks help restrict compliance interventions. Salespeople out to do the best selling job they can on a stock with which they are thoroughly knowledgeable and convinced the issue is right for his clients and prospects at the current price, can better accomplish their goal by focusing on A-rated, quality stocks. Brokerage house compliance departments properly performing their job of supervision frequently limit salespeople in the accumulation of shares of a low-quality issue, but they seldom restrict the accumulation of shares in high-quality issues.

It makes little sense to learn all aspects of a common stock and start a selling effort, then, *solely because of low quality, be limited as to the number of people as to whom the issue can be sold.* Limits by watchful compliance officers may also be placed on the number of shares being bought.

The business of selling securities is tough enough without your creating unnecessary barriers to attaining sales success.

Compliance departments must do their very best to protect firms from lawsuits and also to protect their firms' capital and clients' capital. Time after time, their careful watch over the accumulation of low-quality issues has proven its value. If you concentrate your selling efforts on A-rated issues, you will normally be allowed to sell as much as you can to as many as you can—and that's what the selling game is all about.

Another significant benefit is that you will be able to sleep better at night as a merchandiser of quality stock shares. Your own self-respect is a fragile but necessary ingredient that can best be preserved through knowing you are a purveyor of quality. When clients lose money, you will suffer along with them, but your distress will be less if you have full knowledge that a profit was sought with a prudent eye toward quality. When high-quality investments lose value, their holders are less likely to litigate, by the way, than they would be with similar losses in low-rated issues. Investors who lose money on high-quality issues frequently direct their anger more toward the market than toward the broker who recommended the stock. Investors who lose on low-quality issues tend to direct their anger toward the broker, and they may seek redress through court action.

Stock Selection Criterion 3:
Seek Cash Dividend Income

Regular cash dividends are bonuses to the investor who is seeking capital gains. It is important to recognize that many investors measure their returns on investment solely by the cash dividends paid to them as shareowners. Therefore, in selecting a stock in which the goal is to build a significant position, give careful consideration to the cash dividend: its amount, its security, and the likelihood of increase.

You will find that it is much easier to sell larger quantities of a given investment vehicle to more investors if the yield approaches or exceeds the rate currently being paid for bank passbook accounts (5½ percent at the time of this writing).

By purchasing shares that pay good dividends, most investors persuade themselves of their prudence, based on the expected income. They feel the gain potential is a significant added benefit. Should the stock fall in value from their purchase level, they console themselves that the dividend provides a return on their cost. The regular dividend stream makes the losing investor a more patient holder and often a fairly eager, willing purchaser of more shares with only the slightest encouragement from the salesperson.

I know there are some doubting Thomases in the financial community who decry cash dividends as being meaningless to the high-bracket investor. It has been my experience that very rich investors who talk about the low value they place on cash dividends because they are in such a high tax bracket do so just to impress the listener. *Those same highly taxed grumblers will often move their money from one bank to another to gain one-quarter percent more in taxable interest!* The cash dividend *is* a plus when you are trying to get the wealthy to buy. Also, a cash dividend may act as a yield anchor in falling markets, keeping the stock from slipping as much as stocks that pay lower dividends.

In selecting a dividend-paying stock for sales focus, I look for a stock (1) that has maintained or raised its dividend in each of the previous five years and (2) for which future forecasts are equally optimistic. Good dividend income just makes it easier for the majority of prospects to buy.

Stock Selection Criterion 4: Focus on Low Risk

No rational person wants to lose money. Most investors want to be able to perceive themselves as profit chasers who recognize, understand, and exert some control over risk. Given the choice between seeking a profit from a high-risk, high-potential-gain investment and a low-risk, high-potential-gain investment, they will most often choose the latter, convinced of their prudence.

As you strive to achieve sales stardom and client retention, make every effort to recommend stocks that you believe at the time are low-risk, high-potential-profit situations. By so doing, you expand the number of clients and prospects for whom the proposed investment is suitable. You also expand the share quantity that each might prudently buy.

All these factors nicely dovetail with the objective of selling as much as you can to as many as you can as quickly as you can. Of course, the question arises, How do you judge whether or not a stock is a low risk at the time of purchase? A very fair question.

In order to be able to use the powerful selling words "low risk" when you try to convince a prospect to buy, some substantiation for the statement must exist. That substantiation may be available in an excerpt from the fundamental research report that the analyst wrote or from a projection furnished by the technical analysis section of the research department. Value Line estimates and projections are often helpful for determining the risk potential. If none of the above are available for use in risk estimation (hardly likely, but possible), reasonable assumptions might be determined by carefully studying past high-low price history, past high-low price-to-earnings ratios, and extrapolations into the future based on year-ahead estimates of earnings.

Accenting a legitimately determined, expected low-risk feature develops large sales and many substantial referrals. Isn't that what you want?

Stock Selection Criterion 5:
Pick a Company Whose Name or Product Is
a Household Word

Stockbrokers should try to make their task—creating commission sales—as easy as possible. The job of selling shares of stock is greatly simplified if you are recommending a company that is well and widely known.

Prospects feel more like buying if they personally know of the company, its reputation, the quality of its products or services, and are familiar with its advertising campaigns. Under such circumstances, prospects' fears are better allayed and they are much less suspicious of the salesperson and much more likely to believe in the profit potential of the investment.

Let's assume that you have been looking at the motel industry as potentially an advisable investment area. In trying to narrow your choice to the single best candidate for purchase, you have carefully reviewed the basics such as earnings per share, dividends, book value, return on invested capital, occupancy trends, projected earnings, current stock prices, and other related factors including balance-sheet statistics. Let's also assume that two companies appeared to be equal opportunities in your eyes:

Holiday Inns

La Quinta Inns

In my view it is axiomatic that Holiday Inns would be the choice. The familiarity of the name alone would make it easier to sell more to more people with less effort expended.

Too many brokers earn less than their abilities call for simply because they have not taken proper cognizance of the "comfortable shoe" feeling that owning shares of a familiar company brings to a prospective buyer.

Concentrate your sales efforts on well-known shares and watch your commissions magnify!

Stock Selection Criterion 6:
Choose a Company That Is Number 1
in Its Industry

Nothing warms an investor's heart so much as picking a winner! Making money on a stock investment is balm to the psyche. The profit create a glow that spreads to the immediate loved ones and extends to practically everyone coming in contact with "the winner." Investors' driving desire to win led me to focus on companies that were number 1 in their industry (the number 1 rating could be for any of several things, including total sales, total profit, return on investments, just to name a few). I found that my sales strength was greatly improved and closes more frequently made if I could enthusiastically, resoundingly tell a prospect: *"This company is number 1 in its industry!"*

That is a power-packed selling statement that conveys the impression to the prospect that the company is a winner because it has that coveted number 1 ranking. "Number 1 in the industry" translates in the prospect's brain into "Investment in the shares will make [the prospect] a winner!"

Selling shares of companies ranked number 1 is just an easier job to perform than selling shares of companies without that designation.

As a salesperson striving for success, the more things you can do to make sales easier to obtain, the quicker and greater the degree of success.

Stock Selection Criterion 7:
Pick a Low-Priced Stock (Under $30)

Understanding investor psychology is a factor extremely important to developing a large brokerage business. The concept of "more is better" is deeply ingrained into people everywhere, almost from birth. The inherent greed that plagues most of the human race is a driving force toward "getting more," "owning more."

A thinking salesperson seeking a stock to merchandise to clients and prospects does more than casually glance at the quoted share price. The share price as a lone statistic can dramatically determine the success or failure of a concentrated sales effort.

It has been my experience (and that of thousands of successful stockbrokers) that the best sales results are obtained from stocks in the price range of $10 to $30 per share. Investors typically would rather buy 1000 shares of a $10 stock than 100 shares of a $100 stock. The prospects for gain from earnings, dividends, and everything else might be equal but the price alone would cause more solicited prospects to choose the lower-priced shares. Crazy? Maybe. But that's the real world.

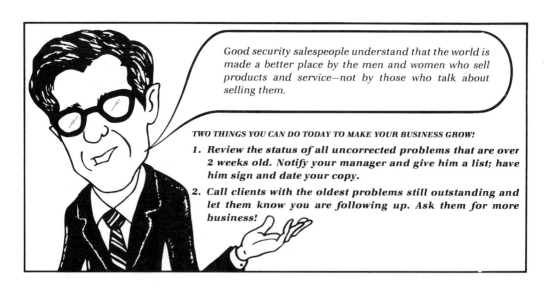

Good security salespeople understand that the world is made a better place by the men and women who sell products and service—not by those who talk about selling them.

TWO THINGS YOU CAN DO TODAY TO MAKE YOUR BUSINESS GROW!

1. **Review the status of all uncorrected problems that are over 2 weeks old. Notify your manager and give him a list; have him sign and date your copy.**

2. **Call clients with the oldest problems still outstanding and let them know you are following up. Ask them for more business!**

234

Some observations may help you understand and use this phenomenon as you try to zero in on a stock to merchandise widely. First, the higher the price of the shares (particularly over $30), the greater the buyer resistance, *no matter how good the outlook for the stock*. Second, if a stock is too low in price (under $10, particularly lower than $5) prospects tend to be suspicious about the company's viability. A very low price invariably causes questions to be asked, like, "Why is it so low? Are they going bankrupt?"

In my experience, the best marketing share price is a stock share priced in the teens. That is a price low enough to assuage most fears of the company's viability and yet allow for some pleasant dreaming about those shares attaining adulthood and perhaps eventually trading at $40, $50, or better.

Stock Selection Criterion 8:
Choose Stock Currently Judged "Buy"
by Your Firm's Research Analyst

If the sky falls down, you don't want to be crushed by the falling debris. Salespeople seeking to survive and thrive in the every increasing competitiveness of the marketplace must be constantly alert to the fact that a lack of judgment can cause fines, censure, or even being forced to leave the industry.

In the stock-brokerage community, bear markets and falling stocks are precursors to client complaints and lawsuits, most of which are based on the suitability of the recommendation for the client. "Suitability" is a catchall covering the client's needs and wants, as well as the grounds on which the recommendation was originally made.

When you choose a stock for mass merchandising and big position building, *restrict your choice solely to issues positively recommended as current buys on a fundamental basis by your firm.*

Should the stock perform badly after purchase, it's the firm's fault! It is the research department's error. It was the analyst who judged incorrectly! You can legitimately direct the customer's ire away from you toward several other sources. You and the client can jointly deplore the bad outcome and still retain a decent relationship, and perhaps the hope of recovery by means of a different analyst's suggestion.

When you are trying to sell in quantity, you want the support of your firm, and the millions the firm normally devotes to research, to back your sales presentation.

There is no more lonely feeling for brokers, carried away by a story of the moment, than to sell the story successfully in a big way to many people and then watch the stock sickeningly slide into low-priced oblivion. Terror strikes, for such salespeople are all alone. No compliance department to side with them. No research analyst to support their buying thesis. Rightfully upset clients may sue, and burden these poor brokers with the guilt stemming from client's losses.

Avoid recommending any stock other than the ones bearing the strongest recommendations of your research department. Sticking to that philosophy can add immeasurable strength to the sales pitch and help multiply the "yes" answers, while making you feel good about what you are recommending and why you are recommending it.

There you have it—my eight criteria for selecting common stocks. If you use my filter system, your chances of doing well will be substantially enhanced as will be your longevity in this business of selling stocks.

Suppose though, try as you might, you don't find a stock that fulfills all eight criteria. What then? I would choose a stock to focus on if as few as five of the eight criteria were present at the time of recommendation. Here are the five core qualities that *must* be present in order to merit your effort at hard selling to position quantities of shares.

1. Seek *high-gain potential.*
2. Choose *high-quality issues.*
3. Seek *cash dividend income.*
4. Focus on *low risk.*
5. Choose *research-approved* stock.

Use my system for one to three years and compare the results to any year in which you didn't seek these criteria. I am confident you will feel inclined to write and thank me for helping build your sales success.

With your focus always on avoiding loss stocks, you can't help but be a winner!

Power-Packed Selling Phrases
for Option Specialists

The listed-options market has blossomed into one of the biggest revenue producers for major retail securities firms. Many account executives have devoted countless hours to learning the intricacies of option activity. The complexities range from margin rules that are incredibly difficult to understand to a myriad of tax consequences that challenge the mental capacity of CPAs and other experts.

The compliance surveillance ladder extends from the Securities and Exchange Commission to the major option and stock exchanges to the individual firms to the salesperson. Before consummating a single option sale, salespeople must have passed a difficult (and growing more so) examination on option rules, regulations, strategies, margins, and tax consequences. The terminology used in the option world is strange enough, and threatening enough, to discourage many would-be participants.

In addition to all the special knowledge salespeople dealing in options must have, they must also monitor carefully to ensure that any option activity undertaken by a client is "suitable" for that client. Suitability is based upon some rather stiff minimum asset guidelines that may or may not be truly useful. The threat of a suitability lawsuit by a client who has lost money engaging in option activity is a real worry for salespeople and their firms, especially since courts and juries continually seek greater protection for the consumer.

Despite all these deterrents and the substantial risks that option

"Be prepared to listen, and listen to be prepared" is a good motto to follow on the road to becoming a top seller of securities.

participants face, the business continues to grow. This growth is fostered by the attractive features that options have for those who buy them and those who sell them.

Option buyers are generally speculators willing to risk total (100 percent) loss of their investment while seeking a return that can be 2, 3, 10, or more times the amount of their investment. Even though an option buyers risks total loss, this loss potential is predeterminable, and it is fixed. Loss can never be larger than the money paid for the contract. Along with the fixed risk and large profit potential, the option buyer enjoys a high degree of leverage. Small dollar investments in option contracts can control underlying stock values measured in thousands of dollars for a finite period of time. Each contract is subject to adjustments as per the actual terms of the contract.

Despite the apparent advantages for option buyers, it has been my experience that salespeople who try to build a clientele oriented to the purchasing of option contracts will not be long-term successes. Losses incurred buying options leave the investor with bitter feelings, despite all prior warnings of the risk involved. Option buyers' trading is frequently frenzied and dictated by emotion. This makes for difficult accounts and causes an inordinate amount of the salesperson's time to be spent in tape watching and hand holding. Additionally, the great majority of option buyers commit only a small part of their assets to the activity (at least that is the prudent road to follow) while committing the balance to other investment areas.

Small losses from buying options will frequently cause investors to switch the rest of their investment dollars to more "conservative" brokers, thereby transferring the commissions away from the option salesperson.

Typical sellers ("writers") of option contracts are percentage-minded folks who seek a high annual return on the capital committed to back the option contracts they have issued. Sellers can go about seeking their high annual return via a variety of strategies, limited only by the sellers' imagination (and capital). They can sell contracts in a conservative or a speculative manner depending on their knowledge, attitude toward risk, and the extent of their collateral to back the contracts issued. The seller's risk varies, depending on the strategy chosen.

If, dear reader, you have gained the impression that I believe writing options is a more conservative, more certain way to earn a return than buying call options, I have conveyed the wrong impression.

Buying options in many instances may be less risky and more conservative than buying stock and writing calls. Other strategies involved in writing options may involve substantially greater risk than option purchase speculations.

As a salesperson out to attract and retain clients of substantial financial means, you will find it much easier to extol the potential benefits that may evolve from issuing option contracts than it is to gain acceptance for call-buying strategies.

A prospect with $1 million in liquid, investable assets might be persuaded to risk up to $50,000 or so in an option-buying program. That same prospect might, under the ministrations of a well-versed option salesperson, commit upward of $500,000 to a regular program of issuing options. With that in mind, it makes sense to concentrate on option writing in order to get large dollar commitments.

My view in approaching wealthy prospects is to get as large a percentage of their investable assets as possible under a planned program utilizing option strategies that are in line with the prospect's investment objectives. Focusing on writing options simply makes the control of assets easier to accomplish.

The salesperson who concentrates on seeking out clients who will regularly, repeatedly, sell option contracts has an excellent handsome living year in, year out, through all the ups and downs of the stock market.

If you obtain option writing clients, you will normally do very well in commission terms for these excellent reasons:

1. *Greater capital investment.* The typical option writer puts more capital to work than the typical option buyer.

2. *Greater staying power.* The typical option writer continues the investment strategies over long-term periods usually measured in years. Compare this to the months or weeks that constitute the usual life span of option buyers.

3. *Greater net earning likelihood.* Among the numerous option accounts I have surveyed, a far greater number showed net year-end profits from their option-selling strategy than did the accounts that were primarily option buyers.

4. *Greater client satisfaction.* In talking to thousands of Registered Representatives throughout the United States, I was informed continually that, in general, regular option writing clients were satisfied with the results of their activity. These clients evidenced their satisfaction by sticking with the procedure. Happy client! Happy salesperson!

The big problem practicing brokers seem to encounter is in obtaining accounts of sizable wealth. After managing to learn the complexities of option margin requirements, option tax consequences, option rules, and option strategies, many brokers find it difficult to acquire and retain clients for whom options are appropriate.

The mysterious jargon used in the Option Clearing Corporation prospectus and in verbal communications makes understanding difficult and often makes a prospect afraid to enter the activity.

As a broker, I learned to simplify the complex in order to make it understandable and therefore more palatable to a prospect or a client. This ability to communicate difficult concepts with ease helped build my production to a high level and to maintain the higher level.

The terms of the option world should be rephrased so that prospects can understand them enough to make a prudent financial commitment. In the rephrasing I developed *power-packed words and phrases* that investors everywhere throughout this country really understood. When these words are used in face-to-face encounters, including investment seminars, people quickly understand, and easily commit funds to, the suggested strategy.

It is important to understand that the word "option" turns off many prospects. To them "option" connotes risk. To many, "option" means outright purchase, speculation in its rawest form. Call writing, an accepted term in the option world, has little meaning to many investors, including a high number of market sophisticates. To them "option" means something complex and possibly time consuming.

In trying to create interest in the writing of options, I found more attentive listening ears whenever I completely avoided the use of the words "option" and "call writing" in my initial presentation.

Here is another LeRoy maxim: *Good salespeople in any field understand that the initial presentation must be well accepted, interesting, and plausible or there will be no second presentation.*

"Starting at a Profit"

The following scenario shows how to use my power-packed selling words to interest a prospect in call writing. Read the presentation words carefully. You will discover that the words "option" and "call writing" do not appear, since they are negatives in an initial presentation intended to develop a prospect's interest. In later conversations their usage is certainly permissible, even desirable. Later, prospects feel they have been admitted to a club with secret passwords when they hear "option" and "call writing."

Assume that Joe Salesman is making an initial call on John Prospect, who is a wealthy investor. Also keep in mind that the decade 1970–1980 was a hectic, volatile, generally unrewarding decade for stock and bond investors. Assume also that the initial greeting formalities have taken place.

Joe Salesman: "Tell me honestly, John, have you been satisfied with how your money has worked for you in the stock market for the past year or three years or five years?"

Top security salespeople know it's more important to get a small order on the books than none at all.

TWO THINGS YOU CAN DO TODAY TO MAKE YOUR BUSINESS GROW!

1. **Compete! Bet a buddy that for this week you can complete more "asking for the order" calls to strangers and open more accounts than he or she can.**

2. **Send each new account opened a personal note thanking them. This note should go out the day the account is opened.**

John Prospect: "Truthfully Joe, I haven't been too pleased. In fact, I would have been better off just doing nothing but owning Treasury bills. Sure, I have had some winners, but they have been more than offset by my losses. I don't mind paying brokers' commissions when I am making money, but it hurts to lose capital and pay out lots of commissions, too."

Joe Salesman: "I understand how you feel. The past several years have really been tough for stock investors. Blue-chip growth stocks and blue-chip basic industry stocks haven't been the money-makers people thought they would be."

John Prospect: "You're telling me! I own IBM, Sears, U.S. Steel, G.M., Exxon, and a dozen others and am sitting on substantial losses despite the fact I have held them a long time!"

Joe Salesman: "Maybe I can help you like I help other clients."

John Prospect: "How's that?"

Joe Salesman: *"How would you like, starting tomorrow morning when the market opens, to begin every stock purchase transaction at a profit [magic power selling words], a profit paid to you cash in advance, a profit that you can count immediately, usually in hundreds, sometimes in thousands of dollars?"*

John Prospect: "That sounds too good to be true. What's the catch?"

Joe Salesman: "No catch. You can do it, too, just as a lot of my clients

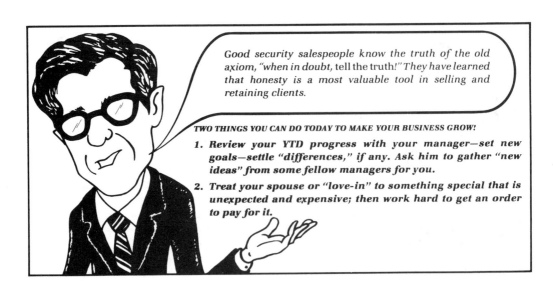

Good security salespeople know the truth of the old axiom, "when in doubt, tell the truth!" They have learned that honesty is a most valuable tool in selling and retaining clients.

TWO THINGS YOU CAN DO TODAY TO MAKE YOUR BUSINESS GROW!

1. *Review your YTD progress with your manager—set new goals—settle "differences," if any. Ask him to gather "new ideas" from some fellow managers for you.*

2. *Treat your spouse or "love-in" to something special that is unexpected and expensive; then work hard to get an order to pay for it.*

are doing. *You can start every stock purchase transaction [repetition sells] you ever make the rest of your investing life at a profit. You can buy a stock and agree to sell your just-bought stock at a higher price than you paid.* For agreeing to sell high what you just bought low, someone will pay you hundreds, maybe thousands of dollars. What makes this even more attractive is that you get to use the money paid you to help pay for the stock you buy!"

John Prospect: "You mean to tell me that for just agreeing to sell at a higher price than I pay someone will give me hundreds of dollars to keep? I don't ever have to pay it back?"

Joe Salesman: "You got it right! And the agreement periods currently never extend for longer than nine months. The agreement periods are often as short as a month or two."

John Prospect: (suspiciously): "What about the dividends?"

Joe Salesman: "You, as the stock owner, get to keep any and all cash dividend as well as the advance money."

John Prospect: "What does the other person get for his money?"

Joe Salesman: "He has hope that the stock will rise above the agreed price by an amount enough to return his original dollars, plus a profit. He is really a high-risk-taker willing to lose 100 percent of his money in a short time period. As long as there is a supply of these willing riskers, you ought to collect some of their money."

John Prospect: "There must be a catch in it. It sounds too good. What risk do I run?"

Joe Salesman: "There really is no real dollar loss risk to you greater than you ordinarily take in owning stock. In fact, your stock ownership risk is lessened by the cash cushion these riskers provide you."

John Prospect: "Well, let's try it on a couple of hundred XYZ. That's a company I like and wouldn't mind owning at the current price."

Read the scenario, and then reread it. If you engage in selling option strategies you will find your "closes" coming easier.

The initial sale is the key sale. That sale converts a prospect into a client. Whether the client becomes a long-term client producing a steady stream of commissions each year will depend on your knowledge and expertise at making, and getting the client to accept, suggestions to lessen risk and increase return.

My power-packed phrases and words are designed to help open accounts. (Account management techniques for retaining accounts would fill another book.) Let's examine other powerful, ear-catching words that can help you change prospects into clients.

"Three Sources of Profit"

The phrase "three sources of profit" carefully uttered in a prospect's presence awakens the natural greed instinct. You can enact the following scenario using those special words to produce orders from prospects.

Learn the phraseology. Use the words daily in your prospecting and you will make sales.

Joe Salesman: "You have told me that you have not been too pleased with the results of your stock market investments."

John Prospect: "That's right. I am dissatisfied with the return, or lack of it, on my stock portfolio."

Joe Salesman: "Starting tomorrow, how would you like to have *three sources of profit* every time you buy a common stock?"

John Prospect: "Three profit sources? What are they?"

Joe Salesman: "First, you could collect a lot of dollars—maybe hundreds, sometimes thousands—for simply agreeing to sell your just-bought stock at a higher price than you paid. This agreement money is paid to you right away, on the very next business day—money that's yours to keep forever. Your second source of profit could be the cash dividends due you as the owner of the stock. The third source of profit would be in the increase in price of the shares from what you paid, to the agreed selling price.

"By agreeing to sell at a higher price than you bought, all you are giving up is the unknown, unknowable profit possibility above the agreed price. In return, for relinquishing some of the profit potential *you collect a handsome amount of cash that you can immediately spend or reinvest, as you choose.*"

John Prospect: "That sounds pretty good."

Joe Salesman: "Not only does it sound good, it is good. You can do it with stocks you already own or stocks you are willing to buy."

If we only wanted to be happy it would be easy; but we want to be happier than other people, which is always most difficult, since we think them happier than they are.

John Prospect: "Well, why don't you look over my portfolio and see if we can't collect some of that advance cash on stock I already own."

This scenario, like others in this book, shows how a typical successful close is accomplished through using *power-packed selling words and phrases*. Don't be naive enough to believe that each time you follow a selling scenario featuring the use of magic words you will make a sale. All you can expect is to increase your batting average, get a higher percentage of "yes" answers per 100 presentations made.

If you use my words and sales techniques as recommended, your commission income will rise substantially. Don't expect perfection. As your skill in using power selling words and techniques grows, so will your confidence and your ability to close. However, you will still have strike-outs, "no sales." Failures are part of sales attempts. So don't let a few failures keep you from steadily using these time-tested selling strategies. Your successes should encourage you to make greater numbers of presentations, and the presentations will eventually build a commission income that will be your pride and joy.

"You Don't Have to Pick Winners to Win"

Here is a phrase to be spoken face to face to an investor who is burdened with losses, and has experienced unsatisfactory results from stock trading activities: "You don't have to pick winners to make money in the stock market." Remember, an eager listener is what you want and need to obtain an order. Let's look at another scenario using these powerful words:

Joe Salesman: "From what you tell me I know that you aren't too happy with your stock investments."

John Prospect: "Disappointed and unhappy would be putting it mildly."

Joe Salesman: "In order to make money as a stock buyer you have to pick winners, and that's hard to do consistently, even for so-called experts."

John Prospect: "You're telling me!"

Joe Salesman: "Would you like to hear how a lot of my clients are making money in stocks *without* having to pick winners?"

John Prospect: "I would sure like to hear about it but I am a little dubious."

Joe Salesman: "A lot of my clients, as well as many other sophisticated investors, buy stocks and agree to sell their just-bought shares at a higher price than they paid. For simply agreeing to sell high what they just bought low they get paid a handsome sum of money. Sometimes hundreds, sometimes thousands of dollars."

John Prospect: "That sounds pretty good."

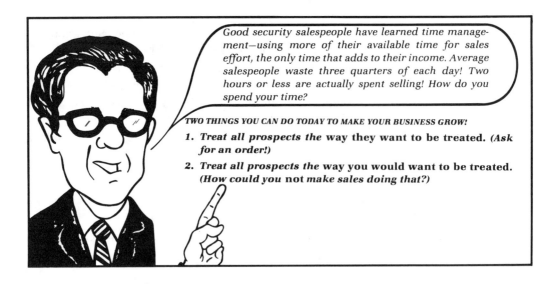

Good security salespeople have learned time management—using more of their available time for sales effort, the only time that adds to their income. Average salespeople waste three quarters of each day! Two hours or less are actually spent selling! How do you spend your time?

TWO THINGS YOU CAN DO TODAY TO MAKE YOUR BUSINESS GROW!

1. **Treat all prospects the way they want to be treated. (Ask for an order!)**

2. **Treat all prospects the way you would want to be treated. (How could you not make sales doing that?)**

Joe Salesman: "It is good. And if you were to do it, too, I can guarantee that *you will make money every single time if you have to sell your shares at the agreed price.*"

John Prospect: "That sounds terrific but supposing the stock doesn't go up to the agreed price?"

Joe Salesman: "Good point. It's possible that you might buy a stock low and collect cash for agreeing to sell it high, and the stock at the end of the agreement period is unchanged from your purchase price. If that were to happen, I guarantee that you would make money every single time.[1] In other words *you don't have to pick winners to make money.* If you can simply pick stocks that stand still you will do well! and if you can't pick stocks that don't move you might follow our Research Department. We have a long-term track record of being able to pick stocks that don't go up [say this with humor in your eyes and voice!]"

John Prospect: "My current broker can pick flat stocks with no apparent effort. Just look at my portfolio."

Joe Salesman: "The strategy I am suggesting for you is even better than I have told you. If you buy stocks and agree to sell them at a price higher than you bought at, they might decline in value. At the end of the agreement period, if your stocks are below purchase price you still might make money."

John Prospect: "That sounds sort of incredible. How can I buy a stock and see it go under my purchase price and still make money?"

Joe Salesman: "If the stock doesn't drop as much as the advance cash you collected you still could make money even though at the end of the agreement period the stock was lower in price than your original cost. The only risk[2] you run is in a stock price drop greater than the advance cash you collected. Even that risk might be reduced by strategies I will go over with you. I just want you to clearly understand (1) *that you will make money every single time that you sell a stock as per the agreement* (assuming the initial facts of buying

[1]The buyer's premium payment would be considered earned as a short-term capital gain upon expiration of the contract. The income would be taxable in the year of expiration, which could be a different year from the year of receipt.

[2]Be sure to explain that you have omitted commission and dividends for the sake of simplicity. Each person prospected for any option activity must be delivered an option clearing corporation prospectus.

stock and agreeing to sell at a substantially higher selling price) and (2) *that you will make money every single time that you buy a stock, agree to sell it at a high price, and have the stock unchanged in price at the end of the agreement period. You don't have to pick winners to make money!"*

John Prospect: "What are we waiting for? Let's get started!"

Carefully review the use of the word "guarantee" in the above scenario. The compliance departments of brokerage firms are leery of having security salespeople using guarantees that might later subject the firm to a lawsuit. However, "guarantee" as used exactly above is factual, not a misstatement or an overstatement. Never guarantee improperly or guarantee something that's not absolutely accurate and true.

Judiciously used, as illustrated, the guarantee is certainly factual, and it produces sales. *With equal emphasis given to the only capital loss risk (a stock price drop greater than the first premium collection)*, a large number of prospects can be converted to regular clients with an initial "testing" of the strategy.

There you have it! Power-packed words and phrases to help sellers of securities expand business through the writing of call options. Use the words and phrases and watch your business grow!

Top security salespeople know that true sales skill consists of telling a prospect all that is necessary—and nothing that is not necessary.

Turning "Zero" into Thousands of Commission Dollars Each Year

One of the most interesting and innovative new investment products available to securities salespeople today is the "zero-coupon" bond. This modern-day investment was first developed by Merrill Lynch, and then heavily marketed and popularized by Salomon Brothers.

Zero-coupon bonds, for those who are unfamiliar with them, are simply bonds that do not pay interest periodically (monthly, quarterly, semiannually). Instead, they sell at a discount from par value and are redeemable by the bondholder at the stated value on the maturity date specified in the bond indenture. (Before beginning a marketing effort on "zeros," the salesperson should become thoroughly familiar with the bond indenture and tax consequences, if any, to buyers.)

Although some zero-bond indentures provide for early redemption by the issuer at less than the stated face value, the zero buyer earns the maximum profit when the bond, purchased at a discount, is held to the maturity date. Consequently, zero-coupon bonds are normally quoted on a true yield-to-maturity basis.

However, zeros are also readily marketable and may be sold prior to maturity. On a resale before maturity date, a profit or loss may be realized. The gain or loss on the resale (after tax liability on prorated interest, when applicable, before redemption) is normally treated as a capital gain or loss. The holding period determines whether the gain or loss is short- or long-term.

Top-flight brokers constantly set goals for themselves—better than the previous year, month, week, but not so high that the goals can't be reached with extra effort. They keep score of how they are doing on commissions, new accounts, new contracts.

TWO THINGS YOU CAN DO TODAY TO MAKE YOUR BUSINESS GROW!

1. *Look at your best day in each of 3 previous months. Average them. Set a goal of having 2 or more days this month that exceed your average best.*

2. *Call spouse (or best friend) and say if you achieve your goal, you will treat to a super-deluxe dinner. Interest the person in your achieving the goal. He or she may even come up with some good prospects.*

There are two benefits to the zero-coupon bond buyer:

1. Known rate of return
2. No "reinvestment of interest" fuss

The knowledgeable salesperson stresses these features as key *benefits* of buying zeros.

A salesperson might focus on three types of zero-coupon bonds. Let's briefly examine the three types:

The Corporate Zero

These bonds are issued by corporations that hope to raise money at a lower-than-normal cost and avoid "debt-service" worries. Unfortunately, most corporate zero coupons bought and held by individuals require the owner to accrete. "Accrete" is a fancy word used to describe a sum representing the prorated share of interest that the zero earned during the tax year. The sum must be computed and reported as taxable income to the IRS, even though it was not actually received. The annual accretion is not only hard for the average individual or broker to compute, but it is quite difficult for the IRS to enforce, since no actual interest payments are made.

Because of possible taxation of the accretion on corporate zero coupons, most securities salespeople concentrate their marketing of corporate zeros to the following appropriate accounts, to which accretion has no, or little, immediate tax consequences:

1. IRA and Keogh Plans
2. UGMA (Uniform Gift to Minors Act) Accounts (if the minor has a large income, taxation of the accreted interest is taxable)
3. Pension and Profit Sharing Plans

Salespersons marketing corporate zeros should restrict their efforts to financially strong issuers. This lessens the risk of failure to pay face value at maturity. In addition, higher-quality issuers normally have a better resale market in the event a sale has to be made before maturity.

The Municipal Zero

These bonds are issued by cities, towns, and other municipal authorities trying to raise funds at more favorable rates while avoiding "debt service" obligations. The big advantage of municipal zeros is that, even though the bonds issued are bought at a deep discount and held to maturity, the profit at maturity is deemed to be exempt from federal income taxation.

These bonds have great appeal to many people who:

1. *Hate* to pay federal tax
2. Want to have a "known" future profit
3. Want to put up a little to make a lot

Note: The viability of the issuer and the ability to pay the bond principal at maturity should be of great concern to the buyer and to the salesperson trying to give proper investment advice.

The Government Zero

The government zero-coupon bonds are mostly "man-made," rather than truly "GI." Here's what happens: Original government bonds with coupons attached are stripped of all the coupons to "call date." These coupons are then sold as a "block," mainly to institutional buyers who want a predictable income stream, represented by the detached coupons. The bond portion (or corpus), representing the principal due on the specific maturity date, is then free to be sold to both individual and institutional buyers.

Salomon Brothers is probably the biggest factor in the government zero market. The firm originated *Certificates of Accrual on Treasury Securities,* known as "CATS." A close examination of CATS is recommended for the following reasons:

1. High volume of trading
2. Large supply
3. Daily pricing of key CATS available by simply perusing NYSE bond tables
4. Bid quotes and volume statistics are available to brokers via desktop computer terminals

Zero-coupon governments have two tremendous advantages for the salesperson trying to market zeros:

1. *Credibility.* The credit rating of the United States Government is the highest possible; there is no doubt about the principal being paid at maturity.
2. *Awareness.* The name of the guarantor, the United States Government, is the most *convincing and acceptable of any zero issuer.*

As with corporate zeros, the individual holder is supposed to "accrete" annually an amount to declare as earned, taxable interest, even though the interest is not received in the tax year.

To avoid this annual accretion, most government zeros are purchased under the same tax-advantaged accounts as corporate zeros:

1. IRA and Keogh Plans
2. UGMA Plans
3. Pension and Profit Sharing Plans

The salesperson desiring to turn "zeros into thousands" of commission dollars each production month and year has an excellent chance to achieve that goal through concentrating on the government zero.

This type of zero can be used in both prospecting by means of public lectures (Approach No. 1) and in "cold" telephone calls (Approach No. 2).

We are born with two ears and one mouth. Some security salespeople think they have to compensate for this by using the latter twice as much as the former. Top security salespeople know that many sales are made by listening!

TWO THINGS YOU CAN DO TODAY TO MAKE YOUR BUSINESS GROW!

1. **Set up a 3-ring binder with samples of all current mailing pieces available in your office, pieces that, when returned, pinpoint a prospect's interest.**

2. **Ask fellow AEs which, if any, are pulling. Call a couple of other branches to find out their mail results.**

For Public Lectures

The following words absolutely electrified (as opposed to electro-cuted!) every public audience where the message was properly delivered:

> "HOW MANY OF YOU IN THE AUDIENCE TONIGHT WOULD BE WILLING TO INVEST APPROXIMATELY $9,000 OF YOUR LIFE'S SAVINGS TOMORROW, *IF YOU COULD GET THE UNITED STATES GOVERNMENT TO ABSOLUTELY, UNCONDITIONALLY GUARANTEE THAT YOU WOULD BE PAID BACK $100,000 FOR EVERY $9,000 YOU INVEST TOMORROW?*"

The italicized words should be spoken slowly, deliberately, with great force and emphasis so that the impact of what you say hits the audience.

The preceding words have been used in public lectures where the audiences have ranged in size from 75 to 500 people. Read these words carefully. If you get the words properly engraved in your memory and deliver them with a high degree of enthusiasm and sincerity, you will be pleased with the results of your efforts. In almost every lecture I have given, every hand went up. When the audience settled down, the speaker continued as follows:

"MANY CLIENTS OF OURS ARE ABLE TO GET PROFIT GUARANTEES LIKE THE ONE I JUST MENTIONED. IF YOU WANT TO KNOW MORE, FILL OUT THE CARD IN YOUR SEAT, OR CALL THE PHONE NUMBER LISTED TO SET UP AN APPOINTMENT."

Please note that there is no mention of "Wall Street" or the term "zero coupon." Also note that you should try to avoid *giving too much* information about the investment. As a skilled salesperson, you should try to "hold back" a lot of information, particularly during a question period. Save most of the details until you can meet face to face or have a one-on-one phone discussion.

For "Cold" Telephone Calls

The cold-phone approach takes place as follows:

Broker: "Mr. _____, this is _____ _____ at _____. We are calling a few key business people (retirees, etc.) like you to tell them about a *most unusual, exciting investment opportunity* that *could produce very large profits* without requiring a very large amount of capital."

"Mr. _____, do you know how to invest approximately $9,000 so that you *will be guaranteed to earn $91,000 and have that profit guaranteed to you* by the United States Government?"

Keep good records if you want to be a top producer. Be ever mindful of the old Chinese proverb: "Even a short pencil is more reliable than the longest memory."

Prospect: "No, I don't know how to do that, and I must say that it sounds too good to be really true."

Broker: "I can understand that you might be incredulous about the large profit possibility from a small investment, particularly since I mentioned that it is *U.S. Government guaranteed.*"

Prospect: "Yes, I am a little leery, having had some less-than-happy investment experiences before."

Broker: "Rather than going into a lengthy explanation on the phone, let's get together late this afternoon or tomorrow at your office (or home). Which would better suit you? This afternoon, or tomorrow, at your convenience?"

Prospect: "How about tomorrow at my office, at 8:30?"

Broker: "Fine. I'll be there, and I know you will be surprised and astonished with the facts that I will present."

Again note the complete avoidance of the term "zero coupon." The stress is placed on the words that sell, which are statements of truth:

1. Large profit
2. United States Government
3. Guaranteed

At the face-to-face meeting, you can explain, with the appropriate literature on hand, just how the largest profit possibility goes with the longest maturity date. Since numerous maturity dates are available, you should be able to make a sale, even if the longest maturity isn't desired. *Double, triple, or ten times your money,* guaranteed by the U.S. Government, are words that do wonders in creating buyer interest and sales.

What a Powerful Marketing Technique!

One of the best marketing strategies to promote the use of zero-coupon bonds was developed by some very enterprising account executives working for my firm.

With the slow sale of condominiums and single-family homes, due to high prevailing interest rates, multiunit builders were advertising price discounts per unit of $5,000 to $10,000.

The brokers approached these builders who were trying to attract

Good security salespeople keep a famous adage in mind when they are talking to clients: "Be sure brain is engaged before putting mouth in gear."

TWO THINGS YOU CAN DO TODAY TO MAKE YOUR BUSINESS GROW!

1. *Meet 2 salespeople who deal in high-priced residential real estate. Try to get their accounts and also try to set up a system so you get their referrals from transfers moving in.*
2. *Call the president of the local chapter of the association of college and university women. Seek her account and ask for the opportunity to present a program at one of the meetings.*

buyers through price discounts and explained to the builders how zero-coupon bonds might be used to create sales: sales at *list price* rather than discount price.

As you might imagine, these savvy brokers found an attentive audience in the builders. What they suggested to the builders was to use face-value, long-maturity, zero bonds as a *gift* to buyers, instead of a price reduction.

For illustration, let's assume that a builder, trying to market $100,000 condominiums, reduced the price to $95,000 in the hope that this modest reduction would encourage buyers to commit to the purchase.

Our sales-minded brokers suggested advertising the condominiums at the original list price of $100,000 and *offering each buyer a $100,000 face amount* zero-coupon bond with each consummated sale. The zeros could be tax-exempt, corporate, or Government (for the highest iron-clad guarantee).

Imagine the impact on a buyer at the closing when gifted with bonds that at maturity would return the entire purchase price of the condominium! Needless to say, the broker sold millions of face-value bonds to the marketing-oriented building community.

This is another idea that you might find helpful in your search for new business. Be sure to clear this marketing strategy with your own Compliance Department. Certain states have tried to have zero "gift givers" be declared security dealers in an effort to discourage the use of zeros by parties other than licensed security dealers.

Index